THE SPECTACULAR CITY

A BOOK IN THE SERIES

Latin America Otherwise: Languages, Empires, Nations

Series editors: Walter D. Mignolo, Duke University;

Irene Silverblatt, Duke University; Sonia Saldívar-Hull,

University of California, Los Angeles

The Spectacular City

Violence and Performance in Urban Bolivia

DANIEL M. GOLDSTEIN

Duke University Press   Durham and London 2004

2nd Printing, 2005

© 2004 Duke University Press. All rights reserved.

Printed in the United States of America on acid-free paper ∞

Designed by Rebecca Gimenez. Typeset in Minion by Keystone

Typesetting. Library of Congress Cataloging-in-Publication

data appear on the last printed page of this book.

FOR CLAIRE

Contents

About the Series

Latin America Otherwise: Languages, Empires, Nations is a critical series. It aims to explore the emergence and consequences of concepts used to define "Latin America" while at the same time exploring the broad interplay of political, economic, and cultural practices that have shaped Latin American worlds. Latin America, at the crossroads of competing imperial designs and local responses, has been construed as a geocultural and geopolitical entity since the nineteenth century. This series provides a starting point to redefine Latin America as a configuration of political, linguistic, cultural, and economic intersections that demands a continuous reappraisal of the role of the Americas in history, and of the ongoing process of globalization and the relocation of people and cultures that have characterized Latin America's experience. *Latin America Otherwise: Languages, Empires, Nations* is a forum that confronts established geocultural constructions, that rethinks area studies and disciplinary boundaries, that assesses convictions of the academy and of public policy, and that, correspondingly, demands that the practices through which we produce knowledge and understanding about and from Latin America be subject to rigorous and critical scrutiny.

Daniel Goldstein's *The Spectacular City* bears witness to the social decay provoked by neoliberal reforms and the public response of Bolivia's poor, rural immigrants to the city of Cochabamba. Through figures of performance and spectacle, Goldstein takes us to the profoundly creative—and often profoundly disturbing—rejoinders of these urban dwellers to the indignities and alienation of contemporary Bolivia. *The Spectacular City* is a story of dance as well as a story of lynching.

Goldstein's striking perspective puts community ritual and community justice in the same analytic lens, and, in the process, excavates surprising relations shaping the cultural politics of Cochabamba's dispossessed. Cochabambinos on the margins of political society have appropriated public spaces to perform justice denied—whether in the form of ritual dancing or in the form of summary executions. *The Spectacular City* presents marginalized politics "otherwise" and, unflinchingly and humanely, tenders its majestic and its troubling configurations.

Acknowledgments

The writing of this book was made possible by a Grant for Research and Writing from the John D. and Catherine T. MacArthur Foundation and by a Richard Carley Hunt Postdoctoral Fellowship from the Wenner-Gren Foundation for Anthropological Research. Additional support was provided by the College of the Holy Cross, including a Charles and Rosanna Batchelor (Ford) Foundation Grant and a faculty research award from the Committee on Fellowships, Research, and Publication; my thanks to Stephen Ainlay, Charles S. Weiss, Susan Rodgers, and David Hummon for their support. Earlier funding for field research and writing was provided by the Wenner-Gren Foundation, the Inter-American Foundation, the Fulbright IIE, Sigma Xi, the Central States Anthropological Society, and the Department of Anthropology and the Graduate College of the University of Arizona.

At the University of Arizona, my deep gratitude and fond affection go to my dissertation advisor, Susan U. Philips, who has read multiple versions of this work and has supported my career through all its phases. Jane H. Hill guided me through my anthropological training from the very beginning, and this work has benefited from her insights and thoughtful commentary. Billie Jean Isbell has provided valuable intellectual and professional support. I hold in my memory the late Robert M. Netting, my first advisor, and the late Daniel Nugent, both of whom influenced this work in important ways.

During my fieldwork in Bolivia I was affiliated with the Centro de Estudios de la Realidad Económica y Social (CERES) in Cochabamba; I thank Roberto Laserna, Alberto Rivera, and Humberto Vargas for their help. Others in Bolivia who have helped me along the way include Rose Marie Achá of Acción Andina; Kathryn Ledebur of the Andean Information Network; Chaly Crespo at Centro Universitario de Ecología, Medio Ambiente y Desarrollo (CUEMAD), who introduced me to Villa Pagador; Carmen Zabalaga at Instituto de Formación Femenina Integral (IFFI); and Sonia Fuentes of the Ministerio Público. For assistance with research I thank Lee Cridland, Rubén Perez, and Laura Peynado. Other friends in Bolivia who have helped me in ways too numerous to list include Carlos and Anna Aliaga, Pamela Calla and Tom Kruse, Gustavo Gordillo and family, and my friends and *compadres* in Villa Pagador.

This book has benefited from the close and careful readings given it by many people in various stages of its production, in addition to many of the people mentioned above. I am especially grateful for the comments and suggestions of Laura Adams, Robert Albro, Andrew Brown, Philip Coyle, Diana Fox, Carol Greenhouse, David Guss, Elizabeth Krause, Aldo Lauria-Santiago, Ann Marie Leshkowich, Ben Penglase, Nancy Postero, Susan Rodgers, Ralph Saunders, Cathy Stanton, and Kay Warren. I have presented sections of the book in conference panels and colloquia, where it has benefited from the comments of Lesley Gill, Kevin Healy, Bruce Mannheim, JoAnn Martin, Sally Engle Merry, Elizabeth Mertz, and David Nugent. My cousin, Lisa Berg, contributed some wonderful photographs for the book. I am also appreciative of the work of Valerie Millholland and Kate Lothman at Duke University Press and to the anonymous reviewers for their constructive commentary.

I am ever grateful for the love and support of parents and siblings: Judith Berg, Richard and Carolee Goldstein, Jonathan and Jamie; my in-laws, Henry and Julie Berkowitz; and, above all, Claire, Benjamin, and Eli, whose love, support, and companionship make it all possible.

Any errors or omissions are my responsibility alone.

A version of chapter 1 was previously published as "*Desconfianza* and Problems of Representation in Urban Ethnography," *Anthropological Quarterly* 75, no. 3 (2002): 485–517. Portions of chapter 4 formed part of the essay "Performing National Culture in a Bolivian Migrant Community," *Ethnology* 37, no. 2 (1998): 117–132; and some of chapter 5 appeared as part of "In Our Own Hands: Lynching, Justice, and the Law in Bolivia," *American Ethnologist* 30, no. 1 (2003): 22–43. Some of my original photographs were published in "Dancing on the Margins: Transforming Urban Marginality through Popular Performance," *City and Society* 1998, 4: 201–215.

Introduction: Becoming
Visible in Neoliberal Bolivia

FIELDNOTES, 29 September 1996. *Don Fausto and I walked up to the health clinic, the concentration point where the different dance groups would gather for the* entrada, *the entry parade that begins Villa Pagador's annual folkloric festival, the* fiesta de San Miguel.[1] *We were among the first to arrive, though it was well past one o'clock, the official starting time. The* Diablada *(devil-dance) group from neighboring Valle Hermoso was supposed to lead the parade, as they historically have done, but they were unaccountably absent. This made our group the first and, by default, the leaders of the entrada. Little by little our people kept arriving, until finally Don Fausto just said, "Let's go," and the band began to play and off we went. The fiesta had begun.*

The entrada followed the usual parade route through the barrio, out across Valle Hermoso, and finally up the hill to the little chapel where San Miguel is housed. I had been dancing along with the fiesta sponsors at the head of the group when suddenly our attention was drawn to a commotion behind us. The Diablada from Valle Hermoso had finally arrived, joining the entrada as it neared the end of its route. The dancers from Valle Hermoso were now pushing right through our group, elbowing the clumsy Morenada *dancers in their heavy costumes off the road, drowning out our band with their own, as they shoved ahead to take their place at the front of the procession.*

Don Fausto stood in the middle of the road watching this disruption, arms folded across his chest, furious and swearing bitterly. The rest of us in the sponsors' group gathered around him, forming an imposing barrier so that the arriving flood of diablos broke over us like waves, spilling around to the sides of the reef we formed.

Then suddenly there was San Miguel himself, a young man from Valle Hermoso dressed in the gold helmet, knee-high gold boots, and winged costume of the archangel to whom the event was dedicated. Sword raised high, San Miguel stood marking time before us, gesturing with his weapon that we should part and allow him to pass through. We held our ground. San Miguel shrugged and crashed through our line, blowing his whistle as he forced his way between two of Don Fausto's comadres stationed at one end of our formation. One of these women began swinging at the saint as he pushed through the line, whacking him on the side of his gold helmet with the flat of her hand, screaming abuse.

At daybreak on the morning of 18 December 1994 . . . I was ordered to the zone of Alalay, Villa Exaltación, to investigate a case of FIGHTING; arriving at the place, great was my surprise to find that a person later identified as MARCOS SAMUEL A., 20 years of age, was hanging from a dead willow tree around which stood approximately 100 people, agitated and blind with fury, screaming: "WE WILL MAKE JUSTICE WITH OUR OWN HANDS." . . . Thanks to the timely and effective intervention of Radio Patrol "110," even worse was avoided, though the mob shouted that they were going to puncture the tires of the police car; clearly it was impossible to identify any individuals given the dangerous circumstances of the moment and besides that no one present, neither men nor women, would give out their names and what's more they shouted: "WE ARE ALL RESPONSIBLE." (Report of the investigating officer, Policía Nacional, Case no. 311758, Cochabamba, Bolivia, 29 December 1994; emphasis in original)

On the urban periphery of Cochabamba, Bolivia's third largest city, lynchings and attempted lynchings like the one described in the above police report have become increasingly frequent, as residents respond to rising crime rates and lack of police attention in their neighborhoods. In recent years, as the Bolivian state has undertaken extensive neoliberal restructuring of the national economic and political sectors, worsening poverty, lack of basic social services, and the state's refusal of accountability have led to heightened levels of violence and social tension throughout Bolivia. The social and economic crisis of the first few years of the new millennium, a period that Bolivians have come to refer to simply as *la Crisis,* has had particular consequences in the country's rapidly growing cities, whose populations have burgeoned with the influx of indigenous people from the countryside seeking new opportunities following the closure of state-owned mining operations and the failure of agricultural livelihoods over the past several decades. In the so-called marginal communities that these migrants have created on the city's outskirts, crimes against persons and property are frequent, and the neoliberal state is widely perceived as having failed in its obligations to protect its citizens from predators. In Cochabamba, attempted lynchings of suspected criminals, often accompanied by denunciations of the state and its representatives for their failure to provide security in the marginal communities, have been widespread.

This book is an examination of one dimension of this phenomenon, an effort to explain what it means to "make justice by one's own hands" in contemporary urban Bolivia. I analyze attempted lynchings of thieves in this context as a form of spectacular cultural performance, a means for people ordinarily excluded from the political, economic, and social mainstreams of Bolivian society to force themselves violently into the public eye. Like other public events performed in the same localities (such as the fiesta described in the fieldnote excerpt above), lynching in Cochabamba today can be conceptualized as a kind of spectacle, a visually arresting and attention-getting display by which the invisible and ignored make demands on a state that has shown itself unable or unwilling to provide order and security to their communities.[2]

The focus of the present study is one particular locality situated on Cochabamba's periphery, a so-called marginal barrio (*barrio marginal*) known as Villa Sebastián Pagador. Settled predominantly by migrants from Bolivia's *altiplano* department of Oruro, Villa Pagador was the site of one of the first of these lynchings in Cochabamba, which took place during my fieldwork there in 1995. By the time of the lynching I had already been at work in Villa Pagador for some seven months, studying processes of community formation and collective action in a context of migration and marginalization. What struck me most about the lynching (apart from the graphic horror of it and the deeply felt rage exhibited by its participants) was the way it seemed to have a great deal in common with another large-scale public performance event in Villa Pagador, the barrio's annual fiesta de San Miguel. Both the fiesta and the lynching were vivid, visual displays of collective identity for barrio residents; both represented appropriations of cultural or legal domains typically designated as arenas of state control; both revealed the deep tensions and antagonisms underlying the ordinarily placid façade of daily life. And significantly, both events expressed a demand for inclusion in the national bodies politic and social by a group of people who had been systematically excluded from full membership in the Bolivian nation. While at first a seemingly odd approach to take—how can one compare a festival to a lynching, anyway?—the similarities between these two events pointed me toward the idea of spectacle as a critical yet often overlooked aspect of political action in a contemporary urbanizing context. As Davis (1986: 14) reminds us in her seminal study of parades as communicative political action, performed street ceremonies take place in relation to all other performances, both contemporary and historical, and must be understood in terms of the "generic context" of their performance (see also Handelman 1997; Shaw 1981). Such comparison can reveal the "logics of meta-design" of public events (Handelman 1990: 7), helping us to see past the graphic visual imagery of both the fiesta and the lynching to the underlying political logic that they share. By placing both fiesta and lynching in Villa Pagador under the same analytical lens, I am able to suggest that each represents a claim to citizenship and a demand for citizens' rights in a context of political, legal, and socioeconomic exclusion.

To consider the political potential of collective violence by examining its spectacular aspects is not to excuse or justify vigilante lynching, to suggest that because people are poor and marginalized they therefore have the right to pursue, prosecute, and brutalize those whom they regard as threats. I do not claim that lynching is, in fact, a just form of retribution against people whose crimes have placed them beyond the pale of humanity—an argument advanced by some of the vigilantes whom I interviewed (echoing in frightening ways the discourse of lynch mobs in the southern United States; see, e.g., Dray 2002). Rather, my aim is to explore the political content and performative dimensions of such violence and to relate it to other spectacles of citizenship, community, and identity being enacted in the same localities, often by the same people, in order to achieve the goals of fostering publicity and inclusion for a marginalized group. In Cochabamba and, more specifically, in Villa Sebastián Pagador, people are struggling not to "resist" state authority but in protest against a perceived failure of the state (see M. Brown 1996; Ortner 1995); what they desire is not autonomy but greater inclusion beneath the rhetorical umbrella of citizenship so as to gain the very practical benefits that membership in the modern city and nation is said to entail. In people's efforts to attain this kind of inclusive citizenship, performances both violent and festive play critical roles in publicizing their predicament and mobilizing the resources to change it.

The modernist Latin American city of Cochabamba is the site and stage on which these spectacular "dramas of citizenship" (Holston and Appadurai 1999: 14) are performed. The city has figured prominently in the history of Latin America as both vanguard and symbol of cultural "progress," economic prosperity, and political power. Particularly in the twentieth-century modernist period of urban planning and design, cities throughout the hemisphere (including Cochabamba) borrowed from European urbanistic philosophies in an attempt to create orderly, "rational," carefully controlled and managed urban utopias (Hardoy 1992). These plans were dashed, however, as rural-to-urban migration transformed the cityscape, undermining the carefully laid schemes of the city planners and municipal authorities by the expansion of unregulated, informal economies and "chaotic" settlement patterns. The story of Cochabamba city in the second half of the twentieth century is very much the story of the competition to define and control the city itself, as the authorities struggled to manage or erase the unwanted migrant presence in the urban landscape, while at the same time these migrants fought for recognition, infrastructural improvements, and their rights of belonging in the city itself (Sassen 1999).

This book, then, is about the city and the spectacular attempts of marginalized people to assert their claims to it. I explore the politics of urbanization and municipal development in Cochabamba and the efforts of local actors in one urban community to perform citizenship and national belonging as they have worked to transform the conditions under which they live. In this process, urban Cochabamba has become not only the stake for which different social groups are competing, but also the stage on which their competitions are displayed. First, I introduce the idea of the city in Latin American history and the problem of urbanization in Latin America more generally, focusing on efforts to define and control the city in a context of migration and urban expansion. I then present some key points to an understanding of spectacular performance in a context of neoliberalism and urban transformation, on the way to a more detailed discussion of Cochabamba history and the ethnography of Villa Pagador in the chapters that follow.

For all of the apparent chaos, disorder, and violence that today seems to characterize it, the Latin American city did not come into being without a tremendous amount of planning and forethought.[3] So much is apparent from a brief glance at the very beginnings of urbanism in Spanish America. The Spanish colonizers confronted the "new" South American continent as though it were a blank slate, conveniently ignoring (and, where necessary, erasing or superimposing their own settlements over) existing indigenous urban centers to assert their own vision.[4] Colonial cities were planned and constructed to reflect ideal notions of urban life impossible to create in Europe, where the "stubbornly material sediments" of the Spaniards' own cities stood in the way of the urban planners' fanciful designs (Rama 1996: 2). In the "New World," the Spanish designed urban centers whose physical organization would reflect the hierarchical racial and political-economic organization of society itself. These cities were to be highly ordered, regular, and governable, their streets uniform, and the functions assigned to particular areas of the city (e.g., housing, commerce, government) predetermined and restricted to those areas. Thus emerged the famous grid pattern of the Latin American city, which persists to this day: the ideal of rationality, of order reflected in the physical layout of the city.[5]

The establishment of political order through the creation of ordered cities was foundational to the colonizers' civilizing mission as well (Stern 1982). The town itself symbolized order, religion, and justice to the Spanish colonizers, an emblem of civilization amid the barbarians whom they had set themselves to conquering and bringing into productive service (Hardoy 1975; Kagan 2000; Szuchman 1996). At a practical level, it was impossible to educate, Hispanicize, and Christianize an indigenous population scattered about the countryside in dispersed hamlets. If they were to have any hope of learning the ways of civilization and becoming good Christians, the "unlettered barbarians," ignorant of justice and reason, would first have to be "reduced" into bigger, more orderly urban centers or townships, what the Spaniards (under Francisco de Toledo, viceroy of Lima in the 1570s) called *reducciones* (Fraser 1990: 24). One benefit to the colonizers of the reducciones system (and one that appears in later, more successful forms of state-sponsored urbanization) was that concentrating the conquered population in towns made them easier to count and control, limiting their potential to revolt (Spalding 1984: 158). But beyond the pragmatics of population management, living in reduced urban centers had an important civilizing function in and of itself, as the Spanish colonizers believed that the mere act of living in an orderly settlement would produce civilized people (Zimmerman 1938). Curiously, for the Spaniards it seemed to be the grid plan of the town itself that would produce this civilizing effect: the physical orderliness of the town would somehow translate itself into the social orderliness of the town's inhabitants. It would also make them amenable to religious conversion: barbarian souls could not be Christianized if their bodies were not first reduced to orderly regulation (Spalding 1984: 216). Consequently, through urbanization and Christianization, the reduced population would serve as a docile labor force for service in mining and agriculture devoted to enriching the coffers of the Spanish Crown.

The key to the Spanish urbanizing project is captured in the idea of *policía*, a term usually translated by historians as "polity" but one that actually indexes a much wider range of meanings associated with the civilizing mission of Spanish colonialism (see the discussion in Kagan 2000: 26–39). Derived from the Aristotelian conception of the polis, policía in sixteenth-century Spanish America referred to citizens organized as a republican community, in which individual desires were subordinated to the collective will, and prosperity and peace were enforced by laws and good government (27). In addition, policía had meanings connected to the Greek conception (derived from Cicero) of *urbanitas*, signifying refinement, politeness, and individual morality (Lechner 1981). Policía, therefore, referred to qualities both public and personal; grounded in "a civil society with a just form of government," guaranteeing "order and justice," it also implied "a broad range of attributes of civilized life such as politeness, cleanliness and rationality" (Fraser 1990: 23; see also Staples 1994).[6] In the Hispanic New World, these qualities became associated specifically and inseparably with urban living. Those residing outside of cities (in other words, the majority of the indigenous populations of the Americas) were described by the Spanish conception of policía as living "like Arabs" (*vivir al árabe*), like nomads or gypsies, "barbaric, bestial, almost sub-human" (Kagan 2000: 27). Policía thus had an architectural dimension as well, for it was achievable only within an "ordered town," which, by the early sixteenth century, "was generally understood as one laid out according to a gridiron or checkerboard plan, that is, in symmetrical fashion with a series of straight streets emanating from a central plaza or square endowed with a church, a town hall, a prison, and the *picota*—each representing a different yet essential component of policía itself" (31–33).[7] This last element of policía—that the norms of civilization and proper comportment would be guaranteed by the state, with force if necessary—in later years would come to the fore as the principal definition of the term: policía as policing, the enforcement of law and order by the state.[8]

The postcolonial or republican period in Latin American urbanism saw an intensification of the effort to rationalize and order the now independent national landscape. Efforts to classify different varieties of settlements (particularly to distinguish among different levels of urbanization) across Peru in the 1870s represented a new kind of drive for order, one that Orlove (1993: 314) identifies as the "administrative impulse" to organize and govern a populace. In the same period, republican geography firmly established the association of particular racial groups with particular regions of the country, so that Indians became identified as "the people of the highlands, the highlands the place of the Indians" (325; see also Flores Galindo 1988; Kristal 1987). This program to establish classificatory order based on population size, density, and race across the national terrain represents a distinctly Andean form of modernity, one that reflects concerns with racial classification and the hierarchical ordering of races across rural and urban space. Just as the Spaniards of the colonial era viewed urban living as producing civilized persons, so in the republican period did Indians come to embody the negative qualities attributed by white Andeans to the rural landscape: a supposed "sadness" and "silence," an antiquated "isolation" and "ruggedness," an imperviousness to the civilizing effects of urban living. These associations would continue to inflect Andean urbanism in the high modernist period of the twentieth century, which in itself showed surprising parallels to earlier urbanistic theories and ideologies.

For the renowned urban planner and architect Le Corbusier, the goal of high-modernist urbanism was to make "the city the reflection of a single, rational plan" (J. Scott 1998: 111). Intended to make the city more economically productive, healthier, and more amenable to state control, modernist urbanism aimed to create cities whose design would also express the planners' commitment to order, rationality, and progress. Like the Spanish colonial planners and, later, such Enlightenment visionaries as Descartes, from whom twentieth-century modernism was descended, Le Corbusier and his followers expressed a preference for straight lines and city blocks laid out according to a grid pattern. The layout of the modernist city would reflect the extant social hierarchy, with one's social status being directly readable in the distance of one's residence from the center of town (Frampton 2001). "Functional segregation" was the watchword, with the establishment of separate zones for work, residence, recreation, and government, and the separation of pedestrian and vehicular traffic. The modernist city would be highly centralized: Le Corbusier's city needed central guidance and administration to maintain the harmony that was so essential to its efficient operation. In addition, through the creation and strict application of a formal plan in the development of the modernist city, planners would eliminate the chaos, poverty, and misery of the unplanned slums of the typical city, which by the early twentieth century had already begun to develop according to the whims of its inhabitants (Mumford 1961: 391–394). This "organic city," the city that emerged over time without central coordination, would be replaced in Le Corbusier's conception by a "Contemporary" or "Radiant City," one created through the "scientific" principles of city planning. For the modernist city planner, "The design of cities was too important to be left to the citizens" (Fishman 1982: 190).

Through centralization and careful planning, the design of the modernist city was intended to reflect and extend the power of the state by increasing what James C. Scott (1998) calls the "legibility" of the subject population and its arrangement in space. The highly ordered modernist city would theoretically enable state officials to count, identify, and locate in space the people under its authority and to tax and otherwise expropriate their resources and their labor more effectively. Additionally, the modernist city would be a more efficiently policed city: police and military personnel can surveil an ordered city better than a randomly organized one, and they can quickly find an address to pursue an investigation because the houses all have numbers and the state knows the identity of the legal occupants of those residences. Unlike cities created without preconceived planning, whose dark, crooked, narrow alleyways were viewed as "abettors of crime" (Mumford 1961: 348; see Low 2000), the modernist city was designed to permit the state an almost panoptic clarity of official scrutiny (see Piccato 2001). Modernist planners also aimed to eradicate popular political protest against state authority by designing the "geography of insurrection" right out of the cityscape (J. Scott 1998: 61; see Holston 1989). The redesign of Paris by

Baron Hausmann under the regime of Louis Napoleon between 1853 and 1869, for example, aimed to curtail opportunities to foment organized political resistance by eliminating the spaces in which such rebellions could be organized. By breaking up the densely settled and chaotically organized working-class sections of the city and constructing a network of roads and rail lines to facilitate the movement of military troops around the city, Hausmann's design was intended to create a city in which insurrection was denied the space within which to become manifest. The imposing monumental architecture and the public spaces that served only for formal displays of state power reinforced this sense of control and overwhelming, unassailable central authority.

In Latin American urban planning of the 1930s and later, the influence of European modernism was pervasive, though only occasionally implemented in wholesale design schemes (e.g., in Brasília; see Holston 1989). However, city planners and municipal leaders were often trained abroad by modernist architects (including Le Corbusier and his disciples in North and South American universities), and these students incorporated various modernist principles into their redesigns of many Latin American cities. But European modernists had no conception of the realities of life in urban Latin America (Hardoy 1992: 40; Peattie 1987). Their idealized, universally applicable models could not respond adequately to an urban scenario that included rapid population growth, particularly the tremendous demand for housing that urban migration would create in the second half of the twentieth century, in cities from Buenos Aires to Bogotá, Mexico City to Cochabamba. As migrants arrived in unprecedented numbers to the cities of Latin America, urban planners and administrators were unable to respond to these people's demands for housing, employment, and municipal services and found themselves desperately trying to defend their original modernist visions against the shifting realities of contemporary urban life.

MIGRATION AND MARGINALITY IN THE ANDES

Imagine a city map. The diagram of the city center is rich with detail, the tangle of streets, plazas, and landmarks so complex that a close-up inset view may be provided to enable one to find one's way through its convolutions. As one moves from the center to the periphery the spaces open up, so that by the time one's eye reaches the outskirts of town the map shows large open spaces, voids sliced only occasionally by an unnamed roadway. There are no plazas in this part of town, no named landmarks or congested business districts that require careful mapping. In contrast to the fullness of the center, depicted so vividly on the map, the city's periphery appears almost empty. But as Gary McDonough (1993) has pointed out, we should not regard "emptiness" in urban space as a void or an "absence of urbanness," but as an indicator that something significant is in fact going on there. The bare spots on the map are often the sites of "intense competition" between groups attempting to define the nature, function, and meaning of these supposedly empty spaces (13).

The empty spaces on the map coincide with what have long been called the "marginal" or peripheral zones of the modern city, and for more than half a century urban anthropologists have been attempting to fill in these blanks with sociocultural understanding (Altamirano 1985; Barragán 1992; Peattie 1968). Previous anthropological work on squatter settlements in Latin American cities (variously referred to as *barrios, favelas, barriadas, colonias populares,* "squatments," or just shantytowns) documented the cultural life of marginal urban communities, exploring the social organization of the new urban settlements (e.g., Gutkind 1974; Hardoy 1972; Mangin 1969, 1970; Roberts 1978), adaptive strategies through kinship networks (Lomnitz 1977), and the extent to which urban migrants had maintained attachments to the countryside in the rural-to-urban transition (Buechler 1970; Isbell 1985; Paerregaard 1997; Sandoval, Albó, and Greaves 1987; Skar 1994). Some of this work was a response to sociological conceptions of urban migrants as alienated and anomic, relegated to the margins of society and lacking any power to effect change over their circumstances (Lewis 1966; Park 1928; Powell 1962; Simmel 1950). Anthropological writings dismantled these assumptions, exploring the ways supposedly "marginal" people were in fact fully integrated (economically and culturally) into the greater urban society and often engaged effectively in struggles to improve their living conditions and expand their political and economic opportunities (Albó, Greaves, and Sandoval 1981; Lomnitz 1977; Peattie 1974; Smith 1989; Velez-Ibañez 1983). More recently, the focus has shifted to the explicitly political, with anthropologists now studying urban social movements based on such themes as religion (e.g., Burdick 1992), racial identity (e.g., Gomes da Cunha 1998), gender (e.g., Jelin 1990), sexuality (e.g., Wright 2000), and the local assessment of felt needs (e.g., Díaz-Barriga 1996). Others (Auyero 2000; Gutmann 2002; Paley 2001) have begun to study efforts by the politically excluded to challenge the very "parameters of democracy" that designate the limits of the political arena in contemporary Latin America (Alvarez, Dagnino, and Escobar 1998: 1).

The trend in anthropological study of "marginal" peoples and places in urban Latin America has thus been in the direction of demonstrating the deep integration of the marginalized into mainstream urban society, examining efforts to overcome the imposed exclusion that characterizes urban marginality. Despite this academic work debunking the "myth of marginality" (Perlman 1976), however, the *idea* of marginality continues to figure prominently in popular and official ideologies of spatial and cultural identification and categorization in urban Latin American society (see Auyero 1999; Wacquant 1995, 1999). In Cochabamba, for example, people of all social ranks use the term "marginal" to refer to a particular type of person and the space he or she occupies on the city's periphery. Marginal barrios are seen by mainstream *cochabambinos*—by which I mean the nonmigrant residents of the more central, well-to-do zones of the city, as well as the municipal authorities who run the city— as dirty and unhealthy places, dangerous, disorganized, and threatening to the established order of the greater urban area. The inhabitants of marginal barrios are themselves seen as marginals: backward, aggressive, and primitive or uncivilized in nature, qualities that their geographical position on the urban periphery supposedly reflects. As such, marginal barrios are frequently identified as "no-go zones," spaces of violence, danger, and crime (see Merry 1996). Residence in such a place, regardless of one's occupation or social standing, is sufficient to label one a criminal. The criminalization of the poor is consistent with Mary Douglas's (1966) famous definition of dirt as matter out of place: as violators of society's norms, criminals are dangerous to social order, antagonistic to social health, propriety, and decency. This criminal element is reflective of the marginal spaces that supposedly produced it: "Excluded from the universe of the proper, they are symbolically constituted as spaces of crime, spaces of anomalous, polluting, and dangerous qualities" (Caldeira 2000: 79).

In the Andes, rural-to-urban migrants are troubling to dominant social categories of race and space that have long served to organize not only the urban but the national landscape as well. Andean cities, as described above, were originally founded on notions of the urban derived from Europe. The city in this foundational vision is a place of progress, of learning, and of light, images derived by explicit contrast with the city's alter, the countryside, "a place of backwardness, ignorance, limitation" (Williams 1973: 1). The division of national space between the rural and the urban, light and shadow, modernity and primitiveness, is accompanied by a corresponding racial distribution that locates people of purportedly European descent (typically glossed in the Andean racial hierarchy as "whites") in the cities, with people of indigenous origin ("Indians") located in the countryside (see Orlove 1993). These "racialized imaginative geographies" (Radcliffe and Westwood 1996), with their juxtapositions of modernity and tradition, progress versus backwardness and stagnation (Weismantel 2001: 5), are thus not only spatial but temporal. The countryside, defined in terms of an "Indianness" that is threatening and dangerous to whites, stands for the national past, contrasted with the urban centers that represent the nation's future. White urbanites, in this not-always-unspoken nationalist ideology, must defend their cities against the contaminating effects of the insurgent Indian masses, *la indiada,* whose attempted entry into the modernity of the city threatens to undermine it. Efforts to keep the indigenous out of the city proper have often been undertaken in the name of "hygiene," part of a declared attempt by urban elites to defend or improve the sanitary conditions of the Andean city by excluding "unclean" people from its precincts (see Colloredo-Mansfeld 1999: 60; Cueto 1991; de la Cadena 2000: 68–67; Piccato 2001: 27; Stephenson 1999; Zulawski 2000).[9]

Indigenous people, of course, have always been a presence in Andean cities (in Cochabamba, e.g., see Larson 1988: 178), but as migration has escalated in recent decades, the threatening and always potentially transgressive nature of the indigenous countryside has begun to demonstrate its power to transform urban reality (see Calderon 1984; Sandoval, Albó, and Greaves 1987). By their very presence, indigenous rural migrants challenge the basic premises on which the modernist cities of Latin America have been founded; likewise, the haphazard nature of marginal migrant settlements threaten the long-standing impulse to social, architectural, and administrative order of these societies. Particularly in recent years, as neoliberal restructuring in the Andean nations has provoked unprecedented levels of "pestilential" (Rotenberg 1993: 28) migration to the Andean metropoles, the sense of a modern city under assault by rural invaders has reached almost crisis levels (see Beyer 1967). In Cochabamba, where the urban population grew from approximately 80,000 in 1950 to nearly 800,000 in 2001, urban migrants have been criminalized as thieves of public land and destroyers of urban order and rationality, their settlements deemed "illegal" and "clandestine" under municipal law. The disorder and "chaos" that these settlements have engendered, the threat they are believed to pose to the health, security, and very identity of the city itself—to a kind of orderly perfection that the Spanish once summarized with the term policía—is today conceptualized as a form of criminality, one that the police, the uniformed enforcers of social order and protectors of society's propertied classes, are now called on to control.

The history of Villa Sebastián Pagador, explored in detail in chapter 3, provides one particular example of how a community formed in the interstices of criminality, exclusion, and fear could become the staging ground for both violent and festive public displays of social inclusion. As one of the clandestine barrios of Cochabamba's southern zone, Villa Pagador was founded at a time when the municipality's strategy for dealing with rapid and uncontrollable migration to and urbanization of Cochabamba was to exclude new barrios formally and legally from membership in the city proper. As such, Villa Pagador was rendered invisible in the eyes of the municipal government and the national state, the needs and demands of its residents unaddressed by the legally constituted authorities. Recognizing that their only hope for gaining such services as running water, public illumination, and police protection was to achieve some kind of inclusion within the municipality and the nation, leaders and residents of Villa Pagador undertook to demonstrate their belonging through a variety of means intended to call attention to their predicament and to protest the unjust denial of "citizenship" that they had experienced. As I detail in later chapters, these demonstrations frequently took on spectacular, and sometimes spectacularly violent, dimensions. In the next section, I consider spectacle as an instrument for cultivating inclusion through establishing control of urban space by parties both authorized and insurgent (see Rosenthal 2000).

SPECTACLES OF CITIZENSHIP IN THE MODERNIST CITY

In the new city, or in the formal additions made to old centers, the building forms a setting for the avenue, and the avenue is essentially a parade ground: a place where spectators may gather, on the sidewalks or in the windows, to review the evolutions and exercises and triumphal marches of the army—and be duly awed and intimidated.

The buildings stand on each side, stiff and uniform, like soldiers at attention: the uniformed soldiers march down the avenue, erect, formalized, repetitive: a classic building in motion. The spectator remains fixed. Life marches before him, without his leave, without his assistance: he may use his eyes, but if he wishes to open his mouth or leave his place, he had better ask for permission first. (Mumford 1961: 370)

Thus urban historian Lewis Mumford imagines the experience of the average citizen in the formally designed space of the modernist city. Envisioned by its architects as a visual display of sociopolitical order, the modernist city was at the same time to be an instrument for achieving that order. According to the modernist philosophy of design, social control and state supremacy are achievable only in an ordered urban space, and the ordered urban space symbolically and pragmatically reinforces and facilitates state power. In Mumford's description, the glory of the nation, the repressive power of the state, and the city itself all become spectacles for the citizen's consumption. The buildings and streets become "soldiers" and parade grounds, the soldiers marching in unison become "buildings in motion": city and state merge indistinguishably into one another, continuous and entwined like a Möbius strip, the one producing, yet impossible without the other. In Mumford's vision, only the spectator—the object of state and city projects of ordering and control—"remains fixed," passive, without agency, infinitely malleable.

Mumford describes the city itself as a kind of spectacle, one whose very architecture and spatial organization perform, and allow for performances of, state power and rational, orderly domination. But this spectacular city, despite its aggressive displays of its own potency, is not in fact a space within which individuals are reduced to mere passive spectatorship. The spectacular city is also a staging ground for other forms of public display, produced by different actors for audiences other than those described by Mumford. In Cochabamba, the city never became the full-fledged spectacle of order that its modernist planners envisioned. Cochabamba's history has been one of conflict between social groups vying to shape the form and destiny of the city, and rather than passive observers, most urban residents (and urban migrants in particular) have been active agents in the organization and operation of the city. At the same time that the city has been ordering them and their communities, urban migrants, by their very presence in the cityscape, have disordered and reordered the city; their continual agitation for improved services and expanded rights of citizenship has shaped the ways the municipal government has had to organize itself as it has tried to respond to their habitation of the city. Analyzing the varieties of spectacle through which the mutual engagement of city and citizens has unfolded in Cochabamba is the goal of this book; doing so requires an understanding of spectacle as a means for producing and overcoming invisibility in the contemporary urban landscape.

Spectacles, like other public events, are systems for not only the performance but also the creation or transformation of social order; they are "locations of communication that convey participants into versions of social order in relatively coherent ways. . . . Their mandate is to engage in the ordering of ideas, people, and things" (Handelman 1990: 15–16). From this perspective, such forms of cultural performance as ritual, drama, carnival, and spectacle do more than merely "reflect" the social system of which they are a part; by calling explicit attention to things or relationships that often escape notice in the flow of everyday life, they can also operate as a critique of the existing social system by presenting alternative forms of living and social ordering (Guss 2000; Mendoza 2000; V. Turner 1986: 22). For many scholars of cultural performance, it is the ability of such performances to serve as both symbolic "models" for and "mirrors" of (to use Handelman's terms) cultural reality that gives them their powerful resonance as instruments for maintaining social order and producing social change (see Babcock 1978; Bakhtin 1981, 1984; Bateson 1958; Bauman 1986; Bauman and Briggs 1990; Burke 1966; Butler 1990; Connerton 1989; Debord 1995; Freitag 1989; Schechner 1988, 1993). Spectacles are often intensely visual, and it is in part through the manipulation of symbolic objects that spectacle performers create meaning, offer critiques, or suggest alternative readings of social reality, often through mimetic reference to other objects or events (Bakewell 1998; Calkowski 1991: 644; Mitchell 1994; Palmer and Jankowiak 1996).[10] And while the spectacle is obviously an attempt to make certain things dramatically visible, it is also, by extension, an attempt to render other things invisible. The spectacle is as much about obscuring what performers wish to conceal as it is about putting on a display: controlling what is to be seen, when, and by whom (Himpele 1996). Like the magician's sleight of hand, the spectacle distracts the audience by calling dramatic attention to a particular referent, overdetermining what is to be seen while masking that which the performers wish to observe.[11]

The spectacle, then, "is about seeing, sight, and oversight" (MacAloon 1984: 270), but it is also about being seen: calling attention to oneself or one's group by means of public display. This is particularly important in urban settings, in which people are marginalized or otherwise rendered invisible in the public eye, yet are in close geographical proximity to the loci of official power. In such a context, the audience for spectacular performance may be quite distinct from the group to which the actors belong, a point not frequently noted by analysts of spectacular performance. In most discussions of culture-as-spectacle, it seems as though the actor putting on the performance is society itself, at the same time that "society" or "the public" stands as the audience for these same performances, thereby draining the spectacle of any explicit political content or potential for creating political change. Most discussions of spectacular and other kinds of performance events derive from the Geertzian conception of culture-as-text, interpretable stories that people tell themselves about themselves; these stories or events (like the Balinese cockfight, perhaps the most famous cultural performance in the ethnological literature) offer "metasocial commentary" on what it means to live in and be a part of a particular society (Geertz 1973: 448; see Roseberry 1989). Some scholars have conceptualized spectacular performance in these terms as a kind of public performance of shared culture, without identifying who or what actually constitutes a particular "public" (e.g., Beeman 1993: 380; MacAloon 1984: 247). Numerous ethnographic examples illustrate the tendency of scholars to seek holistic, culture-building functions in spectacular performance (e.g., Dundes and Falassi 1975; Handelman 1990). In DaMatta's (1991: 26) conception of Brazilian carnival, for example, the parades and processions of carnival are "fundamental means whereby what we call 'Brazilian reality'— following the famous Geertzian formulation—unfolds before itself, looks at itself in its own social and ideological mirror, and, projecting multiple images of itself, generates itself like a Medusa as it struggles with the ongoing dilemma of changing or remaining the same."

"Itself," repeated mantralike, homogenizes that which requires differentiation. To speak of society or the public performing itself for itself is to miss the very thing that makes these performances invaluable as sites of social analysis: their availability to differentially empowered groups, operating with vastly different agendas, to produce alternative visions of the social world. Rather than regarding spectacle as a performance by "society" in "public" in some generalized way, we can instead consider it a form of political action based on visual display, undertaken by specifically positioned social groups and actors attempting to stamp society with their own agenda. This is most evident in spectacles of state formation, the ceremonies, celebrations, and parades like those described by Mumford, in which state power and authority are displayed to citizen-spectators. In these events, spectacle is not simply the way society speaks to itself, but a critical technique of modern state formation; it is through spectacle that national political communities are imagined and projected, indeed created, and their reality persuasively communicated to their subject-citizens (Anderson 1983; G. Joseph and Nugent 1994; Taylor 1997). The nation-state is an ongoing and ever-unfolding political production, the reification of an "essentially imaginative construction" masking an elaborate ideological project of self-legitimation (Abrams [1977] 1988: 76). As such, state formation requires large-scale ceremonial displays and rituals of incorporation to produce and portray "its" domination as legitimate and disinterested (Corrigan and Sayer 1985). In ways that some observers have characterized as "magical" (Coronil 1997; Taussig 1997), the nation-state produces and projects its own reality through such spectacles as parades and processions (Abercrombie 1991; Davis 1986), anniversary celebrations (Kertzer 1988), and other festivals of national unity (Sheriff 1999), as well as through more quotidian rituals of national loyalty and incorporation such as initiation ceremonies (Bowie 1997) and bureaucratic procedures (Herzfeld 1992), to produce collusive relationships between subjects and the state. And as they serve to construct and incorporate a particular collectivity as citizens of the nation, these spectacles of national unity also serve to identify and exclude the foreign, the alien, the unincorporatable other.

But it is not just the state or elite social groups that are able to orchestrate the complexities by which spectacles come into existence. Precisely as some modern nation-states have entered into the crisis of the neoliberal moment, losing their ability to regulate, order, and control society and their subject populations, groups among these populations are searching for instruments to reimagine social order, re-presenting themselves and their social worlds in local efforts at transformation and restructuring. To this end, spectacle provides a kind of vivid political protest for groups of people ordinarily excluded from the mainstream of urban public life, an instrument for their own self-imagining that Appadurai (1996) identifies as an emerging possibility of everyday life under globalization. Spectacular performance is interesting not merely because it is performed in public, but because spectacular events enable groups of people to establish themselves *as* a public, to define themselves as part of the public or as a special kind of public in a particular society. Performed for an audience that includes the political, economic, and social elite, "the public of importance, the 'political public' " (Lee 2001: 1), spectacles produced by marginalized groups are an effort to construct another kind of public, a "popular public" to which officeholders and other authority figures should hold themselves accountable (see Albro and Himpele n.d.).

At the same time, spectacle serves as a device to restructure patterns of inclusion, a technique by which the marginalized insist on their own incorporation within national structures and systems from which they have previously been excluded. For many, these efforts are articulated through the idiom of citizenship, long the rhetorical cornerstone of the state's inclusive politics (Trouillot 2001; see Jelin and Hershberg 1996; Lagos 1997). By calling on their rights as citizens of the nation, those rendered silent and invisible to the ears and eyes of the state can find a stage from which to demand their inclusion through displays of national belonging (M. Joseph 1999). These alternative "dramas of citizenship" (Holston and Appadurai 1999: 14), composed of parades, marches, speeches, and other, more quotidian forms of public demonstration, are critical means by which those ordinarily cast as the audience for state-sponsored performances of the nation take the stage themselves (Newman 1997). Sometimes these dramas assume spectacular dimensions, becoming big, bold displays able to catch and hold the attention of a large audience, which might prove receptive to the demands that the demonstrators articulate (see Albó 1994; Lehm Ardaya 1998; Ticona, Rojas, and Albó 1995; Van Cott 1994).

Apart from the de jure laws governing formal citizenship are ritual expressions of belonging that underlie them. Public displays of citizenship may be particularly critical for migrants, those displaced or deliberately relocated from their places of origin, and the children of these migrants, the first generation of native-born in a new locality. In a world

dominated by transnational capitalism, commodities and cultural arti-
facts flow with much greater ease than the bodies of the displaced, and
structures of racism and inequality inherent in national social and political hierarchies hinder the incorporation of new arrivals into the national formation (Appadurai 1996; Harvey 2001). Defined as alien to the
nation and so continually obliged to demonstrate their belonging, migrants (whether transnational or, as in the case discussed here, internal)
may call on the visually dramatic to forge community in a context of
displacement while at the same time fostering their own membership as
citizens within this new context (see Postero 2000; Roberts 1995). As
May Joseph (1999: 11) puts it, "The expressive stagings of citizenship in
the culture of new immigrants enact the need to reinvent community in
the interstices of political visibility." But (as Joseph also reminds us)
such stagings need not imply blind embrace of the nation by those
seeking to enhance their own visibility. Rather, what public displays of
legitimate inclusion often conceal is the profound ambivalence of the
actors, whose faith in such institutions as "the nation-state" has been
tempered by long experience of subordination and violence, and who
recognize the heterogeneity that such inclusive political communities
strive to mask beneath a homogenizing ideal of citizenship. These actors
collude in strategic ways with the state, donning the mantle of subject-
citizens for what it will gain them, while remaining skeptical of official
promises and guarantees.

Spectacle provides migrants and other groups, displaced and powerless to control ordinary forms of social inclusion, with a mechanism for
transforming their condition and making claims on the nation. Rather
than producing a harmonious kind of social solidarity out of conflict
(as, for example, Victor Turner's [1986] social dramas were supposed to
do[12]), spectacles of social inclusion often result in temporary mediations
of the social disarticulation engendered by migration and marginalization. They also can produce heightened levels of tension between different groups and classes in the urban milieu in which they are performed, as actors and spectators debate the meanings, methods, and
outcomes of particular public events. The discourse about the spectacle
may be loud and divisive, with no sort of consensus being reached
among the different parties to the conversation. This ongoing discursive
engagement problematizes the potential outcome of any given spectacular performance, suggesting that discord, ambiguity, and conflict may
be any spectacle's eventual result.

As Mumford's description of the modernist city reveals, the urban setting provides the theater par excellence for the performance of national and other identities (see also Guano 2002). As Mumford implies, this is due in part to the spectacular nature of the city itself, whose very architecture is an expression of the grandeur and might of the state that built or inherited it. In the modernist city, the dominant theme of the spectacle is order and control, the imposition of rationality and regulation over the chaos of everyday life and the power of the state to superimpose its vision of the future over the reality of the present. But the city also contains within it numerous spaces for the performance of other kinds of spectacles, large and small, authorized and insurgent (Holston 1999). The former includes the spectacles of state power that Mumford describes, whose pomp and splendor are indistinguishable from the very setting within which they are performed. But others are orchestrated by unauthorized parties attempting to express a different vision of the future from that imagined by the state, and in their performances violence may play a critical role.

In the contemporary context of neoliberalism and the expansion of globalizing capitalism, in which many postmodernist nation-states are increasingly confronting their own inability to live up to modernism's promised future of order, prosperity, and peace, violence is not just a symptom of this failure but a spectacular response to it. As free flows of wealth, labor, and industry extend around the globe, Andean nations are increasingly dependent on extranational forces that penetrate their borders and impact their economies (Gill 2000). At the same time as their ability to regulate their own money supplies, credit ratings, and labor flows diminishes, national governments are preoccupied with regulating markets, attracting foreign investment, repaying foreign debt, and maintaining stable environments for the operations of transnational capital. Meanwhile, the state's ability to provide adequately for the needs of its citizens is eroded. Efforts to comply with externally imposed schemes of structural adjustment, as in Bolivia, have led to the privatization of state-owned industries, rising unemployment, and the withdrawal of states from already limited and circumscribed social welfare initiatives and provision of basic infrastructure and services (Comaroff and Comaroff 2001; Dunkerley and Morales 1986). While academics debate the continued relevance of the nation in an era of globalization (e.g., Hirst and Thompson 1996; Lukacs 1993), many within these national societies experience the disarticulation of the nation as a loss of security and economic opportunity, the failure of the state to provide for and protect its citizens from the vicissitudes of the world economy.

In Bolivia, the return to democracy in the 1980s (following decades of authoritarian rule; Klein 1992) and the subsequent failure of the state-run economic model was followed, in turn, by the return to power of the MNR (Movimiento Nacionalista Revolucionario) party in 1985 and the imposition of a stringent new economic program, the Nueva Política Económica (Healy and Paulson 2000).[13] This plan stabilized the plunging national economy by delivering an "orthodox shock" of neoliberal economic reform, halting hyperinflation, privatizing state-owned industries (including mining, long the base of the national economy), and adopting a free-market program of deregulation of production and the import/export sector and increased labor "flexibilization" (Gamarra 1994; García Linera 1998; Gill 2000). The costs of this restructuring have been borne largely by the poor and working classes of Bolivians, though more recently the middle classes have begun to feel the effects as well. Displaced miners and other unemployed workers and ex-peasants have migrated to the cities in search of economic opportunity, inserting themselves into the nation's expanding informal economy. Many of these former residents of the highland altiplano region have relocated to the lowland Chapare, joining in the production of coca leaf (the raw material for cocaine) for processing and export to consumer nations (Healy 1988; Sanabria 1997).

Despite efforts at political reform (through the Law of Popular Participation; see chapter 2), levels of dissatisfaction with the state's handling of the mounting economic and social problems in the country have led to increasingly violent clashes between state authorities and participants in popular social movements, especially coca growers and the urban poor. Levels of violence have worsened at the turn of the millennium, as the ongoing national economic emergency (la Crisis) has become more intractable. A seminal moment came in 2000 with the so-called Water War in Cochabamba, in which masses of urban residents mobilized to denounce the proposed privatization of the city's water supply (which would have subsequently raised the cost of domestic water provision to levels beyond the reach of most people). This uprising led to the termination of the state's contract with the multinational Bechtel Corporation, and has been widely hailed as a defeat of the forces of globalization at the hands of a "popular majority" (Schultz 2000), though many injuries and several deaths resulted from street clashes between protestors and police. In February 2003, striking police officers and their supporters protesting low wages and a proposed tax hike clashed with the military in the Bolivian capital of La Paz, leaving over thirty dead and destabilizing the regime of President Sanchez de Lozada, whose tax proposal was a response to IMF urgings to reduce the national debt. In October 2003, a cross-section of "popular" groups organized massive social protests against the Bolivian state's plans to sell natural gas to foreign-owned companies for export to the United States. The casualties of the "Gas War" included more than eighty people killed by the Bolivian military, and the Sanchez de Lozada regime itself, which collapsed in the face of protestors' demands for the president's resignation.

Thus, even as the Bolivian state has adopted a formally democratic stance, its own historical weakness, coupled with the debilitating pressures of compliance with international debt repayment schemes and the demands of globalizing capitalism, have meant that substantive democratic reform has been impossible to implement (Drake and Hershberg 2001). Even as state violence against citizens mounts, local actors increasingly interpret state neglect of social services as a denial of civil rights, including the right to a life free from crime and violence. In this context, the state's inability (or unwillingness) to provide security to its citizens is one of the strongest sources of the delegitimation of the state in Andean nations today. This is particularly evident in the area of personal security, the protection from crime provided to citizens by the state (through the instrument of the police) and the adjudication of criminal cases by the court system. As the material resources available to the state to provide such services diminish, police personnel adopt extralegal measures to enhance their income and frequently turn to violence as a means of punishing or controlling perceived criminals without having to rely on a judiciary that they neither trust nor regard as effective. In Bolivia, the escalation of these measures by those charged with administering official justice has coincided with rising crime levels nationwide, as those unable to find work in the globalizing economy seek opportunity in the underground economies that parallel the official one. In such an environment, the average citizen has no recourse to protection under the law, being unable to distinguish the criminals from the security providers. People frustrated by this state of affairs voice their condemnation not only of thieves who prey on the innocent, but of the Bolivian national state and its representatives, the police and judicial officers, who are perceived to be complicit in allowing this situation to exist.

It is not surprising, then, that residents of Cochabamba city are themselves increasingly adopting extraordinary measures to confront their vulnerability to crime and to exhort the legal authorities to conform to their responsibilities. Middle-class residents have fortified their homes against invaders, and in many neighborhoods have banded together to hire private security firms to police their streets. Lacking the resources to hire others to do the job, residents of poorer communities, notably in Cochabamba's peripheral southern zone, are taking matters into their own hands, exacting what they call "justice" through attempted lynchings of those presumed guilty of crimes in their neighborhood. Such actions can usefully be read as attempts by those marginalized from the benefits of national citizenship to exert some control over their precarious situation, compensating for the absence of official security providers: "To wit, when communal action is taken—in the name of informal justice, cultural policing, or whatever—against those who ply the immoral economy, it is often in the millennial hope of restoring coherence and control in a world run amok, of filling the void left by the withdrawal of the state and making good on its sundered obligation to the nation" (Comaroff and Comaroff 2001: 36).

In addition, vigilante lynching in Cochabamba today represents a kind of "pragmatics of inclusion," a practice by which political actors attempt to "claim new rights and negotiate structural transformations that enable them to enact those rights" (Lazarus-Black 2001: 389). By decrying the state's neglect of their rights as citizens to security and safety in their homes and communities, vigilantes in Cochabamba are calling attention to their predicament, attempting to insert themselves forcibly into the official justice system of the state by their insistence not merely on formal citizenship but on what Holston (1999) has identified as "substantive citizenship," which includes the legal and civil rights that people expect as full members of the polity. At the same time, vigilante lynching poses a challenge to and rejection of the state and its official justice system by proclaiming for people themselves the right and the ability to make justice "by their own hands" (see Rosenbaum and Sederberg 1976). If a monopoly on the "legitimate use of physical force" is the defining characteristic of the modern state (Weber [1918] 1958: 78), then efforts to privatize the administration of justice and the exaction of punishment pose direct challenges to state authority and legitimacy.[14] So-called self-help justice making thus represents a simultaneous embrace and rejection of the official order; it calls on the state to enforce the law, at the same time suggesting that justice may be attained apart from the law, that the two are perhaps separable and indeed may at times be in opposition. If Bolivian vigilantes are "autonomous citizens" (Johnston 1996), then they are also "insurgent" ones (Holston 1999), for their actions suggest that legitimate citizenship itself may be derived outside of or apart from the state, which through its own inaction has forfeited the moral authority to bestow it (Pardo 2000).

In its visceral, inescapable visual immediacy, vigilante lynching in Cochabamba is a kind of spectacle, a performance whose audience includes both potential criminals and the state itself. For people long excluded from the official realms of political and social life and unable to have their demands registered by the legally constituted authorities, taking "justice" into their own hands is a dramatic way to capture the attention of an inattentive audience. This is what might be called the pedagogical function of spectacular violence: whether state-sanctioned or unauthorized "mob" execution, "the spectacle of the scaffold" is an instrument for capturing and educating an audience, "an organized ritual for the marking of victims and the expression of the power that punishes" (Foucault 1977: 34; see Osiel 1997). At the same time, as mentioned earlier, violent spectacles have a great deal in common with other—more celebratory, less violent—spectacles of inclusion, large-scale public events employed by the socially and politically marginalized to assert their belonging in the national social formation. In Cochabamba, events both violent and festive operate in the language of citizenship: by their very actions, and by the interpretations they make of their actions after the fact, lynch mob participants and folkloric dancers offer a critique of the neoliberal state for its failure to count them among its citizens. For many in Villa Pagador, and in other communities where similar incidents have occurred, lynching is seen as an attempt to secure the rights of citizens to safety and security in their homes, asserting their willingness to do the job if the state cannot (see Speed and Reyes 2002). Fiesta participants (who, on another day, may also join a lynch mob) express similar sentiments, explaining that their command of national folklore proves their belonging to the nation and highlights the injustice done them by a state that denies them the benefits of membership. The intersections of these very different yet thematically similar events are explored more fully in the chapters that follow.

The chapters of this ethnography are organized in such a way as to provide the fullest context for understanding the spectacular performances that lie at its core. This context includes both the historical and ethnographic background against which these performances took place, as well as the process of participant-observation by which I came to learn about them. Thus, chapter 1 presents an inquiry into the practice of ethnography in an urban context characterized by suspicion and mistrust, under the ever-watchful eyes of unfriendly observers. I relate the history of urbanism discussed in this introduction to the practice of ethnography in a context of spectacular performance. Though in later chapters I discuss the role of state and municipal authorities as audiences for "unauthorized" performances, anthropology, too, can function as a kind of audience for spectacles of power and identity, and in thinking about my fieldwork in Villa Pagador I have had to examine my own role as spectator of the very processes about which I write.

In chapters 2 and 3, I provide an overview of the history and growth of Villa Pagador within the urban context of greater Cochabamba. In chapter 2, I turn to an examination of the history of the city of Cochabamba, focusing particularly on the period since 1950, during which time the city experienced its greatest population growth as a result of increased migration from the Bolivian altiplano. I examine in detail the efforts and failures of Cochabamba's urban planners to create a "modern" city, against the perceived threats posed by migration and illegal settlement to urban order, civic identity, and municipal authority in Cochabamba. I focus on the changing nature of the relationship between the marginal migrant barrios and the municipal government, beginning with the municipality's strategy of simply ignoring the illegal settlements that escaped its control, to the creation of a decentralized system of municipal authority that has enabled the municipality to finally penetrate and regulate marginal barrios like Villa Pagador.

I then turn in chapter 3 to a consideration of Villa Pagador itself and its emergence in this context of struggle between the municipality and the "illegal" settlers of the urban periphery. I trace the history of the barrio from the time of its founding in the late 1970s to the present, discussing the problems that resulted from the illegal sale of land in Villa

Pagador and the corruption of the barrio's "traditional" authorities, which paved the way for acceptance of "legitimate" municipal authority in the community. Throughout, I consider the ways in which residents of Villa Pagador have worked to construct a sense of community in the barrio and to represent themselves as an organized and unified collectivity to the municipality and to development groups with the potential to improve their quality of life. This struggle is waged against the stigma of being labeled illegal and hence excluded from membership in the city proper.

Taken as a whole, chapters 1 through 3 provide the indispensable historical, legal, and sociocultural context within which spectacular practices of both folkloric dancing and lynching in Cochabamba can be understood. The horrific nature of lynching in the marginal barrios of Cochabamba's southern sector is more fully comprehensible when it is placed in a context of several decades worth of exclusion, wherein indigenous rural-to-urban migrants were pushed out of the city proper, systematically denied the rights of members of the urban polity, and left to create their own society on the margins of the state and the municipality. It provides a measure of understanding to realize that the people who today are taking the law into their own hands in an effort (in their words) to create justice and security have themselves long been labeled illegal, constructed as criminals in official discourse and governmental practice, literally "planned out" of the city by urban theorists who saw no place for them in the world they were inventing. If we are to understand the lynching of thieves in contemporary Cochabamba, a practice widely viewed as criminal and "barbaric," it is essential to fully historicize the people whose practice it is.

Chapter 4 takes up the process of identity performance by residents and leaders of Villa Pagador as they attempt to insert themselves into the national community through folkloric spectacle. I provide a detailed ethnographic examination of the organization, history, and motives for participating in the barrio's annual fiesta de San Miguel, an event modeled on the nation's folkloric Carnaval de Oruro. I argue that by basing their own local fiesta on this national cultural event, barrio residents labor to produce and publicize a collective identity derived from their self-proclaimed mastery of national folklore, in order to enhance the legitimacy of their community and to foster integration with the Bolivian nation.

Chapter 5 takes up the question of vigilante justice, focusing on the attempted lynching that took place in Villa Pagador in 1995. Analyzing this incident and local and citywide responses to it, I explore the ways vigilantism acts as a moral complaint against state inadequacy, challenging state legitimacy and redefining ideas about justice, citizenship, and law in the process. The chapter also analyzes the range of discourses that surrounds lynching in contemporary Bolivian society, exploring the interpretive conflict that results as barrio residents attempt to counter official representations of the meaning of vigilantism in their community. In this analysis I focus on the spectacular dimensions of vigilante justice and the ways it operates to perform images of community to outside audiences. These themes are summarized in the conclusion, as I draw out more explicitly the common features of the two spectacular events discussed in chapters 4 and 5.

1

Ethnography, Governmentality, and Urban Life

One irony of life on the margins is that a person can feel both completely invisible yet closely observed.

As I discussed in the introduction, invisibility is the critical condition facing marginalized people in urban Bolivia. Having occupied land and constructed housing illegally on the urban periphery (a process detailed in chapter 2), residents of barrios like Villa Pagador have been politically, legally, and socially excluded from membership in the city and the nation, an exclusion that they experience as a denial of citizenship and basic civil rights. The spectacular displays of belonging in which many of these people participate are efforts to reverse this exclusion, to make themselves visible to the legal authorities and to demand a response to their requests for services, including the desire for order and security in their communities.

Despite this legal and political invisibility, residents of marginal barrios are nevertheless subject to a variety of forms of official scrutiny, as the state endeavors to count, measure, and otherwise know and hence regulate the populations of the urban periphery. Such forms of official knowing have intensified in recent years, as neoliberal reforms and expanding democratic rhetoric have replaced the politics of exclusion as the state's official doctrine in dealing with marginal communities (see chapter 2). In Villa Pagador, for example, barrio residents are subject to the official gaze of a variety of state agents and agencies engaged in the production of local "legibility" (J. Scott 1998). A project of state formation premised on the transformation of "chaotic" social reality into orderly governability, this "legibility effect" (Trouillot 2001: 132) attempts to subordinate subject populations to state control through a host of normalizing techniques intended to count, assess, and otherwise render citizens "knowable" to the state (in a manner reminiscent of Foucault's [1977] disciplinary techniques of knowledge and control, what he elsewhere calls the "arts of governmentality" [1991]). Ultimately, the goal of such techniques is to inculcate norms of proper comportment and self-discipline in subjects, framing their subjectivity to make them responsible for their own conduct and thereby reduce state responsibility for their management (Gupta and Ferguson 2002: 989; see also Burchell 1996; Merry 2001).

The ubiquity of census takers, tax collectors, and land legalization officials in the marginal barrios of Cochabamba attests to the prevalence of government efforts to render these areas legible to the state by gathering information and ensuring local compliance with state ordinances and procedures. The transformation of squatters into citizens through the land legalization process (detailed in chapter 3) is especially critical in the effort to increase the governability of the margins. At the same time, nongovernmental organizations (NGOs) are also operative in marginal barrios like Villa Pagador, producing their own kinds of legibility as they attempt to determine where and how to create development opportunities for local people. The proliferation of these NGOs under the neoliberal regime also points to the effort to reduce state accountability by devolving governmental responsibilities for such institutions as schools and police to private or nonstate enterprises (Gupta and Ferguson 2002; see Gill 2000).

Under neoliberalism, then, even the invisible barrios of the margins are being closely watched. But the people subjected to these forms of official observation do not readily reveal themselves, nor do they passively submit to these new forms of governmentality or their agents. This is particularly true in the case of tax collectors, whom barrio residents fear and go to great lengths to avoid and deceive. At the same time, though, people in Villa Pagador also recognize that the increased scrutiny to which they are subjected has the potential to undo the invisibility to which they attribute so much of their misfortune.[1] Barrio residents have a special interest in NGOs, which many regard as their best hope for gaining needed services for themselves and their neighborhood, and to whom they want to present a particular view of themselves that they

1. A police officer observes the entrada parade in Villa
Pagador's fiesta de San Miguel. Photo by the author

believe conforms to the expectations that NGOs have of their client populations. Caught up in this contradiction of resenting yet welcoming
outside observation, barrio residents are very much concerned with
manipulating the ways they appear to official enumerators, as individuals and as a group, for the specific ways they are rendered legible
will have powerful economic consequences for themselves (e.g., in the
form of tax assessments) and for their community (e.g., in the form of
development projects). The performance of individual and collective
identity here has two faces, one intended to attract resources into the
community, the other designed to limit the information available to
those trying to take resources out.

Thus, in Villa Sebastián Pagador, people want to control the production of ideas about and images of themselves and their community and
recognize the benefits available to them if they can effect such control

(see Warren 1996, 1997). In such a context, even the most quotidian of interactions can be performative, a miniature spectacle of individual or collective identity (Butler 1990; Goffman 1959). As the following chapters more thoroughly explore, people in Villa Pagador hope to elaborate a reputation for their locality as an organized and politically mobilized community, a reputation that will bring economic benefits through government investment or by attracting development projects to the barrio; one that will scare away thieves and keep the cops honest; one that will force the local authorities and the national state to pay attention to their needs, to legalize their land claims, and to provide them with needed infrastructure. Publicity, or the power to represent themselves in specific ways to a wider audience, is a vital, material force in people's lives: if they can portray their community as an organized, homogeneous collectivity, local people recognize that they will be good candidates for development assistance from the Bolivian state and international NGOs; if they can portray themselves as poor, they will be less likely to receive an onerous tax bill from city assessors; if they appear to harbor revolutionary potential, they may have a stronger hand in negotiating with the municipality. Barrio residents therefore regard control over images of themselves and their community as absolutely vital to their survival, and good publicity as critical in making these images available to a wider public (see Battaglia 1995: 87; Ginsburg 1995; T. Turner 1991).

Into this environment of observation, suspicion, and self-presentation steps the anthropologist, a different kind of observer (a participant-observer, in fact) come to do ethnographic research in the marginal barrio. The anthropologist arriving to do field research comes with the intent of authorship, ultimately aiming to produce a written ethnographic account of his or her research findings. But from the very outset of fieldwork, the anthropologist-as-author must contend with the attempted self-authoring evidenced by the people about whom he or she hopes to write. The anthropologist enters a milieu in which he or she becomes incorporated as actor, audience, and resource in local representational programs (Battaglia 1995: 83). The ethnography the anthropologist intends to write can take on important implications in local identity-building projects, for the politically savvy regard the anthropologist as a medium of communication previously unavailable to them, and ethnography as a means to present a version of themselves to a wider, perhaps even an international, audience. Many of these people recognize that the anthropologist who has come to study them will ultimately produce a written report about them, one that represents them, their needs, and their desires to a larger and more powerful world beyond their immediate domain, and they will attempt to exert some kind of influence over that final product. Actively engaged in their own ongoing projects of community representation, local people may see in the anthropologist a potential ally in their efforts to broadcast their message of community reputation to the wider world; they also may perceive the anthropologist as a potential threat, a wild card whose writings about the community could jeopardize their local initiatives.

In this chapter, I explore the conflicts that arose during my attempts to write the ethnography contained herein, a process that I came to discover was fraught with political and economic significance for the people of Villa Pagador. One indicator of this significance is the level of mistrust or suspicion that I encountered in doing research, what people in Villa Pagador call in Spanish *desconfianza*. In the many conversations I had with friends and informants[2] in Villa Pagador about my activities in the barrio, it became clear to me that many in the community were concerned about what I was going to write about them and whether my ethnographic work would benefit or damage local reputation and related initiatives, whether it would bring resources into or take resources out of the barrio. This uncertainty colored my field experience and contributed to feelings of unease, of desconfianza, about me and my work in the community. Such desconfianza is not attributable to some inherently suspicious nature of *pagadoreños* themselves, nor simply to my own intrusion on their community as an outsider. Rather, desconfianza for many in Villa Pagador is a rational response to the anxiety and uncertain conditions of life in contemporary urban Bolivia. Always on their guard against unfriendly eyes and the hegemonic projects they represent, people on the margins must themselves be ever watchful and wary.

And yet, anthropological research in such a context is not only possible: for me it was remarkably fruitful, fascinating, and, I hope, an important tool in the political lives of the people whose struggles I have documented. Again, however, the process has two faces. The intersections between the kinds of performances offered to "official" observers and those played for anthropologists—and between anthropological and other, official forms of observation and knowing—suggest that the subjects of anthropological research may regard ethnographic inquiry as another kind of extractive enterprise, another means of producing legibility, whose benefits to the local community are difficult to discern. But their willingness to participate in ethnographic research and the collaborative ethnography that is ultimately produced suggests that anthropology can be a form of publicity, and as such a useful instrument in advancing the causes it studies.

ON ETHNOGRAPHIC AND
OTHER FORMS OF REPRESENTATION

I'll begin, as ethnographers do, with an arrival story.

The first thing I noticed about Villa Sebastián Pagador was the dust. Cochabamba is an arid city, to be sure, and even in the better parts of town the dry, brown air is a visible, palpable presence. But in Villa Pagador the dust is almost stifling. The barrio's many unpaved streets and frequent bus transit combine to produce an oppressive cloud of haze that stings the eyes and burns the throat. Most of the trees and low vegetation on the hillside were removed years ago to make way for mud-brick housing, so little plant life remains to hold down the eroding earth against the strong winds that whip up the valley from the south. The dust gets into people's cooking pots and clings to their drying laundry; it enters their homes like an unbidden guest and resists eviction, even against a regular program of sweeping and wet-mopping. Stepping down off the bus from the city center, I pulled the collar of my T-shirt up over my nose and mouth and, like a masked desperado, trudged toward the marketplace, where the leaders' group was holding its weekly meeting.

I had been attracted to Villa Sebastián Pagador because of its reputation in greater Cochabamba as an organized and politically active community. I knew Cochabamba from earlier experience, having gone there to study Quechua in 1993, and when I returned for extended fieldwork (1994–96) my intent was to study migration to and political organization in the peripheral barrios of the city. As I cast about for a field site, my attention was repeatedly drawn to Villa Pagador. Friends in the city spoke of the barrio as being highly mobilized and active in its own development, and Pagador's reputation as the most organized and progressive barrio in all of Cochabamba was frequently broadcast in the local news media. This reputation for organization and political activism made the barrio particularly appealing as a site for the study of migration, community formation, and political action in an urbanizing context.

2. Villa Pagador's main avenue. Photo by the author

I had been rehearsing in my head what I was going to say to these people, the leaders of the community in which I hoped to do fieldwork. Though by this time I had already been coming around Villa Pagador for a few weeks, visiting acquaintances and making gently probing inquiries into the possibilities of doing research in the barrio, I had not yet secured official permission from the local authorities to work there. In many ways, this was a formality: many other people were already doing different kinds of research in Villa Pagador, and they hadn't bothered to ask anyone for permission. But I would be the first anthropologist to do fieldwork in the community, and in the tradition of good Latin American ethnography, I felt it would be polite to seek permission before I began in earnest. It also seemed important to have the local authorities on my side, even if they weren't actually in a position to keep me out. As I neared the house where the meeting was being held, I practiced the complex Spanish constructions I would employ to present my case to the authorities and win them over in support of my project.

I was quite surprised, therefore, to discover that not only was I to be allowed to work in Villa Pagador, but that my presence there was regarded by some of the local leaders as potentially useful. Though the meeting began with discussions of regular business, attention soon became focused on me. Doña Lidia, then president of the leaders' group, posed me a direct question: What are you here to study, she demanded, and how will it benefit us? I had come prepared to explain myself, but even so I was nonplussed. Haltingly, I began by saying that I would like to write a study of the barrio, but Doña Lidia interrupted. *No*, she instructed me, *un libro*, putting me on notice that nothing short of a book would be acceptable to the community. A book, she explained, would put the name and the history of Villa Pagador before the eyes of the world.

Thus I began my work in Villa Pagador with a commission to represent that community to the outside world. This charge gave me something of a unique position in the community, one that was open to various interpretations by different people in the barrio. As a "professional" from the United States, I was regarded by some as a potential resource in their efforts to gain national and even international recognition for the community. For some people I represented a possible connection with USAID or some other, unspecified development organization (not an unrealistic expectation, given the prevalence of international development workers in the community; see below). Others, like Doña Lidia, recognized my potential as a mouthpiece for community reputation, that is, as a resource for publicity, the dissemination of images of the local group to a mass audience.

Being perceived as the person who was going to represent Villa Pagador to the rest of the world had its advantages and its drawbacks. From a fieldwork perspective, my efforts to write a book about the community served to open a number of doors that would otherwise have been closed to me. People often invited me to attend meetings and community events, taking the time to clarify what was going on and to explain how particular incidents or individuals figured in the broader history of the barrio. Others willingly submitted to my requests for interviews or shared documents they had in their possession. At times, however, I felt that people were putting the best face on things for me, emphasizing those aspects of local history that they felt reflected most favorably on the barrio, particularly on its image as an organized and unified community. By the same token, I occasionally felt excluded from discussions or meetings that revealed certain negative aspects of barrio life, such as conflicts or disunity among community members, or events that touched on aspects of local politics deemed sensitive by some of the local leaders. Particularly in the early days of my fieldwork this limitation felt problematic, and I worried about the comprehensiveness of the understandings I was reaching, whether I was not just being played as a puppet by the local spin doctors. It was as though I were trapped in some sort of Goffmanesque house of mirrors, in which I could never find my way into the "backstage" that lay behind the public face of the community.

This state of affairs, I later realized, was the result of the factionalism and divisiveness that existed in the community, as some people clearly feared the depiction of the community that my book would offer. As I discuss in chapter 3, Villa Pagador has a history of antagonisms among various groups within the community, and the anger, tension, and occasional violence that these strained relationships created provided an unavoidable backdrop to my fieldwork. Concerned as they were with constructing a community reputation as organized and unified, local leaders of various factions worried about the potential of my work to reveal the dark underbelly of this reputation.[3] From a fieldwork perspective, these divisions raised issues of preference and point of view, what Mannheim and Tedlock (1995) have characterized as the problem of "collusion" (see, e.g., Behar 1995; Burns 1995). In writing ethnography, the anthropologist must make choices about whose perspectives to represent and how to represent them in print. This can be a particular problem for anthropologists writing about such homogenizing concepts as community, especially when working in an environment that is politically divided and fraught with competing interpretations of the social world (see chapter 3; García 2000; O. Harris 1994). How is one to depict community, a supposedly unified, homogeneous collectivity, when the members of that community themselves can't agree on its definition, or hold very different conceptions of its history? In choosing whose perspectives to represent in their writing, anthropologists run the risk of privileging some voices (usually those of our friends and key informants) while suppressing or neglecting others.[4] And though anthropologists may be slow to recognize this conundrum, for many in the study population the problem of collusion is quite evident. In Villa Pagador, it meant that people on opposite sides of issues would react to me differently at different times, depending on their perception of my allegiances.

I don't mean to create the perception that my field experience was a negative one, or to suggest that I was not privy to the troubling realities of barrio life. To the contrary, as evidenced below, I established many close friendships and fictive-kin relationships (*compadrazgo*) in Villa Pagador, which were both personally enriching and professionally rewarding. As in all fieldwork experiences, the initial suspicions held by people began to fade as time and my persistence in participating in the affairs of the community made my presence there expected and even welcome. Friends and key informants from all factions in the barrio often sought me out, inviting me to participate in important family and community events, including the fiesta de San Miguel (see chapter 4). After the terrible disruption created by the lynching incident (see chapter 5), many different people were concerned to explain to me their version of events, to make sure that I recorded accurately and honestly (from their perspective) what had actually occurred and what it signified in the larger scheme of things. Even people who initially feared or distrusted me in time came to feel that their own participation in my research was essential: as I came to know and to interview more and more people in the barrio, it became increasingly important to those who originally had refused me an interview to participate in my study, so as not to have their perspective excluded. These people seemed to recognize the potential problem of collusion and tried to ensure that their voices would not be left out of the final product.[5]

My acceptance in the barrio was greatly expedited when I took up residence there, which began a few months into my fieldwork. Finding a house to rent in the barrio was not easy, and we had to wait until Doña Lidia had finished the renovations on a spare room in back of her pharmacy before we could move into the community. My wife, Claire, had accompanied me to the field, and her presence helped to counter the effects of desconfianza as well. Additionally, about four months into the field period Claire became pregnant, and people in the barrio were active in their speculations about the sex of the child (everyone said it would be a girl; they were all wrong). Once Benjamin was born and came to live with us in the barrio (we returned to the United States for his birth, but went back to Bolivia shortly thereafter), we felt very much accepted in the community. Our willingness to bring our newborn child to Villa Pagador was as great a demonstration of our commitment to the community as anything we could have planned (though people frequently chided us for not naming the baby Sebastián, in honor of the barrio). Whenever possible, I tried to perform what services I could for barrio residents, including teaching English classes and frequently serving as *padrino de fotos*, taking pictures of important barrio events and leaving copies for the local archive. Claire, a certified teacher in the United States, taught her own English class to elementary school children during their school vacations and volunteered her services teaching in one of the barrio middle schools.

Thus, levels of mistrust or suspicion fluctuated during the course of my fieldwork experience. To some people I became a trusted compadre and close confidante, a friend who could tell them of the world outside Bolivia and who might in turn tell the world about life in Villa Pagador. Other people could never give up the idea that I was some sort of globalizing agent, perhaps a scout for a multinational enterprise, or a spy for the CIA or the DEA;[6] others never really accepted my claim that I was not with USAID and had no access to funds to support a project they had in mind.[7] For others, I came to be perceived as a friend of the barrio (albeit a mildly eccentric one), kind of like a community mascot (L. Adams 1999). At public events, friends jokingly presented me to outside visitors as "the first *gringo* citizen of Pagador." Don Lucho, a local leader, once responded to a whispered inquiry about my identity with a huge laugh and the comment, "He's studying us!" ("¡Nos está estudiando!"), which everyone in earshot found hilarious. But even amid the laughter there were cautious glances, and despite my continued presence in the barrio some people studiously avoided me, refusing even to greet me in social situations, the height of rudeness in a place that values civility even toward known enemies.

Encountering a certain level of mistrust, or desconfianza, is not an uncommon experience for fieldworkers in the Andes (see Starn 1999: 12). In response, some have found themselves resolutely focusing on ritual, or politics, or other public domains of social life (e.g., Abercrombie 1998: 83), finding that, in addition to their accessibility, these are in fact the topics that their research consultants would most prefer them to study. My own study of spectacular public events fits this paradigm. This emphasis on the public domain is not necessarily attributable to the inherent reluctance of native Andean people to open themselves to outsiders, a confirmation of the stereotypical closedness of the indigenous Andean. Rather, I think the desconfianza that impacts the work of many anthropologists, in the Andes and elsewhere, is the result of a political stance taken by the subjects of anthropological research themselves, who view ethnographic research in the same context as other types of investigation being conducted by outsiders at work in their communities, the results of which they fear may have negative consequences for themselves and their ongoing politics of representation.

It is a measure of the success of people's efforts to construct and publicize local reputation that Villa Pagador has become the object of attention of external agencies and individuals interested in the problem of urbanization in Bolivia. Researchers doing all kinds of work in urban Cochabamba, whether for academic or applied purposes (see below), somehow inevitably seem to end up in Villa Pagador. I include myself in this assessment. During the year and a half that I lived in the barrio, I met a number of students, development practitioners, government functionaries, evangelical missionaries, and other "outsiders," both foreign and domestic, walking the streets of Villa Pagador. Many of these outsiders working in the barrio were Bolivians. For the local university, the Universidad Mayor de San Simón (UMSS), Villa Pagador serves as a kind of laboratory for undergraduate and graduate students doing social science research in urban Cochabamba. Attracted by its reputation for strong political organization and cultural homogeneity, students come to Villa Pagador to carry out short-term surveys and questionnaire-based sociological research. (As mentioned above, I myself was drawn to Pagador by this same reputation.) Most of these students are sociologists and architects. Most of the foreigners working in the community while I was there were from the Netherlands; like their Bolivian counterparts, none stayed for more than a few days, lodging in downtown hotels until their work was completed. These investigators also carried out survey-type research, employing questionnaires and formal interview techniques to gather large quantities of data in a rapid-appraisal mode. The foreigners usually arrived with a company of students from UMSS, whom they had hired to help administer the surveys. I was the only North American in the barrio and the only anthropologist.

The barrio's reputation as an organized and homogeneous community appeals to investigators in a number of ways, several of them told me. For the applied researchers and NGOs, interested in perhaps starting some sort of project in an urban barrio, a community that is known to be organized and active in its own development is vastly more appealing than one that lacks any preexisting organizational structure and would therefore require greater capital investment to bring it to the point where it could sustain the management of a development project without external support. The more academically inclined, especially the university students, view Pagador as a model site for the study of the transformations the country has experienced over the past thirty years, as rural populations have been displaced and migrated to the cities in search of new lives and livelihoods. The more idealistic among them see in Pagador a hope for the future of Bolivia, evidence that urbanization need not mean dissolution and loss of tradition and community. The purported ethnic homogeneity of the barrio is another attractive feature of the place as a research site, facilitating the conceptualization of the barrio as a coherent unit of study.

Pagadoreños have thus become quite familiar with the presence of outsiders in their community, many of them doing research for various purposes, perhaps in the employ of the government, or an NGO, or the local university. Though most people doing research in urban barrios like Pagador come with benign intent, the purposes of these investigators (*investigadores*, a term used to refer generally to researchers of various stripes, from government workers to anthropologists) are often unclear to barrio residents, and people are left to speculate as to the true nature of the investigator. In a place like Villa Pagador, where conflicts with the state are a daily affair and the struggle simply to earn enough money to feed one's family is ceaseless, people view outsiders as both possible threats and potential resources. A stranger asking questions might be a tax collector or other government functionary, an architect working for the municipality, or a cop; he might be a DEA agent, or a journalist, or a missionary; he might be a *kharisiri*, a supernatural being come to steal away their vital essence (their fat/*grasa*: Canessa 2000; Weismantel 2001), or someone come to steal their children, to sell their organs abroad for transplants (see A. Adams 1998); or he might simply be a student, an architect with an interest in housing design, or an anthropologist come to study *la cultura*. On the other hand, this stranger may work for a development organization or NGO and so have access to funds to support a long-coveted project in the barrio, or possess formal or informal connections with agencies and resources beyond the reach of barrio residents. In any case, assessing an outsider's true motivations is a subject of much concern and discussion among barrio residents, and the unresolved doubts about an investigator's identity and purpose often result in desconfianza.

Indeed, some investigators at work in Pagador come with dubious purposes. Anthropologists in Latin America are often mistaken for tax collectors, and in the urban barrios of Cochabamba, at least, there is good reason for people to make such an association. The municipal government has a staff of investigators working out of the Department of Revenue, which makes house-by-house visits in barrios throughout the city to determine each household's tax base. Understanding that property and income taxes are levied on the basis of house size, composition, occupancy, and whether the structure has a business or purely residential function, people routinely misrepresent themselves to these tax investigators, claiming that their house has fewer rooms than it actually does, or that fewer people live on the premises, or that a space used for a workshop is just a storage room. The subtleties involved in this kind of public performance are captured in an excerpt from my fieldnotes:

10 October 1995. *I was just about to leave Nestor's house when Nestor himself pulled up in a truck and unloaded a great electric generator from the back. Then he invited Gustavo and me in for a drink. "A beer," he promised as he left, but he came back with a bottle of carbonated apple juice. Nestor said that some investigators from the University had come by that morning, asking all sorts of questions about his house: How many rooms does it have? how many people live there? is it made of brick or adobe? and the like. They may be students doing independent research, Nestor says, but when they are finished they will turn their data over to the municipality, which will use them to determine taxation levels for his household. Nestor says that he and everyone he knows routinely lie to investigators who come around, because they are afraid that whatever they say will be used against them.*

Gustavo says that in his case, when the tax investigators come around he denies that he uses his house as a workshop to make clothing. He shows them an old identity card from his days in the construction business, and claims that while he bought the house from someone who used it as a workshop, he doesn't use it for that purpose. As a result of this lie he is working clandestino, *without paying the proper taxes on his home and workshop, and without holding the proper* padrón, *which is a document from the municipality certifying that you have paid your taxes and have the right to work in your established business. Gustavo says that everyone lies about their work in the same way they lie about their houses.*

Nestor, too, lies. When the investigators come around, walking into his yard as if they own it, he manages to persuade them that his workshop consists of just the space underneath the little aluminum awning in one corner of the yard. All the rest he says is just a junkyard (and so it would

appear to the untrained eye, with twisted metal lying in heaps around the
dirt patio). Since taxes on home businesses are determined by the size of the
workshop, his strategy is to persuade the investigators that his space is much
smaller than it actually is.

For social scientists aspiring to do "purely" academic research in the barrio, desconfianza and the impulse to lie can obviously be highly problematic in collecting data. As Nestor's comments reflect, university students engaged in scientific research are perceived as being in league with the tax collectors, collaborating with the state in its attempts to know and regulate the population of the marginal barrios. People express fear of a new tax code based on the research done by universitarios in their community, which they say will tax people more accurately on the basis of their property. This desconfianza is heightened by the fact that social scientists and state functionaries typically rely on the same techniques of data collection (usually the survey and census), are not resident in the study community, and do not share with barrio residents the results of their research. Indeed, the problem is in part a methodological one: the close correspondence in methods used by investigators of various kinds, from government officials to development groups to university students, tends to ally them all in the minds of those being studied, the poor and illegally settled residents of Villa Pagador. Even the seemingly most innocent questions, the staples of anthropological-type surveys, can inspire multiple interpretations when viewed from a position of desconfianza. Questions about household size and the gendered division of labor, for example, are regarded with skepticism, for they hold implications about household income, as do questions about the level of education of household members and the composition of the daily diet (someone who eats a lot of meat, for example, might have an unreported source of income). Similarly, the number of rooms in the house, the materials used in construction, and the uses to which rooms are put, though relevant to anthropological interest in household organization and family economics, are also directly implicated in tax assessment.

Reliable data on household income and economics generally may be impossible to collect in urban barrios of Bolivia, and the effort to do so may only enhance the climate of desconfianza. This is due to the sometimes illegal occupations and money-earning strategies of household members. Many people who sell in the downtown market or on street corners, or who are involved in the manufacture, sale, and transport of merchandise around the country, do so without the proper permits or licenses that the state requires (Gustavo's lack of a padrón being a case in point). Even more problematic, the coca production industry in Bolivia pervades every aspect of economic life in the country, reaching even into the marginal barrios of Cochabamba, La Paz, and elsewhere. Many people may work seasonally in the coca fields and processing areas, earning enough money through intermittent labor to buy a new truck or to make improvements to their house (Laserna 1997). People are obviously reluctant to share any information on the subject, and suspicions of investigators asking questions about household economics and income-generating strategies are extremely high, limiting the possibility of fully understanding the dynamics of the household economy.

The unwillingness to cooperate in the data collection efforts of outside investigators can have contradictory results for barrio residents, as in the case of the national census conducted throughout Bolivia in 1992.[8] The results of this census are locally believed to underestimate the population of Pagador by a vast number, owing to people's reluctance to state accurately the number of individuals living in their household. This underestimate has had the unfortunate effect of making the barrio appear much smaller than it actually is, thereby reducing the political might of the community in the eyes of the state. Population size is a key factor in community self-representation strategies: the bigger the population, the more seriously barrio residents believe they must be taken in their claims for a voice in local politics and in their demands for city services. For this reason I have known people to become extremely angry when discussing the national census figures, which put the barrio population at around 10,000 people, a number locally regarded as far below the actual size (local estimates have the population at around 30,000, a number supported by other, nongovernmental studies; see Dirección Social Universitaria [DISU] 1996; Liebson 1995). The desire to underrepresent individual household size, while advantageous for personal tax purposes, conflicts with the desire at the community level to overrepresent the barrio's population. People's anger at the census in part reflects their frustration with being forced into this catch-22 predicament.

Even the most seemingly quantitative methods thus have implications for the production of representations by and about barrio residents. What the examples above suggest are the ways people in Pagador use their encounters with outsiders, particularly with interested investigators like state officials, to produce and perform representations of themselves which they hope will entail direct economic benefits (in the form of lower tax assessments, for instance), or at least will enable them to avoid trouble with the government. The conducting of a survey is not the simple transmission of "data" from surveyed to surveyor; rather, it is part of the complex performance of a perceived local reality negotiated between a barrio resident and a city official, or a social scientist asking similar questions. When an investigator comes to call he or she encounters not a neutral subject willing to divulge information about herself (because surveys are conducted during the daytime, the people interviewed are usually women), but a threatened and suspicious person who knows full well the consequences of giving the wrong answers in response to survey questions and who therefore answers the door with a profound mistrust of the investigator already in place. In responding to his questions she tells him what she thinks he expects to hear, so that he will go away satisfied and not report back to the authorities that something unusual is going on in that household. The enclosed household compound, surrounded by a mud wall topped with broken glass and guarded by a ferocious dog that serves as a defense against petty thieves, also serves to deter unwanted entrance by local investigators (something lacking in the case of Nestor's open workshop/yard). This wall limits the investigator's own view of the inside of the household, forcing him to rely on the answers given to him by the woman at the door. The written report that results from this performative encounter stands as another kind of negotiated representation, rather than the straightforward and objective study that its authors intend it to be. As the example of the census demonstrates, however, strategies of individual self-presentation may have unanticipated negative consequences for the politics of collective representation as these are practiced at the level of the community.

PARTICIPANT-OBSERVATION IN THE CITY

Though always cognizant of the politics of representation that colored my fieldwork, on a daily basis I was more concerned with the practicalities of doing ethnographic research in a complex and often confusing urban social context. Given the many problems associated with "objective" urban research, I dispensed entirely with survey techniques, instead pursuing a participant-observation approach to urban fieldwork. Despite criticism suggesting that participant-observation in the city necessarily perpetuates an outdated "community studies" approach (see chapter 3), I found that participant-observation need not necessarily contribute to an artificial bounding or isolation of the locality from the greater society in which it is embedded (see Leeds 1994; Mullings 1987). On the contrary, it was through direct participation in local life that I came to learn about the city outside the barrio, how people perceive and experience the city, and how it impacts their lives. Through observing the activities within and surrounding the Casa Comunal, the local branch of the municipal government, I learned about the kinds of legal and bureaucratic impositions the city authorities place on barrio residents, and how these poorly understood laws and requirements negatively affect people in Pagador. I saw the missionaries and development people and university students come and go, the police inspectors and salt vendors and journalists and mobile vaccine clinics and visitors from the countryside, even a traveling circus with some sort of rangy monkey and a blue-faced dwarf; and I observed the kinds of responses they encountered among the local population. I witnessed the local protests against state neglect of the barrio, and was there when the mayor came to visit to address residents' complaints. Nor did participant-observation confine me to the barrio: I followed people as they went about their daily search for work downtown; I accompanied them on visits to the credit union in search of loans, to the market to sell their wares or to do their shopping, to the *alcaldía* to make denunciations against the land speculators for illegally evicting delinquent tenants, to the *prefectura* to denounce the local police for their ineffectiveness and collaboration with thieves. In short, through participant-observation I gained an understanding not of the barrio's isolation from the city, but of the intense and all-pervading integration of the marginal barrio within the city, and of the way the city is experienced by the barrio residents with whom I lived.

As critics of urban participant-observation have noted, the highly mobile nature of urban populations and the character of urban barrios as bedroom communities (*dormitorios*) to which people return only at night can hamper the effectiveness of participant-observation (Foster and Kemper 1974; Gulick 1973; Gutkind 1974). I found this at times to be a problem in my own work, particularly on Wednesdays and Saturdays, market days in the city's *Cancha*, when many barrio residents go downtown to the enormous outdoor market to buy or sell. At such times I would find myself the only person on the streets of Pagador and would retreat to my compadre's workshop to sit idly watching him do his metalworking. Nevertheless, the problem of the bedroom community seems to me to be greatly exaggerated. It is true that the barrio population by necessity is highly mobile: people often spend their days wandering about the city in search of employment as construction workers or seeking customers to buy their vegetables, or they travel about the country, transporting items to sell or resell. All of these occupations are sporadic, however, and people often find themselves in the barrio for long stretches between jobs or money-making opportunities. Local bureaucratic demands also keep people home; though unfortunate for them, it was a positive boon for me to hang out in the Casa Comunal talking with frustrated landowners attempting to legalize their claims, or to wait for hours outside the school with parents hoping to enroll their children in the already overcrowded classes. In addition, many people make their living locally, and some of my best and most consistent collaborators were people who had a shop or home-based livelihood in the barrio: the local market women, the barber on the corner, Doña Lidia in her pharmacy, my compadres the welder and the pants maker and the homemaker, the shoe repairmen, the bureaucrats in the Casa Comunal, the many local shopkeepers. Sundays in particular were always productive: on Sundays most people stayed home, attended meetings, played soccer, or hosted weddings, and these were the best days to find people in the barrio.

As I came to focus more on the political dimensions of local life, however, it became apparent that I would need a more systematic and in-depth means for acquiring large amounts of information on specific topics of interest within the amount of time I had allocated (or which circumstances had allocated me) for completion of fieldwork. Therefore, about eight months into my fieldwork, I began to conduct informal interviews with individuals who were knowledgeable about the history of the barrio or were currently involved in local politics, either as leaders or as participants in local political or community-based organizations, such as the water cooperative or the various local churches. Though wide-ranging and conducted without any preestablished or pretested set of questions, these interviews focused on certain specific themes, including the personal life history of the respondent, community history from that person's point of view, his or her perceptions of the barrio and of the city and its authorities, and his or her ideas about how the barrio is viewed by outsiders. I also collected a great deal of documentary information pertaining to Villa Pagador, the southern zone of Cochabamba in which Pagador is located, and the problematic of marginal barrios in Bolivia in general. This material included newspaper and other media reports, government documents, and a number of secondary studies conducted by other researchers working in marginal Cochabamba, offering an interesting perspective on the various representations of barrio residents and their communities being produced by outsiders.

These three subsidiary projects—participant-observation, intensive interviewing, and collection of documentary materials—together constituted a "triangulated" methodology through which I have produced my own representation of Villa Pagador. Triangulation, though, is a fancy term for what amounts to a flexible and adaptive approach to fieldwork. As Hannerz (1980: 310) says, urban life, by virtue of its complex and politicized nature, requires a high degree of methodological flexibility on the part of the researcher. The urban anthropologist needs to be circumspect about the uses of the data collected and how this collection takes place, and open to the multiple interpretive avenues that present themselves, in order to arrive at an understanding of a locality in and of itself and as situated within a translocal, urban, and even global totality (see Appadurai 1996).

CONCLUSION: BECOMING PART OF THE STORY

Many crucial facts lie beyond the time and place of interaction or lie concealed within it. . . . When the individual is in the immediate presence of others, his activity will have a promissory character. The others are likely to find that they must accept the individual on faith, offering him a just return while he is present before them in exchange for something whose true value will not be established until after he has left their presence.—Erving Goffman, *The Presentation of Self in Everyday Life*

The struggle to control representation lies at the root of desconfianza in Villa Pagador. As an outsider stepping into this milieu with the goal of producing my own representation of local experience, my presence in the barrio was a source of constant mediation and interpretation by local people. Concerned as they are with reputation and image and identity, for some pagadoreños it was never fully possible to forget that I was going to go home and write a book about the community, and that

3. Barrio leaders toast the ethnographer at a lunch in Villa Pagador's marketplace. Photo by the author

anything they might tell me could end up in print. This could mean that people exaggerated the positive aspects of a situation to cast the best possible light on themselves, or else they downplayed a negative situation out of fear of retaliation by others in the barrio or an unwillingness to make the community appear disunified. For many in the barrio, I think, it was difficult to determine the extent to which I might be a community resource—an instrument of publicity for local struggles— or a liability, someone who would betray local secrets, converting my knowledge of the community into a resource to advance my own career. My role as scribe and interpreter, armed with tape recorder and laptop computer, made me a notable figure in the barrio, sometimes popular, at other times a pariah, and sometimes, unexpectedly, an unwitting participant in the local struggle for self-representation.

29 September 1995: *Día del San Miguel. It was the morning of the* entrada, *the start of the big barrio fiesta de San Miguel. I was walking up the main avenue of the barrio, heading towards Nestor's house. The parade was due to start in an hour, and people were beginning to gather by the health clinic, the concentration point for the dance groups to assemble for the parade. In the street I encountered a group of men dressed in suits with colorful sashes across their chests. They were the* Comité de Festejos, *the organizing com-*

mittee for the fiesta, whose three members were all important community leaders and key participants in my research. They were accompanied by two other men, introduced as engineers but whom I later learned were heads of a local political party and honored invited guests who had come to the barrio for the fiesta.

One of the members of the committee, Don Nelson, seemed especially pleased to see me. He grabbed me by the arm and led me along with them to a nearby bar, where we all gathered around a small table and were served several tall bottles of beer. The pagadoreños in the group toasted the Pacha-mama (Earth Mother), pouring offerings of beer on the ground as is customary before drinking. One of the engineers, a large man with a thin, scraggy beard, bulbous nose, light skin, and receding hairline, told me he was from Cochabamba, "one of the few original cochabambinos left in the colony," a reference to the large population of immigrants that now live in the city. The second engineer, a sandy-haired man with light eyes in an ill-fitting leisure suit, looked unfocused and said little.

To my great surprise, accustomed as I was to being politely ignored in such gatherings, I suddenly found myself the object of attention in this small group. My Pagador friends introduced me again to the invited dignitaries. I was described by Don Ignacio as a great friend of the barrio who had done much to help the community by donating photos of important events and teaching free English classes to children of the barrio, and who was going to go home and write a book about the community. Don Nelson also described me as being like a community member, though he joked that I was really a mal-pagadoreño, a complex pun referring to my lack of a salary for the work I was doing (i.e., poorly paid, malpagado) and to the fact that I am from the United States and so not really a pagadoreño at all. Nelson thought this joke hilarious, and repeated it several times in the course of the day.

In this incident, the attention paid to me, the description of me as an outsider come to help the barrio and be part of the community, is perhaps best understood as an attempt to demonstrate the importance of the barrio itself, that a gringo should come and live there and work with the people. That the barrio's story should warrant inscription in a book by a foreigner, to be written in English and read by an international audience, was held up as another indication of the barrio's importance. By pointing me out to the distinguished guests, the other outsiders whom they were trying to impress, the authorities of the barrio were making a comment about their own significance in world affairs, the centrality (rather than the marginality) of their community and its history to the life of the city and the nation. This incident represents one of the ways I myself was incorporated and transformed into a community member, albeit an imperfect one (a mal-pagadoreño), and the ways this identity was at times strategically deployed in the service of community reputation building. In this instance, I was taken out of my ethnographer role by my friends in the community and momentarily transformed into something like a native, "the first gringo citizen of Pagador." Accustomed to being part of the audience for local-identity performances, it was with some surprise that I found myself suddenly up on stage with the rest of the cast.

In a way, this one small incident summarizes the themes I have attempted to set forth in this brief foray into methods and reflexivity: local self-representation as a site of intense political negotiation and the contradictory role of the anthropologist as both audience for and author of collective representations. What should be clear from this discussion is that representation is, for those represented, a matter of fundamentally material significance, with political and economic consequences that extend to all aspects of daily life. I have also attempted to illustrate the dialectical nature of identity performance in this conflicted and politicized environment, wherein local people at once perform for and yet hide from the official, normalizing gaze of state authorities and other powerful observers. The local production of collective and individual identity is directly implicated in this multifaceted struggle, simultaneously an attempt to attract resources into the community while limiting the extraction of resources (including information) from it. Ethnographic research in this context partakes of both sides of this dialectic: although they may recognize ethnography as a resource, local people also may view it as another form of exploitation to which they are subjected. The parallels between the kinds of observation and interrogation employed by both anthropologists and tax collectors serve to highlight this contradiction: though anthropologists may hope to make our work a resource to the local community, our research practice may require us to "see like a state" (J. Scott 1998), despite our best intentions.

The bright side of this situation, of course, is that despite their misgivings, many people were willing to take me on trust, to offer me a "just return" against the promise of some possible benefit to themselves in the long run and to offer me friendship and collaboration in my research endeavors. Despite the desconfianza that anthropologists encounter, most fieldwork experiences are also characterized by the formation of such warm and productive working relationships with a variety of people whom we call informants, consultants, or just friends. These people are willing to share with us the intimate details of their lives and struggles, hoping perhaps that in some way their collaboration with us will do more than merely advance anthropological knowledge. The present work, like so many others, would not have been possible without this generosity; I hope this book that Doña Lidia envisioned will serve to publicize the struggles of my friends in Villa Pagador. In this sense, the anthropologist, already perceived by many in the study community as some sort of agent of globalization, can serve to enhance the visibility of that community in the eyes of a wider, even a global audience.

2

Urbanism, Modernity, and
Migration in Cochabamba

At first glance, the city of Cochabamba appears to have been created without any intentionality whatsoever. The city's contradictions are everywhere and abundant, as a brief stroll along any of the downtown streets reveals. The streets themselves, for example, are narrow and clogged with buses, taxis, and private vehicles, their exhaust griming the façades of the two- and three-story buildings that line the streets of a grid laid out in the sixteenth century. But many of these streets, colonial-era holdovers never intended for automobile traffic, intersect others developed in the 1950s precisely to accommodate the heavy flow of vehicles required for the booming economy of a modern city. The extremely narrow sidewalks that at points disappear entirely into the sides of buildings are similarly "modern" in design, the barest of concessions to pedestrians in a downtown that was planned to segregate foot from vehicular traffic. Glittering shop fronts, their entryways decorated in brightly colored awnings and banners depicting popular Disney characters, stand incongruously alongside buildings constructed in the eighteenth and nineteenth centuries. On the Prado, a park-like boulevard that joins the city center with the suburban residential neighborhood of Cala Cala to the north, stand elegant homes built of concrete and glass, their gardens closed off from the street by high walls topped with razor wire and shards of broken bottles. But the Prado, though stately with age and importance, is of fairly recent vintage, a product of the first modernist push of the prerevolutionary era in Cochabamba. At the Burger

King on the Prado's northern end, Mitsubishi Monteros idle at the drive-through window, while women in traditional dress, their children held in *aguayos* across their backs, beg for coins from the passengers inside. The impression one gets is of a city striving for modernity but not quite achieving it. "My Cochabamba," sighs an architect friend of mine. "Mi ciudad híbrida." My hybrid city.

It is not just in the relatively prosperous city center that this incomplete modernity is evident. The battle for the future of Cochabamba is and for decades has been unfolding on the urban periphery, in that zone known to locals as the "margins" of the city proper. All around the city, thousands of migrant settlers have been setting up homes, schools, and churches, arriving from the countryside and from other cities throughout Bolivia and challenging the old order of Cochabamba, its sense of itself and its familiar urban landscape, by the transformations their presence has engendered. As one moves away from the downtown's tree-lined avenues and shaded sidewalks that were intended to identify Cochabamba as the "Garden City" of Bolivia, past the quiet residential suburbs with their high, white walls, tiled roofs, maids' quarters, and fenced gardens, out toward the urban periphery, one begins to catch glimpses of this other side of Cochabamba's contemporary urban problematic.

Board a local bus, for example, southbound out of the city. The "P" to Villa Sebastián Pagador stops at the corner of Lanza and Honduras, one block from the city's immense outdoor market called la Cancha, and a mass of people heading home from a day of buying or selling typically boards at that intersection. As the bus heads south out past the Cancha and around the boggy, algae-choked Laguna Alalay, the paved road gives way to cobblestones and then to dirt as the bus makes the turn toward Villa Pagador. Though this was once farmland, it is now a dry and barren dustbowl. What little greenery exists is found creeping up the steep sides of the gullies, carved by erosion from the hillside above the barrio, that slice maliciously across the unpaved roads. Houses here are made of adobe, sun-dried mud bricks of local manufacture. The flat roofs are covered in corrugated tin sheeting, and the house lots are surrounded by six-foot-high mud walls, their tops, like those of their more prosperous neighbors to the north, ringed with broken glass and jagged bits of metal to keep out intruders. The occasional pig or chicken can be seen foraging in the ravines or in the garbage along the roadside.

From the perspective of longtime resident cochabambinos, the peo-

4. Cochabamba, with a view toward the southwest. Photo by Lisa Berg

ple living in the old city center and its near-in suburbs, the migrant settlers of the periphery are a threat and an affront, intruders on Cochabamba's urban landscape, thieves of public land and destroyers of urban rationality. These migrants appropriated land not intended for urban development, and through patterns of illegal settlement intervened in the architects' efforts to transform Cochabamba into the imagined Garden City of Bolivia, a modernist utopia of ordered streets, shady parks, and stately homes. Instead of a garden, the migration boom of the second half of the twentieth century has created what from the planners' perspective is a sprawling urban jungle, crowded, dirty, and chaotic. The rationality of the planners' utopia has been disrupted by the brute realities of life in the marginal barrios, including the poverty and violence endemic to the periurban communities, and by the intrusion of their residents into the economy, politics, and society of the old downtown.

Of course, from the perspective of the migrant settlers things seem rather different. For these people the city has always been a hostile place, antagonistic to their desire to make a living and raise a family in peace. Having come to the city in search of economic opportunity and a better life, they found their ambitions thwarted at every turn. They have endured the neglect and then the harassment of the municipal bureaucracy, whose ceaseless norms and regulations make the basic privileges of citizenship unattainable. They have suffered the racism of urban dwellers, of city bureaucrats, of police and priests and teachers, all of whom seem to regard them as a variety of subhuman. And they have been victimized by the predations of violent criminals, who roam seemingly unchecked through the unlighted streets of their communities. The "modern" Cochabamba envisioned and partially implemented by the city's planners, politicians, and professional elites was never meant to include them, the squatters and settlers of the margins.

The experience of urbanization from the perspective of urban migrants themselves is the subject of chapter 3; the present chapter explores Cochabamba's urban history and the impact of migration on the city itself. In the introduction, I provided a brief survey of urbanism and the idea of the city in Latin American and Andean history. The dominant urbanistic themes traced therein—the city as the seat of civilization, of what the Spanish called policía, a combination of civic citizenship, order, cleanliness, and polite comportment, achievable only through urban living—are clearly exemplified in the history of Cochabamba that I present below. I focus on the city's latter-day transformations, particularly the migration boom of the second half of the twentieth century and the period of "urbanistic delirium" (Solares Serrano 1990: 346) that accompanied it, as a dedicated group of planners attempted to transform Cochabamba into a modernist urban utopia, only to meet with failure as their plans for orderly, rational development confronted the reality of massive in-migration of ex-peasants and ex-miners from the Bolivian altiplano. I then turn to a consideration of Cochabamba in the 1990s, as the attempt to create urban order through architecture and city planning gave way to an administrative approach to rationalizing the city and transforming illegal squatters into urban citizens. The attempt to establish order—and the way this attempt symbolized for many the struggle of light against darkness, rationality against chaos, civilization against barbarism—is the constant theme of this history.

MIGRATION AND URBAN FORMATION IN COCHABAMBA

In 1571 Francisco de Toledo, viceroy of Lima, granted the right to found a city in the agricultural high valleys of Alto Peru to Captain Gerónimo Osorio, who initiated construction and settlement of the Villa de Oropesa in 1574 (Urquidi 1949). The name of the town was soon changed to Cochabamba, the Spanish pronunciation of Qhochapampa, the original

Quechua name for the area, meaning "flood plain of the lake" or "flat area subject to flooding" (Guzman 1972). The city was founded in an area of extremely fertile and productive agricultural land at the eastern end of the Valle Bajo (Lower Valley) of Cochabamba department and provided the seat of Spanish control of the surrounding valley lands and pueblos. Situated at an altitude of 8,360 feet (2,550 meters), Cochabamba is nestled between the peaks of Tunari and the Cordillera Occidental to the north and west and the lower San Pedro chain to the east; to the south, the city is bordered by the lake known as Laguna Alalay and sheltered by small hills that form a corridor leading out to the towns and farmland of the higher Valle Alto. The entire Cochabamba valley was known for its rich soil, mild year-round climate, and rainfall adequate to the needs of its agrarian economy. In addition to the natural advantages of the site, the founding of Cochabamba was motivated by the presence of a sizable indigenous population to perform agricultural labor and provide tribute to the Spanish colonizers, the same criterion that guided the creation of other Latin American cities, including Puebla, Lima, and Arequipa (Hardoy 1975: 20). Laid out in a typical grid pattern based around a central square fronted by church and town hall, the city of Cochabamba at the time of its founding was a physical symbol of emerging Spanish domination in this rich agricultural region (Larson 1988: 76).

The department of Cochabamba in the seventeenth through the nineteenth centuries became the major grain-producing region of Bolivia, serving as a kind of breadbasket to the highland mining regions of the country. Production of maize and its elaboration into *chicha* (fermented corn beer) for local consumption as well as for export to the highland mining centers was a principal occupation of valley agriculture (Gordillo 1987). In addition, through the *mita* system imposed by the Spanish colonial regime, Cochabamba became a major supplier of forced peasant labor to work in the mines of Potosí (Larson 1988; Sánchez-Albornoz 1978). The city of Cochabamba itself served as administrative and mercantile center of the valley's political economy, supervising relations of production and distribution throughout its hinterland. Land in the Cochabamba valley was concentrated in large feudal landholdings, *haciendas* or *latifundias* owned by a white Creole oligarchy, many of whom maintained urban residences while their holdings were managed by mixed-race (*mestizo*) supervisors and worked by indigenous Quechua sharecroppers (Rivera 1992). As an urban center, Cochabamba experienced very slow growth throughout this period of

Map 1. Bolivia

almost three centuries, a period described as one of "provincial som-
nolescence" (Honorable Alcaldía Municipal [HAM] 1987), during which
time the city was "static, traditional and conservative, surrounded by
manorial haciendas" (Guzman 1972: 8).[1]

The public identity of the city changed little during this period. Despite the revolutions of the early part of the nineteenth century, which
culminated in the overthrow of Spanish colonial rule in 1825, Cochabamba maintained its role as agricultural center and marketing town
(Solares Serrano 1986). Unlike most other regions of Bolivia, where the
hacienda system went into decline after the revolution, the Cochabamba

valley saw a flourishing of haciendas under the control of a Creole aristocracy, helping Cochabamba to retain its prominence as agricultural supplier for much of the country, particularly to the mining centers of Oruro and Potosí (Klein 1992: 124). Though the second-largest city in Bolivia at the time of independence, Cochabamba had a small population of just over twenty thousand and continued to experience very slow growth for the remainder of the nineteenth and the first part of the twentieth centuries.

Until the mid- to late nineteenth century, small-scale commerce in agricultural products provided the economic mainstay of most urban residents. An important point of articulation between the city and its hinterland was the large and bustling *feria* or peasant market, known by its Quechua name, la Cancha.[2] Historically, the Cancha provided the space in which the city and the surrounding countryside met, as valley agriculturalists brought their goods to town to market them to the Creole and mestizo urbanites.[3] This became particularly important in the early twentieth century, as peasant smallholders (*piqueros*) began buying parcels of land and fragmenting the old haciendas of the central valleys (Larson 1998: 313). Many of those involved in marketing were themselves ex-peasants, men and women without adequate savings to enable them to purchase land and who had migrated to the city and entered the urban marketplace as a way to escape from the exploitive relations of production in the countryside (Rodríguez Ostria and Solares 1990). As the market grew in size and the diversity of items sold, a new class of dealers emerged to buy from the rural producers and to market their wares in the urban Cancha (Guzman 1972). Many of these marketpeople were indigenous or mestiza urban women, or *cholas,* who occupied this emerging economic niche as retail specialists in food products and other domestic goods.[4] Another key element of this commerce was the sale of chicha in the many locally owned brew shops, or *chicherias,* set up throughout the city, including many in the city's main Plaza Principal. Usually run by cholas, the chicherias were famous hives of revelry and drunkenness in the very heart of the city itself (Rodríguez Ostria and Solares 1990: 74). The demand for chicha further linked city to countryside, as hacendados and small-scale agriculturalists competed to provide the market with raw materials for chicha elaboration, and "mestiza entrepreneurs" established networks of supply and exchange with indigenous valley producers (Larson 1998: 364–365).

By the 1870s, the ruling elites of Cochabamba had begun to imagine a future for their city that would depart from its long-standing ties to the agrarian economy and society of the hinterland, envisioning for themselves a more refined and progressive city, predicated on a European model. Agriculture continued to serve as the economic basis for the Cochabamba valley, but the urban elites were expanding into more diversified commercial enterprises, especially banking and import/export commodities exchange with neighboring Chile and Peru. From the perspective of Cochabamba's white middle class, the bustling markets and chicherias, with their indigenous and cholo entrepreneurs, boisterous revelry, and decidedly "rural" aspect, were a grave problem for a city with incipient aspirations of modernity. Though the chicherias were patronized by a wide cross-section of Cochabamba society (including men of the white middle class), for an elite with the nascent goal of "europeanizing" (*europeizarse*) themselves and the city, both economically and culturally, the association of chicha, "the nectar of the valleys," with agrarian tradition was a drag on modernization, one that brought rural practices of sociality right into the city's Plaza Principal (Rodríguez Ostria and Solares 1990: 75). Public debate began to focus on questions of urban health and sanitation, with many in governmental and elite economic circles arguing that the city must be cleaned of the many contaminants that were making Cochabamba congested and unsanitary. As the city began to expand with the increasing commerce in the Cancha, many complained that the city lacked the infrastructure to provide water and sanitation services to its population. In addition, by the late nineteenth century the city was experiencing a number of disease epidemics, particularly typhoid and diphtheria. In the minds of many in Cochabamba at the time, the source of this disease was not the conditions in which people were living but the people themselves, indigenous and of rural origin, marketpeople and vendors of chicha. Seizing on a new diphtheria outbreak in 1878, the *sanitaristas* (members of the municipal elite bent on cleaning up the city) successfully lobbied the city government for the removal of the chicherias from the city's Plaza Principal, requiring them to relocate to a distance of at least four blocks from the center of town.

Over the next decade, subsequent disease epidemics provided the occasions for the further removal of chicherias from the city center, ultimately requiring them to set up shop on the urban periphery (compare with Albro 2000a). The effect of this displacement was to reconfigure the city center as exclusively a place for "modern" economic activity (i.e., banking, import/export, and marketing of imported manufactured goods), business conducted by the city's middle and upper classes and in service to these classes (a process that intensified with the arrival of the railroad to Oruro in 1892, which linked Cochabamba more closely to the highlands and the ports of Arica and Antofagasta beyond). The economic and sociospatial transformations that occurred "served to modify the daily life of the middle and upper classes and along with that, modified their conception of the traditional city, refuge of ancestral customs, habits and values, covering it with a varnish of 'modernity,' that began to be applied in the city center" (Rodríguez Ostria and Solares 1990: 79). Meanwhile, the southern zone of the city continued to grow in spite of, or in response to, the reinvention of the city center, as artisanal production expanded and commercial activity in the Cancha continued to flourish. At the same time, the chicherias, displaced to the urban periphery, served to "urbanize" the city's suburbs, drawing more people from the countryside into the orbit of the city itself.

The Beginnings of the Boom
The official population of the city of Cochabamba in 1900 numbered 21,866 people, inhabiting an area of the city later known as the Casco Viejo, the old city center (Escobar de Pabón and Ledo García 1988). The official limits of the city at this time did not extend beyond the zone delimited by the Plaza San Antonio to the south (site of the Cancha) and the Rio Rocha, a river that curves around the city center bounding it to the north and west. The city grew slowly during the first half of the century, and by 1950 the population had grown only to about eighty thousand. The Rio Rocha, prone to seasonal flooding, was channeled and bridged in the early 1950s, enabling the expansion of the city and the founding of the suburban zones of Cala Cala, Queru Queru, and La Recoleta to the north of the old city center. Between 1900 and 1950, the city experienced slow, tentacular growth to the north and south, facilitated by the arrival of motor vehicles and the expansion of the transport network, enabling automobile transit around the city (HAM 1987). During this period the city's northern zones became more closely integrated to the city center, providing residence to well-to-do urbanites. The southern zone of the city beyond the Cancha had experienced growth in the early part of the twentieth century following the relocation of the chicherias, and the expansion of artisanal activity and small industry beginning in the 1940s saw the establishment of some new neighbor-

hoods in this zone. None of the population counts from 1900 on made mention of the many rural migrants squatting around the urban periphery. Attracted to the city by the possibility of a life outside of agriculture, these people created an unregulated settlement (known locally as the Barrio Obrero, or workers' neighborhood) on the south side of town, whose existence was not officially recognized by the municipality.

The population growth of the city prior to 1950 can be attributed in large measure to the migration of peasants from the rural provinces and small towns of Cochabamba department to the departmental capital, seeking to integrate themselves with the growing industrial economy based in Cochabamba city (Centro de Estudios de Población [cep] n.d.). A significant moment in this process came with the cessation of hostilities in the Chaco War (1932–35) between Bolivia and Paraguay. Large numbers of discharged peasant soldiers returned from Bolivia's disastrous defeat in this conflict politically radicalized and critical of prevailing political and economic relations in the country (Arze Aguirre 1987; Farcau 1996; Rivera Cusicanqui 1986). Many of these former peasants determined not to return to their conditions of *pongueaje* (indentured servitude) in the countryside, entering instead into vertical clientelistic relationships with mestizo ex-combatants in towns and urban areas around the valley (like those in Ucureña described by Dandler [1969]). In what has been called "the first rural-urban migration" of the twentieth century in Cochabamba (Solares Serrano 1990: 309), many of these peasant ex-combatants came to the city to find employment and establish residence. The effect on Cochabamba was to precipitate a housing crisis in the city, as the new arrivals quickly filled up what hotels, lodgings, and rental properties existed. The influx of rural migrants was a shock to the established middle class of Cochabamba city, reflected in the words of one writer for the newspaper *El Imparcial*, who in 1935 editorialized, "A high percentage of indigenous people went to the war and came back from the Chaco, representing a most dangerous threat to social security" (cited in Solares Serrano 1990: 309). The fear of indigenous migration reflected in these few words would again appear with greater force during the postrevolution migration boom of the 1950s and 1960s. Many of these new arrivals set up temporary residences on the southeastern fringe of the city near the Barrio Obrero, where resided the poorer residents and workers who serviced the market economy of the city center.[5]

This first wave of migration of *ex-combatientes* into Cochabamba and the housing crisis it precipitated was to renew the process of self-reflection on the part of urban politicians, planners, and residents about the future of Cochabamba, invigorating a debate that many would attempt to resolve over the next several decades. In 1937, the main questions on the municipal agenda were how to incorporate the rapidly expanding suburban zones to the north of the city with the old city center, and how far, ultimately, to extend the limits of the city itself. Recognizing the need for a regulatory plan (*plano regulador*) to coordinate the growth of the city, the Municipal Council of Cochabamba invited Miguel Rodríguez, an architect from Argentina, to assess the needs of and to recommend plans for the expansion and modernization of Cochabamba. The plan Rodríguez proposed was focused mainly on the question of incorporating the northern residential zones into the city proper by extending existing streets from the city center northward and constructing two new diagonal streets (which together would comprise the Prado, or Av. Ballivián) connecting the suburban zones of Cala Cala and La Recoleta to Plaza Colón and Plaza 14 de Septiembre downtown. The guiding architectural theme of Rodríguez's proposals was that the old city center should serve as the "center of attraction" for the greater urban area, a central nucleus around which all the suburban areas (particularly to the north, northeast, and west of the city) would be articulated. The eastern part of the city Rodríguez deemed to be "of very little importance"; as for the southeastern zone, home to many of the poorest residents of Cochabamba, Rodríguez viewed it as a "veritable gypsy camp" that would require "the diligent attention" of the municipal authorities to impose "better organization and better physical and moral hygiene on these miserable people [*desgraciados*], who are packed into dense and dirty housing, with no other example [of how to live] than degeneration and vice" (quoted in Solares Serrano 1990: 360–361).

Creating the Rational City

Drawn plans have always been the best examples of operative cultural models. Behind their ostensible function as neutral registers of reality lies an ideological framework that validates and organizes that reality, authorizing all sorts of intellectual extrapolations on the model.—Angel Rama, *The Lettered City*

By the early 1940s it was clear to the political leaders of Cochabamba that their city was beginning to experience unprecedented growth and increasing complexity. The mounting presence in the city of indigenous ex-peasants, whose purportedly deficient physical and moral hygiene had long been confined to the countryside, now was perceived to threaten the already precarious health and well-being of urban Cochabamba. The unregulated construction and prolongation of streets throughout the city (in both poor and middle-class neighborhoods) seemed to be leading to the creation of a transportation system that lacked any centralized coordination, an arterial network with no "heart" to control the flows within it. Additionally, the lack of housing for the newly arrived indigenous ex-combatants and other urban migrants was creating a problem that would continue to plague Cochabamba's city fathers for decades to come: land speculation. In the absence of any formal mechanism for regulating the sale and development of open land in and around the city, by the early 1940s *loteadores* (land speculators) had begun to exploit this opportunity to get rich quick. Advertising the sale of lots in "modern urbanizations," the loteadores sold undeveloped parcels of land at astronomical prices, promising buyers that it was only a matter of time before city planners would provide them with the streets, parks, and urban services they required. The practices of the loteadores were creating "tiny but problematic urban islands amidst an agricultural sea" on the urban periphery (Solares Serrano 1990: 320), particularly to the south, which served to complicate further the city's attempts to plan for its own future and to define the limits of the city itself. Enriching themselves at the expense of the city's order and physical attractiveness, the loteadores were labeled (in the words of one local newspaper) "enemies of Cochabamba" (*El País* 24 February 1940; cited in Solares Serrano 1990: 370). However, given the high demand for housing by new arrivals to the city, many of whom were ignorant of the ways of the city and willing to pay any price to obtain a home, the activities of the loteadores proved extremely difficult to control.

Troubled by this unregulated urbanization that obeyed no scientific principles of planning or organization, the alcaldía and the city council set about legislating the urbanization of Cochabamba to control its growth and ensure the establishment of order in the city.[6] By 1946, city officials (under the leadership of architect Luis Muñoz Maluschka) had drafted the General Law of Urbanization, which defined urbanization as including the municipal administration of all city services, the improvement of hygiene in the city and the "sanitizing of its zones," and the technical reorganization of the municipal administration in charge of regulating construction and urban planning (Solares Serrano 1990: 389). The city government organized a team of architects to devise a technical plan to implement the requirements of the General Law of Urbanization. Coordinated through the Office of the Director of Municipal Public Works (which later became the Department of Urbanism and finally the Urbanism Service of the Honorable Municipality) and the city's Department of Architecture, this team labored through the second half of the decade of the 1940s to prepare a new governing Regulatory Plan, or Plano Regulador.[7] The strategy for urban growth and development laid out in the Plano Regulador was adopted by the municipal government upon its completion in 1950 (and updated in 1961 and again in 1985) and put into effect through a series of laws, ordinances, and programs designed to direct the future growth and composition of what planners called the "urban fabric" (*tejido urbano*) of the city.

Thus began in Cochabamba what Solares Serrano (1990: 220) has called "the arduous process of transforming the village [*aldea*] into a city and hacienda society into modern society." The person in charge of implementing this transformation (and more specifically with developing the Plano Regulador for Cochabamba) was an architect named Jorge Urquidi Zambrana (1986), a native cochabambino and a committed modernist whose goal for Cochabamba was "to rationally direct the growth of the city, in this new stage of its evolution" (16). Urquidi and his team (which included other young architects such as Gustavo Knaudt, Franklin Anaya, Daniel Bustos, and Hugo Ferrufino) were trained in modernist principles, having studied architecture at the Universidad de Chile and visited such modernist architectural shrines as Paris and Buenos Aires, and they approached the creation of a planned Cochabamba with a distinctly modernist agenda. For these architects and their political backers in the city's municipal council, the goal of urban planning was to create an efficient and industrious city, based on the modernist principle of functional segregation as a means to create order, balance, and economic productivity (Anaya 1947). In practical terms, this meant "zonification," the establishment of specific zones within the city for residence, recreation, administration, and economic activity, with the last divided into industrial, commercial, and artisanal subzones. The guiding metaphor was derived from the natural world: the city was to be conceptualized as "a living organism—understood in a completely biological sense—that contains and enables the harmonious development of the functions of collective life" (3). The health and well-being of this "organic reality" depended on its ability to perform all of its functions in a balanced and efficient manner, with each zone operating in harmony with every other, the totality integrated into a single functional system. To coordinate and execute such a complex and neatly balanced plan required strict adherence to the rules of "scientific urbanism." In the words of the alcalde of the time, Carlos D'Avis: "We want to open up the horizon of Cochabamba and envision for the future a prosperous and scientifically structured city. To do that . . . we will pursue the norms of the urbanistic sciences that are, without doubt, one of the disciplines that has benefited most from recent technological advances and that has been applied to the development of the great world centers" (quoted in Solares Serrano 1990: 391).

While obedient to the dominant modernist themes then prevalent in architectural and city-planning circles worldwide, Urquidi's team was also heavily influenced by the Garden City movement most associated with the work of Ebenezer Howard in Europe and Ernst Neufert in Latin America. An alternative to the highly centralized urban core so favored by other varieties of modernist planning (including that of Le Corbusier, though Howard's work preceded his by some twenty years), the Garden City was envisioned as small and decentralized. Consisting not just of suburban dormitories but of actual cities that contained all aspects of life—including work, residence, and recreation—required for the well-being of its residents, the Garden City would serve to draw people away from the congestion of the city center. However, the Garden City would be integrated as part of a larger system of other such urban units, the whole being linked together by a network of interconnected transport, such that the Garden City designation ultimately would be applied to this greater conurbation (P. Hall 1990: 87). The greater urban area would be surrounded by a permanent agricultural "greenbelt," which not only would provide the city with inexpensive fresh produce but also would serve as a kind of horizontal wall to heighten the sense of unity among residents of the Garden City, while bounding the urban settlement from the rural areas surrounding it (Mumford 1961: 516). Finally, urban growth required a public authority to manage and coordinate its many aspects, including control of land and regulation of construction to ward off rampant speculation (Howard 1902). For Howard, the main point was "to establish the possibility of a more organic method of city growth, which would reproduce, not unrelated fragments of urban order, but unified wholes" (Mumford 1961: 521).

The Cochabamba architects of the early 1940s sought to integrate elements of the Garden City approach with other modernist tenets deriving from Le Corbusier's Radiant City model (see Holston 1989). Their architectural schemes and innovations were encoded in the Plano Regulador and its accompanying Plan Regional, intended to govern and coordinate all aspects of urban expansion and development in the Cochabamba valley. From the Garden City model, Urquidi and his team derived the idea of a close integration between countryside and city that would also maintain a distinct division between these two zones. They also wanted to discourage centralization of population by fostering "balance" in the population distribution (*población equilibriada*) in the Cochabamba valley, to keep the city from growing too large at the expense of the rural hinterland (Urquidi Zambrana 1967: 23). To accomplish this, the plan proposed the creation of viable "satellite cities" in the immediate vicinity of Cochabamba that would serve as "population nuclei" adjacent to the metropolitan center; these satellites would include Quillacollo to the west, Sacaba to the east, and the farming community of Valle Hermoso to the southeast (40), future site of Villa Sebastián Pagador. Departing from the idea of a centralized downtown around which all urban activity would be articulated (a model proposed by the architect Rodríguez in 1937), Urquidi's team developed the idea of a "cellular organization" for the city, in which a thoroughly modern downtown "nucleus" would be surrounded by a series of "cells" or what the planners called "neighborhood units" (*unidades vecinales*), self-contained and self-sustaining communities of about fifteen thousand to twenty thousand inhabitants (Solares Serrano 1990: 397). These units would be arranged in three concentric rings around the city center, all of them articulated through a sophisticated urban transportation system that would unite them into a single "urban organism" (Urquidi Zambrana 1967: 49).[8] This system would benefit not just the city's inhabitants but urban society as a whole; according to one architect involved in the project, the cellular system would replace "the shacks and hovels, in which the race physically and morally deteriorates, with newly designed, pleasant and beautiful neighborhood units" (50).

It was in the old downtown area, the Casco Viejo of Cochabamba, that the modernist impulse of the design team became most apparent (Knaudt 1947). The old, narrow streets had to be widened and extended to permit the heavy flows of automobile traffic that the modern city required. The old one- and two-story buildings made of stone and earth, many of them dating back to the colonial era, had to be replaced with tall edifices of reinforced concrete, to provide residences and offices for the workers of the modern economy. The plan for the "urbanization of the Casco Viejo" reflected modernist principles in its intention to separate vehicular from pedestrian traffic in the downtown area: streets were to be categorized either as serving rapid, heavy flows of vehicular traffic or as "service streets" (*calles de servicio*) internal to the downtown area, and these streets were to have only very narrow sidewalks or none at all (Urquidi Zambrana 1967). Elsewhere, pedestrian walkways would be created to allow foot traffic in appropriate areas (e.g., in the downtown business district and the marketplace). Planners would also begin a district-by-district reconstruction process through the downtown, expropriating land and pulling down old buildings, replacing them with new, high-rise edifices. New housing construction in the city was to be in the chalet style, employing such modern construction materials as reinforced concrete, metals, and industrial ceramics, in place of traditional materials such as adobe, straw, and wood, which typified the do-it-yourself construction techniques (*autoconstrucción popular*) of the poor barrios (Solares Serrano 1990: 313).

At the same time, following the Garden City model, the planners sought to maintain and integrate nature within the city proper. Urquidi and his team devised plans for creating a green and park-like city, with broad, tree-lined boulevards and numerous public spaces to remain in a natural state for the recreational enjoyment of citizens. Construction of homes would follow this public example, with all new chalets to be built with large front yards and enclosed gardens (the *jardín interior*; Solares Serrano 1990: 311).[9] While bringing nature into the city, the plan also called for the maintenance of boundaries between the urban and the rural areas proper. The city itself (including its neighborhood cells and satellites) was to be surrounded by an agricultural belt, whose land was not to be expropriated or colonized for housing. Nature would be kept in its place: though it was not included as part of the Plano Regulador, Urquidi himself developed a proposal for the creation of the municipal Botanical Gardens on Cochabamba's northeast side, and later (in 1962) was a key proponent of the creation of Tunari national park, an area to remain in permanent forestation on the hills overlooking Cochabamba (Urquidi Zambrana 1999). As for the southern zone of the city, the Plano Regulador stated that the barrios in this part of the city "deserved special attention" under the Plan and would be "the beneficiaries of grand

5. Cochabamba, downtown. Photo by Lisa Berg

parks and services that would in the future transform their present condition" (Urquidi Zambrana 1967: 167). Such parks and green areas were deemed essential to a healthy, modern society: "The public green serves the exalted social function of promoting human sociality [*convivencia humana*] in an elevated and healthy manner, much like a tonic for physical and spiritual health" (154).

Ironically, decentralization of the city through implementation of the Plano Regulador and the Plan Regional required the creation of a centralized administrative bureaucracy (following prevailing tendencies toward centralization in Bolivian national politics; Klein 1969). Under the authority of architect Franklin Anaya, the city expanded the role of the Department of Land Registry (Catastro), to be set up "according to the European model" to enable property owners to register their land with the city by its size and value (Solares Serrano 1990: 388). A newly created Statistics Section within the Department, together with the Office of Control of Construction, would further enable the city to measure, record, tax, and regulate the ownership and use of urban land. Perhaps most significant was the effort to define areas of growth and settlement by setting legal limits to the officially designated urban area, the Radio Urbano, of Cochabamba. By limiting the areas that could be legally colonized and settled by new migrants to Cochabamba, the municipality hoped to be able to control and regulate new settlements and to protect the farmlands that surrounded the city, preserving them as areas of agricultural production (Urquidi Zambrana 1986). At the same time, the municipal government attempted to limit urbanization by establishing legal requirements of new settlements, demanding that land amounting to 39 percent of the total land area of the settlement be ceded to the alcaldía. These ceded lands (*áreas de cesión*) were to be given to the state to be used as "green areas" (*áreas verdes*), that is, as parks and recreation areas for the city's inhabitants, or as public spaces (*áreas públicos*) on which to locate schools, hospitals, or roadways.

Through the establishment of these norms for new settlements, the city hoped to be able to control its own growth, to dictate which areas of the city might be urbanized and to determine how much of those areas could be devoted to housing. Such an approach would serve not only to constrain rampant urbanization of the city's open spaces, but it would also place limits on the overall size of the urban population. Thus, while other Latin American cities seemed to be blindly stumbling into an era of unprecedented expansion, the urban planners of Cochabamba were positioning their city to respond to this impending growth in an orderly and systematic manner. It was with great optimism and self-confidence that the authors of the Plano Regulador set out to institute the "rational use" of resources and the "logical" growth of the city within the specified terrain of the Radio Urbano. Key to this agenda was controlling the establishment of new settlements, to balance the needs of the growing urban population with the economic and ecological requirements and possibilities of the Cochabamba valley.

MIGRATION AND CHAOS

"The practice of migration," notes Thierry Saignes (1995: 170), "is deeply rooted in Andean history." Nevertheless, the migration boom that followed the Bolivian national revolution of 1952 was without historical precedent.[10] The revolution against the old postcolonial order and the political and economic elites who controlled it transformed social relations in Bolivia, and in the years that followed the urban centers of Bolivia began to experience exponential growth. Between 1950 and 1976, the population of the city of Cochabamba more than doubled. According to the national census of 1976, the urban population of Cochabamba had by then grown to 204,684, from about 80,000 in 1950 (CEP 1993).

The nature of this population growth had changed along with the rate of growth: whereas prior to 1950 the greater part of the migrant population had been drawn from the rural areas of Cochabamba department itself, by 1976 the majority of migrants arriving in Cochabamba originated from Bolivia's altiplano departments of Potosí, Oruro, and La Paz (Águilo 1985). This trend continued throughout the 1980s and 1990s, and by 1992 the urban population of Cochabamba had reached 407,825. For the first time, the number of people living in urban areas of Cochabamba department (including the towns and provincial capitals) outnumbered those living in the countryside. Whereas in 1950 only 24 percent of the departmental population was urban, by 1992 52.26 percent of the departmental population was living in urban areas (Instituto Nacional de Estadística [INE] 1992). This trend continued into the twenty-first century, with 58.68 percent of the departmental population in 2001 residing in cities.[11] While Cochabamba today ranks as the third largest city in Bolivia (behind Santa Cruz and the national capital La Paz, with its neighbor El Alto), its rate of urbanization (3.64 percent per year between 1976 and 1992, increasing to 4.19 percent for the period 1992–2001; INE 2001) exceeds that of either of the two larger urban centers.[12]

This explosion in population movement to the cities of Bolivia over the last few decades of the twentieth century stemmed from a number of factors motivating migration out of the altiplano and toward Cochabamba, Santa Cruz, and other metropolitan areas. The peasant smallholders of the Bolivian altiplano had been hard hit by a severe drought lasting through much of the early 1980s, which, coupled with several devastating animal diseases affecting much of the livestock (mainly llamas and sheep) of the altiplano, jeopardized rural livelihoods. This ecological crisis coincided with a national economic crisis that lasted from the late 1970s through most of the 1980s, a crisis characterized by declining agricultural prices, skyrocketing inflation, and mounting international debt (Klein 1992: 271–272). Perhaps worst of all, the price of tin, long Bolivia's major export commodity, bottomed out in the mid-1980s, leaving the country with virtually no source of foreign currency (other than the coca leaf) for debt repayment. The federal government, under the regime of President Victor Paz Estenssoro and reacting to pressure from the United States to liberalize the Bolivian economy, responded in 1985 by instituting a new economic program which included a permanent closure of the nationally owned tin mines, putting thousands of miners out of work (Peñaloza Chej 1991). Many ex-miners came to Cochabamba; known as *relocalizados,* these workers and their families were "relocated" to the city as part of the Bolivian government's agreement (codified as part of Decreto Supremo 21060) with the miners union to provide for the displaced workers (Nash 1992; Taller de Información y Formación Académica y Popular [TIFAP] 1988). Additionally, many ex-peasants and urban dwellers from other parts of the country turned their sights on Cochabamba (Ledo García 1993, n.d.). As a city with a thriving informal economy centered on the small-scale commercial opportunities in the Cancha, artisanal and industrial work, and easy access to the coca fields of the lowland Chapare region (see Léons and Sanabria 1997), Cochabamba offered the promise of economic opportunity in a pleasing climate (Escobar de Pabón and Ledo García 1988).[13]

The Migrant Invasion
The migration boom that began in the 1950s posed an immediate challenge to the carefully laid schemes of Cochabamba's urban planners and their Plano Regulador. The first evidence that all would not go as planned came in the late 1950s, when, as mentioned above, the city began to experience a much greater influx of migrants from the altiplano. In the absence of affordable housing opportunities (what rental properties there were in the city center were beyond the means of most recent immigrants), people began to organize as settlers or renters unions (*sindicatos de inquilinos*) with the intent of securing permanent housing for their members, even if that meant colonizing land deemed "unurbanizable" by the alcaldía. Between 1955 and 1961, these renters unions initiated the first land invasions in the city. The land that these groups occupied—on two hills in the southern zone (Cerro San Miguel and Cerro Verde) overlooking the Laguna Alalay—had been designated as áreas verdes by the municipality, public land that was to be turned into parks and recreation areas or left unsettled as open, "natural" spaces. (Cerro San Miguel had been designated in the Plano Regulador of 1950 as an "area of arborization.") To the urban planners, such green or public areas were essential to the rational growth of the city, in that leaving such spaces unpopulated would serve to limit the number of people that could set up residence in a given area, thus controlling population growth. Such open areas would also provide for the pleasure of the city's inhabitants, as recreation areas and as places for the enjoyment of nature within the confines of the city. To the migrants confronting a grave housing shortage, such green areas represented vacant lots to

be used for residential development. Invasion of land and the "auto-construction" of housing soon followed (see Holston 1991a).

As discussed earlier, human out-of-placeness in the Andean city has often been understood in terms of a threat to the cleanliness and health of the city and its elite inhabitants, dirt and disease being the idioms through which fears about the violation of social, racial, and geographical order are expressed (Colloredo-Mansfeld 1998; Poole 1990b; Weismantel 2001). It is not surprising, then, that the irregular settlement patterns and colonization of the green areas by the migrants unions were viewed by the native Cochabamba population as a contaminating threat to the very life of the city itself. Press characterizations of the land colonizations at this time characterized migrants as a dirty and polluting influence and their unregulated settlement as an attack on the physical body of the city, leaving disease and destruction in their wake. "The green areas," read an unsigned editorial in the daily *Los Tiempos*, "apart from the recreative function that they serve, constitute the very lungs of the city and contribute to maintaining in great measure the ecological balance" of the urban environment ("Enajenación de áreas verdes en Cochabamba, 1" 1974).[14] Thus, the threat of the migrants' invasions was not only to urban order but to the very survival of the city: like bacteria invading a vulnerable host, the migrant groups were portrayed as contaminating Cochabamba with their unclean neighborhoods and irrational settlement patterns. Another unsigned editorial in *Los Tiempos*, describing the illegal settlements of the southeastern zone, depicted the fear of many native urban cochabambinos regarding these new settlements, again echoing the threat of pollution that the migrant settlers posed to municipal health but couched in the logic of orderly urban development: "Not only do [the illegal settlements] do irreparable damage to the city by causing the disappearance of important areas of reserve, but they will also lead to the presence of unhealthy and unattractive neighborhoods [*barrios insalubres y antiestéticos*], given that the topographic configuration of the areas in question poses insurmountable technical difficulties to the delivery of potable water and the removal of sewage and rainwater, creating the risk of gravely contaminating the Laguna Alalay" ("Urge la conservación de las áreas de reserva urbana" 1974).

The migrant settlers were painted as "bad citizens" and selfish violators of the public trust, thieves of public spaces and transgressors of urban rationality, turning parks and farmland into settlements for their own interests. Even the precious greenbelt, which in the Garden City model was supposed to permanently surround and define the urban nucleus, began to be colonized by settlers, who were being pushed ever further to the south and east in search of open areas on which to construct homes. The process of urban expansion and settlement, governed by its own laws of availability and obliging need rather than the bureaucratic rationality contained in the Plano Regulador, was characterized by government officials, media commentators, and native cochabambinos as "irrational," "anarchic," and "absurd," as well as deeply threatening to the city and its inhabitants (Urquidi Zambrana 1995; see Lobo 1982). Again, much of the blame was placed on migrants' colonizing of lands meant for use as green areas. In another article bearing the terrifying headline "Cochabamba Is Being Left without Lungs to Breathe" ("Gonzalo Terceros Rojas: Cochabamba se está quedando sin pulmones para respirar" 1993), the writer editorialized: "Although cochabambinos still call it 'the Garden City,' it is evident that Cochabamba is becoming less and less a garden and more a semi-desert." Emphasizing that this type of invasion posed a great threat to order and rational growth in the city, another editorial commented that with the municipal government's apparent inability to regulate this disorder, "what was in principle an anomaly seems to be becoming a norm, despite its illegality and irrationality. The most grave aspect of this is that this alienation of the municipal patrimony could continue until Cochabamba is left without a single public park" ("Enajenación de áreas verdes en Cochabamba, 2" 1974). The "savagery" of these land invasions was captured in a magazine article that described the invasion of Cerro San Miguel by a renters union as "an act of urbanistic cannibalism without parallel in the history of urban civilization" (Canata 1962, cited in Urquidi Zambrana 1967: 169).

The response of many native (i.e., nonmigrant) cochabambinos to the transformation of the city by migration was informed by a profound nostalgia, an imagined remembrance of Cochabamba's past in which life was simpler, quieter, more refined. As the pace of urbanization continued to quicken during the decades of the 1970s, 1980s, and into the 1990s, commentators reflecting on the past claimed to remember fondly the days when Cochabamba was a "great village" (gran aldea), a genteel community composed of urban elites, a kind of urban parallel to the stereotypical face-to-face rural hamlet or small town of the Bolivian countryside.[15] "The transformation of the old manorial city, residence

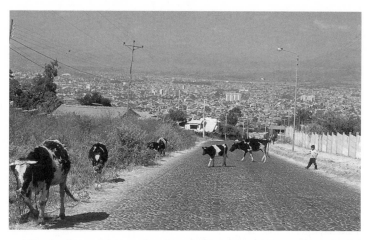

6. A boy herds cows along a city street on Cochabamba's periphery. Photo by Lisa Berg

of *latifundistas*, into the city of today," was a shock to the white upper-class elite, whose families had dominated Cochabamba for centuries (Solares Serrano 1986: 68). The idea of Cochabamba as the Garden City of Bolivia, though more a product of the architectural imaginings of the 1940s than a built urban reality, entered the discourse of urban elites at this time as a romantic ideal of the city's lost past, quickly becoming irretrievable as migration and illegal settlement escalated. At the same time, native cochabambinos began to decry the apparent failure of the municipal government to control the expansion of the city by urban migrants. This mixture of nostalgia and complaint is captured in the words of one newspaper columnist, who returned to Cochabamba after eight years of working abroad in the United States to find her native city "completely changed": "The Cochabamba of my childhood no longer exists. Instead what I encountered is a city in which growth has become a LIMITLESS URBAN EXPLOSION. A city that has grown and probably will continue growing, if care is not taken, with very little suitable Urban Design, with very little regulation or urban planning and I ask myself: Why? What has happened?" (Lopez G. de Page 1993; emphasis in original).

A significant factor compounding the danger that these migrants seemed to pose to Cochabamba was their cultural and linguistic difference from the native cochabambino elites expressing such fears. As discussed above, migration to Cochabamba prior to the 1950s had originated primarily from the Cochabamba valley itself, whose Quechua-speaking *valluno* population had much in common with the urban residents of Cochabamba (including shared ties of kinship, clientage, and fictive kinship). Upper-class cochabambinos were accustomed to dealing with Quechua vendors in the marketplace, having Quechua nannies for their children and Quechua gardeners for their chalets; indeed, many of the middle and upper classes spoke fluent or at least "market" Quechua, being but one or two generations removed from indigenous origins themselves. With the advent of altiplano migration, however, much of it from Aymara-speaking highland communities, the cultural identity of the city seemed to be under assault. Suddenly, women wearing derby hats and the long, multilayered skirts of the *pollera* (in contrast to the shorter polleras associated with the Quechua women of the valley) could be seen on every street corner, as Aymara market women began taking up places in the Cancha. Aymara could be heard on buses and in the market. The altiplano migrant represented a new kind of person with whom white Cochabamba had very little experience (see Albro 1998). Opposed to the stereotype of the Quechua person, who in the Bolivian racial imaginary is regarded as humble and servile, an Aymara stereotypically is viewed in Bolivia as inward-looking and reserved, tradition-bound and antimodern, tough and historically indomitable: "The Aymara were never conquered, not even by the Inca!" is a common claim. For many in Cochabamba, the arrival of this new kind of "uppity Indian" (Guss n.d.) posed a new kind of threat, not just to the health and well-being of the city but to its established racial hierarchy as well.

The pattern of public land invasions in Cochabamba hit its peak during the decades of the 1960s and 1970s. In addition, private sales of land in the agricultural greenbelt began to escalate, as peasant smallholders began to realize that they could earn more from the sale of their land outright than by keeping it in agricultural production. Extending a process that had begun in the 1940s, individual loteadores bought up sections of agricultural land, particularly in the southern and southeastern zones, and divided it into lots to sell illegally to immigrants who continued arriving from the altiplano. To make matters worse, the municipal government seemed incapable of regulating this process. Lacking the means to prohibit illegal land occupations, the municipal authorities were forced to acknowledge the new settlements, violating the terms of the Plano Regulador (which had been updated in 1961 precisely in response to such unregulated growth) by extending the officially recognized Radio Urbano to include new communities that continued to spring up around the city. Settled areas that had originally been part of the city's greenbelt were now incorporated into the city itself and subjected to municipal taxation and offered municipal service provision. The alcaldía hoped that by bringing these settlements into the official body of the city it could better prevent further illegal activities (especially further illegal land occupations) in those zones. To most observers, however, it appeared that the alcaldía had no control over the situation and could not protect the "municipal patrimony" of the city from alien invasion.

By the late 1970s it was clear to the alcaldía and to most observers that the growth of the city was proceeding without regulation by the municipal authorities. The Plano Regulador was declared obsolete by a number of these authorities for its inability to contend with these circumstances; responded the College of Architects, promoters of the original plan: "What is obsolete we believe is the mentality of those who denigrate the Plano Regulador without first proposing other, more efficacious means and instruments for the development of the city" ("El colegio de arquitectos de Cochabamba frente a las arbitrarias cesiones de parques públicos" 1980). Nevertheless, it was clear that the effort to produce an orderly "urban fabric" was a failure. The Plan Director de la Region Urbana of 1985, a successor to the Plano Regulador, attempted to address the "urban chaos" that had arisen from this settlement process, but was forced to admit that "45% of the urbanizations and subdivisions within the city escape municipal control" (HAM 1985: 4). Acknowledging its own failure, the alcaldía for the first time in the mid-1970s began to pursue a policy of exclusion rather than incorporation: instead of attempting to bring illegal settlements into the fold of the Radio Urbano (and hence subjecting them to municipal authority), many of these settlements were simply declared illegal or clandestine and excluded from the body of the city. That is to say, rather than being incorporated as part of the city, these illegal barrios were to be cut off, as the city tried simply to forget that these stains on the urban fabric even existed. These settlements now hovered outside of any type of municipal authority. In the southern zone of the city, where many of the most recent settlements were concentrated, a large sector of occupied land was declared a red zone (*zona roja*), an area composed entirely of illegal settlements. The red zone (which included much of Villa Sebastián Pagador) was considered "frozen" (*congelado*) by the alcaldía, its inhabitants denied even the opportunity to legalize their land claims. Unable to regulate the illegal settlements, the alcaldía closed its door on them, deciding to concentrate its efforts and its resources in the "legal," more established, and well-to-do zones of the city.

Though the public outcry against illegal settlement was deafening, in many ways the real victims of the illegal land transactions were the purchasers themselves, the migrant settlers of the city's periphery. The majority of these settlers knew little of the alcaldía's regulations governing land sales and had no conception of a green area, whose cession the alcaldía required to make the transaction legal. As a result, many were the unwitting victims of the land speculators' fraudulent activities and found themselves owners of illegal landholdings, title to which they were later unable to legalize (compare with Holston 1991b; Pezzoli 1987). Often, the loteadores promised the purchasers a future delivery of infrastructure and services, which they claimed the municipality would soon be providing; many loteadores skipped town following the sale, leaving the purchaser with nothing but empty promises. These transactions sowed the seeds of future conflicts between settlers and loteadores, and between settlers and the municipal authorities who, in the settlers' view, stood by and allowed such transactions to happen (see chapter 3). Today, many settlers express their rage and sense of powerlessness at being duped by the loteadores into purchasing land illegally and decry the state's failure to protect them from the consequences of its own regulations.

In reflecting on the failure of the city authorities to establish a regulatory plan that might actually have served to guide the development of Cochabamba, it is tempting to place the blame on the planners themselves for their lack of foresight and uncompromising dedication to a modernist agenda. Indeed, there is an element of truth to such accusations: uncritical descendants of Le Corbusier and his modernist philosophy of order, integration, separation of functions, and centralized planning and control, the Cochabamba architects were attempting to impose a master plan that did not coincide with the urban reality of Cochabamba and that was inflexible in responding to the demographic changes that the city was to experience. In many ways, the fault of the planners was in being almost perfect modernists, for their implementation of modernist architectural principles was a nearly textbook application of that school's agenda, whose full physical realization was to be found almost nowhere on earth outside of a few Latin American cities (Bullrich 1969: 35). At the same time, however, it is important to recognize that the architects and the politicians supporting them were products of their time and, as Solares Serrano (1990: 403) correctly observes, the plans they developed "in their own way expressed the anxieties about change in a city and society that for centuries had been a bulwark of tradition and centralized state authority." In countering these anxieties, the planners proceeded with the naïve hope that through the imposition of order and the implementation of a rational plan they could create not just a city, but a society characterized by wisdom, justice, and prosperity, with economic, residential, ecological, and infrastructural needs kept in perfect balance.

A NEW PLAN: THE TALLERES ZONALES

By the 1990s, the architectural impulse to produce an ordered city through physical design of the urban environment had failed. After decades of illegal land sales and settlement, the "urban fabric" of the city was more disordered than ever, and the exclusionary politics that the city had adopted in response had created a vast zone of unregulated, illegal settlements on the south side over which the public authorities held virtually no control. Indeed, by 1993 fully 80 percent of all the peripheral barrios were categorized as clandestine or illegal, a figure that encompassed 40 percent of the total urban population ("80% de urbanizaciones periféricas son clandestinas, reconoce Concejo" 1993). By ignoring the legal requirements of urbanization, migrants themselves had taken control of the urban development process, defying the municipality's efforts at regulation. Unable to extract cessions of land, to tax property, or to put its seal of approval on land transactions, the alcaldía was left entirely out of the process and thus could not establish its own authority in the new communities. The unintended consequence of excluding these neighborhoods from membership in the city had been to prevent the state from penetrating and controlling the excluded barrios.

Despite the failure of the architectural approach, the "administrative impulse" (Orlove 1993) to create order remained a powerful driving force for municipal planners and politicians, now operating within the economic and political constraints of late twentieth-century Bolivia.

Migration to Cochabamba from the altiplano had continued at a prodigious rate, escalating after the imposition of neoliberal structural adjustment reforms in the mid-1980s. These economic reforms, which entailed a large-scale retrenchment of state investment in national industry and an opening of the economy to global capital, coincided with an emerging project for political reform focused on decentralizing the national state, which since 1952 had been characterized by a highly centralized administrative authority (Malloy 1989). In 1993, Gonzalo Sanchez de Lozada ("Goni") was elected to the Bolivian presidency on a promise of governmental reform, particularly with the intention of promoting broader political representation and citizen involvement in government. Breaking with the long-standing centrifugal tendencies in Bolivian politics (Klein 1969), in 1994 Goni's administration introduced the Law of Popular Participation, or Participación Popular, to accomplish this objective. Participación Popular required that inefficient, centralized decision making and governmental authority be broadened to incorporate the citizenry at large, who would be involved in determining key issues related to their own development (Secretaria Nacional de Participación Popular 1995). The plan called for the creation of a new stratum of elected political leadership at the local level, recasting rural and urban communities alike as Organizaciones Territoriales de Base (OTBs) in charge of local decision making and development. Rather than a top-down distribution of state resources, development monies would be given directly to these groups, which would administer them through a local Oversight Committee (Comité de Vigilancia). Thus, by fulfilling a series of procedural requirements mandated by the state (see Bigenho 1999), local neighborhood organizations (*juntas vecinales*) in both rural and urban areas could recast themselves as OTBs and receive money directly from the state to carry out their own initiatives. In this way, Participación Popular enabled the national state to identify and regulate local base communities by determining the form such communities must take and the means by which they must operate (Kohl 2003; Van Cott 2000). The plan also expanded the autonomy of local, particularly rural, communities, while drawing resources and authority away from centralized governmental (and typically urban municipal) structures (Medeiros 2001).

In 1993, Manfred Reyes Villa of the Movimiento Bolivia Libre (MBL) Party was elected mayor of Cochabamba. Manfred, as he is popularly known (he also sports the sobriquet "Bombón" [bonbon], "because he's so sweet," people wisecrack), came to power on a platform promising to address the problems of the peripheral barrios of the city by reversing the policies of exclusion adopted by previous administrations. In particular, Manfred pledged to preserve the natural environment and to control the chaotic patterns of land colonization in the agricultural zones bordering the limits of the city ("Reyes Villa proclamó política urbana para una defensa del medio ambiente" 1993). Key to Manfred's plan for asserting municipal control over its chaotic periphery was to decentralize the alcaldía, in an effort to extend the reach of the municipality into the barrios themselves through a system of *subalcaldías*. Only by establishing a local presence in the barrios and working directly with barrio residents, Manfred suggested, could the alcaldía hope to bring those communities under its authority. As one municipal official put it: "We have seen that the Alcaldía can't close its eyes to this brute reality. The Alcaldía must intervene in these barrios in order to regularize [*regularizar*] them. It has to incorporate them, to integrate them to the city, and that presupposes that the Alcaldía must open regional offices, to relocate technical teams to be able to elaborate new plans according to the reality of the situation" ("El 40% de la población está asentada en barrios clandestinos" 1993).

Decentralization of the alcaldía and "regularization" (i.e., legalization) of individual land holdings became a priority of the municipal government under Manfred. Only in this way, his administration asserted, could the chaos of the periphery be transformed into the good working order that is essential to a government's control of its population. In the words of the new Director of Urbanism, Oscar Terceros: "Facing the chaotic and disordered growth of the city of Cochabamba, it is necessary to elaborate a strategy of urban development with a vision towards the 21st century, and a goal of standardizing a process of systematic and ordered growth. . . . One of the priorities will be to introduce a dedicated support system to the marginal barrios in order to proceed with the regularization of the clandestine dwellings and the ordering of the streets and roadways" ("Urbanismo evitará loteamiento de áreas verdes" 1993). This direct approach to confronting the problem of the barrios was a distinct change from the policy of the preceding administrations, whose exclusion and neglect of the marginal communities was motivated by a frustration with failures to prevent illegal colonization and housing construction. It also reflected a new strategy for achieving the goals of order and rationality contained in the Plano Regulador, of "regularizing" or normativizing both the physical structures of the city and its inhabitants. Illegal landholdings would be transformed into orderly, legally sanctioned land titles through an official process of bureaucratic rationalization. At the same time, by undergoing this rationalizing process, landholders themselves would be transformed from illegal squatters into legitimate and fully recognized municipal citizens. In addition to the benefits it would bring to the municipality, such a plan accorded well with the national government's move (through Participación Popular) toward decentralization and citizen involvement in decision making at all levels. Before one could have citizen involvement, after all, one needed citizens.

To accomplish this decentralization of the alcaldía to pursue the goals of regularizing the illegal barrios and rationalizing their inhabitants, in 1993 Manfred and his political ally Gonzalo "Chaly" Terceros, president of the city council, revived an experimental system of sub-alcaldías called the Talleres Zonales (Zonal Workshops) and placed them under the direction of a new municipal department, the Office of Barrio Management (Dirección de Gestión Barrial) ("Concejo creará dirección municipal para atender las zonas periurbanas" 1994). Chaly Terceros's brother Oscar was named to head this new department. The system of Talleres Zonales had first been created in 1990 by a group of architects from the local university, working through the municipality as city planners. These architects had designed an experimental project that attempted to address the problems created by the overly centralized and bureaucratized system of municipal government, which had failed to manage urban migration and expansion. The Talleres Zonales were based in six different marginal barrios deemed most in need of the services of the alcaldía, because they had the highest concentration of illegal settlements in the city and thus were most in need of assistance in legalizing their land claims. By bringing the administrative and technical services of the alcaldía into the barrios themselves, the municipal government hoped to find a new way of regulating the clandestine barrios of the city by doing away with the top-down system of planning and governance that had been in place since the adoption of the Plano Regulador and its accompanying legislation in the 1950s. It was also hoped by some of the more socially and politically progressive people in the alcaldía that this system would help to bring new infrastructure and attention to the needs of the people living in some of the poorest zones of the city (Dominguez 1994). The barrio of Villa Sebastián Pagador was chosen as the site of the first of these experimental Talleres.

In many ways, the Talleres Zonales project was a radical break with the urban politics of the past. Rather than a top-down system of administration, which had attempted unsuccessfully to impose its regulatory norms on the people of the barrios, the Talleres Zonales aimed to enlist the participation of the local population in the process of community development and land legalization. In this way, it was hoped, both the alcaldía and the marginal barrios could benefit, the alcaldía by establishing legitimate authority in the marginal barrios and transforming lawless squatters into honest taxpayers, and the people by having access to the means of land legalization and a mechanism to organize and work for urban development. The "Talleres Zonales approach" was described in this way:

> For the municipality the Talleres Zonales are technical offices of participatory planning at the micro level. They should be decentralized to have better control of the illegal settlements and to protect the permanent deterioration of the environment.
>
> For the people the Talleres Zonales are technical, social, legal and administrative tools that the municipality provides so the population can use their rights of control and participation in the municipal government. The organized participation of the people should make possible
>
> – the reinforcement of grass roots organizations that have been losing their representativeness
> – a local urban planning that gives better answers to the needs of the people. (Dominguez 1994: 86)

To accomplish these ambitious goals, each Taller Zonal was organized into five commissions, each one dealing with a different area of concern to the alcaldía and the people of the barrio and each conceptualized in terms of the rights of municipal and national citizens. These five commissions (as spelled out in a pamphlet distributed to the community by the Taller Zonal) were legal issues ("Know your rights and obligations"); infrastructure ("Plan—to advance"); health and human services ("Health—another of your rights"); education and culture ("Education is another right"); and ecology and forestation ("Concerned citizen, take care of your environment—Plant a tree!"). In addition, a Zonal Council (Consejo Zonal) was organized in the community, whose membership consisted of both barrio representatives and city officials. Consciousness raising and "consolidation of democracy" (Dominguez 1994: 86) through "popular participation" in the barrios were important goals of the Talleres Zonales' idealistic planners. Both the language and the intent of the project signaled it as a precursor to the reforms that would be inaugurated a few years later on the national level, with the advent of Goni's Participación Popular.[16]

This nascent idealism, however, may have been the Taller Zonal's undoing. The attempt to transform the institutionalized means of urban governance through such a radical and sudden change created a stir within the entrenched municipal bureaucracy. After less than a year of operation the Talleres Zonales project began to encounter political resistance within the alcaldía itself, and mounting conflicts over the purposes and management of the project resulted in its suspension in 1991. In 1993, following his election as alcalde, Manfred Reyes Villa reinstituted the Talleres Zonales, renamed the Casas Comunales (Communal Houses), as a means of accomplishing his goal of decentralizing the alcaldía, extending municipal services to the urban periphery, and incorporating the marginal barrios into the city, while responding to the national political movement toward decentralization instigated by the Law of Popular Participation. Manfred declared the southern red zone "unfrozen," once again opening the alcaldía's doors to the marginal barrios, and provided the Casas Comunales as the instrument by which the residents of these barrios could put their papers in order and legalize their land claims.

In the initial stages of this second life of the project, the Casas Comunales seemed to be organized with the same noble intent as their predecessor, the Talleres Zonales. The alcaldía seemed to be in transition from the centralized bureaucracy of the past to a system of governance more integrated within the neighborhoods of the city and more responsive to the needs of the population. The municipality also began to express an interest in building up, rather than undermining, local forms of political action and organization, encouraging the formation of groups that it hoped to enlist as participants in the process of urban development. In announcing the reestablishment of the Talleres Zonales/Casas Comunales system, Director of Urbanism Oscar Terceros observed, "The Talleres Zonales represent not only a factor in decentralization, but also the possibility of participation of the citizenry and strengthening of neighborhood organizations. . . . Emphasis is being placed on the training and organization of the people 'so that they will realize that they are actors in their own development' " ("Oscar Terceros: 'Antes que sea tarde debemos reconducir el desarrollo urbano' " 1993).

For the municipal planners and participants in the project, these early years of the Talleres Zonales/Casas Comunales were incredibly exciting. Trained as architects but with a knowledge of history, sociology, and political philosophy and a rather uncharacteristic (for bureaucrats) ethic of social responsibility, the men and women in charge of creating and staffing this new system were part of a new generation of architects, critical of modernist theses of urban planning and the Plano Regulador. These officials were young and enthusiastic about transforming the system of urban governance under the leadership of the young and dynamic mayor, Manfred Reyes.[17] The Casa Comunal architects (many of whom I came to know personally and who shared with me their memories and writings of this period) saw themselves as dedicated not only to improving the living conditions of the city's poor, but to helping these people to become full citizens and active participants in their own economic, social, and political development. This type of training (*capacitación*) and consciousness raising (*concientización*) was seen by the architects as transformative for the migrant residents of the barrios, who had previously labored under the idea that they were not full citizens, having long been defined as illegal and excluded from or ignored by the municipality. (Barrio residents dispute this interpretation of their consciousness, as discussed in chapter 3.) Becoming a citizen, however, meant legalizing one's land claim and receiving the official approval from the alcaldía recognizing the legality of one's property holding and thus one's right to inhabit the city. This recognition would come in the form of the approved plan, or *plano aprobado*, a drawing of one's property made by an architect and stamped by the alcaldía. For the Casa Comunal architects, the plano aprobado was an icon of legitimacy, physical proof that they could give to the illegal barrio residents to indicate that they had, indeed, become citizens of the municipality. Remembers one of the architects who worked in Villa Pagador on the city's far southeast side:

> In that space of preparation that was given them, we made them see that they were as much citizens as those who live in the city center.

Because they paid their taxes just the same, they were supporting the development of their region just the same, even though they were migrants, no? Because before that they always believed themselves to be marginalized, or that they shouldn't ask for anything, that they should always be quiet. But after we came in they realized that it wasn't like that, that they had rights, too, because they were citizens. And the thing that most made them citizens was the plano aprobado from the alcaldía of Cochabamba. Because that permitted them to say "I live in Cochabamba, and this is my plan approved by the alcaldía."

Once again, however, it was the political radicalism and philosophical idealism of the Casa Comunal architects that led to the project's downfall. The alcaldía, which had originally expressed great interest in capacitación of barrio residents to organize and participate in their own development, began to fear that such an approach would undermine its ability to control the marginal populations. Having finally been able to establish a foothold in the barrios through the regularization requirements and the approved plan, the alcaldía no longer desired the creation of a population who would be participants in the development process and so make demands of the municipality. Retreating from the social component of the program, the Casa Comunal system began to emphasize the legal, bureaucratic elements of its function, fulfilling the requirements of Participación Popular by decentralizing local political decision making while at the same time maintaining control of the system through its monopolization of the land legalization process. The work of the Casa Comunal shifted to focus almost exclusively on helping residents comply with the regulatory requirements for legalizing their land claims. The five social commissions no longer met, and city officials no longer sat as representatives to the Zonal Council, leaving that institution solely to the barrio residents themselves. Most of the original architects in Villa Pagador were fired or transferred to other districts, and the architect who took over the directorship of the Casa Comunal was a pure technocrat with no social vision. The architect quoted above, who took such pride in the work of the Taller Zonal in teaching the residents of Villa Pagador to demand their rights as citizens, was transferred to another office in another barrio and buried in paperwork to manage the steady flow of legalization procedures submitted by residents. This architect views this change of emphasis by the alcaldía as a deliberate attempt to reverse the process of capacitación initiated by the Talleres Zonales:

> DANIEL: Do you believe that the alcaldía doesn't want the people to be so prepared, so active, to complain so much?
> ARCHITECT: Well (laughs). If I told you the opposite I would perhaps be lying to you, no? I think that no governmental institution, none, is interested in having its bases or its people or its citizens demand too much of it.

CONCLUSION

The Casas Comunales became the Casas Municipales in 1996, a change of name (from "Communal Houses" to "Municipal Houses") that reflects their distancing from a progressive agenda toward an increased bureaucratization of their function. The system has expanded to include fourteen different Casas in as many districts of the city and is regarded by the alcaldía as one of its most effective instruments for governing the previously unregulated urban periphery. At its most effective, the Casa Municipal system has begun to accomplish what decades of urban planning and design could not: the production of an orderly urban fabric in Cochabamba. Though illegal settlement continues to be rampant on the margins of the city, increasingly the residents of these settlements are being remade as citizens through the imposition of regulatory norms on land sales and home construction in the barrios. Principally, this has been accomplished through the land legalization process, which requires each barrio resident to go through a number of bureaucratic steps to receive approval from the city. Residents desiring legalization must pay an architect to draw up a diagram of their lot, indicating that their land and the buildings on it meet the city's requirements for a legal residence (buildings have to be of a certain size, situated a certain number of meters back from the street; each lot must be surrounded by a wall indicating its boundaries; construction materials are specified, and so on). They must pay all the back taxes owed on the land, which can go back quite a few years given the long "frozen" period during which people were unable to legalize their holdings. They must verify that an appropriate cession of land has been made to the alcaldía for use as an área verde. And they must file endless reams of paperwork, getting the official stamps and seals on all their documents. Only then can the resident receive the plano aprobado from the city, proving that he or she is, in fact, a landowner and a homeowner. The value of this plano aprobado in the eyes of barrio residents themselves—a key to understanding why this regulatory system has experienced success in the marginal barrios—is discussed fully in the next chapter.

For the municipality, land legalization through the plano aprobado is an instrument of urban governmentality, a way for the alcaldía to assert its control over the marginal barrios by making good citizens out of illegal settlers, using the bureaucratic process as a means to transform the chaos produced through haphazard settlement patterns into good administrative order. By setting up the Casa Comunal as a means to provide access to the legalization procedure, the alcaldía could insert itself into the land sale and settlement process, thus giving it a means to establish its legitimate authority in the barrios. By granting the approved plan to residents who complied with the norms of the state, the alcaldía was able to become a player in the urbanization process from which it had long been excluded. At the same time, through the direct ministrations of the Casa Comunal, the alcaldía could claim to be promoting the interests of decentralization and democratization, as prescribed by the national government's program of Popular Participation.

Both the Casa Comunal system at the municipal level and the Law of Popular Participation at the national level represent efforts to rationalize, order, and render legible a Bolivian population that for decades had proven ungovernable through centralized programs of urban design and political authority. In an apparent contradiction, by decentralizing state authority the Bolivian government seems to have created a more effective system for extending state control. This has certainly been the case in the Bolivian countryside, where rural political organization is being transformed through Popular Participation. During fieldwork in rural Cochabamba, for example, Carmen Medeiros (2001: 413) observed "how the application of LPP [the Law of Popular Participation] entailed the official registration of even the most remote rural communities; the identification of places that did not appear on the maps, municipalities whose boundaries were undefined, and individuals who had never been counted on any census. Today, regional and national state agencies have official listings, bookkeeping, and development plans that further the management of the state's territory and its peoples."

Similar processes have occurred in the cities of Bolivia. In the name of expanding citizen participation in government, chaotic urban communities have been reorganized as OTBS, with Zonal Councils and Oversight Committees, their structure, organization, and composition transformed through the process of receiving official recognition (see Bigenho 1999). Illegal squatters themselves are remade as citizens, transformed through the land legalization process into landowners and taxpayers. The "arts of governmentality" (Foucault 1991) involved in this transformation are subtle, operating at the level of daily routine and bureaucratic ministration, part of what Gil Joseph and Daniel Nugent (1994) call the "everyday forms of state formation." Though apparently reducing its own role in managing the lives and fortunes of its citizens, the state in this process effects a more complete saturation of life in domains that previously it had been unable to regulate. In Bolivia, as the adoption of neoliberal policies reduces state responsibility for the social welfare of citizens, the effects of this process are unmistakable and ironic: "In the movement of shrinking its responsibilities and enlarging civil society participation, the state ended up enlarging the sphere of its hegemonic control" (Medeiros 2001: 413).

Of course, political projects of this sort are never complete, and the effects they produce are contradictory and fleeting. The contradictions engendered by Popular Participation and the Casa Municipal system represent moments of success for the state and municipal authorities in their ongoing quest to establish order and sovereignty in the chaotic spaces of the urban margins. The responses of the marginal citizens themselves to this process are another subject of consideration. This chapter has told the story from the perspective of the authorities and the dominant social factions they represent, focusing on the official concern for creating order and a rational, manageable population on the urban periphery. The next chapter tells the other side of this story, narrating the experience of urbanization and migration from the viewpoint of the migrant settlers themselves, focusing on the formation of Villa Sebastián Pagador on the southeastern fringe of Cochabamba. The efforts of urban migrants to contend with the politics of exclusion and incorporation are the focus of this analysis.

3

Villa Sebastián Pagador and
the Politics of Community

There is a particular variety of experience that people in Cochabamba (as elsewhere in Latin America) call the *trámite,* and understanding it helps us to understand a bit better what life is like in the ever-expanding city. It also helps us to understand the relationship of the city—particularly the city government, its policies, practices, and ideologies—to the people of the urban periphery.

A trámite is translatable into English as a bureaucratic procedure or business transaction, but such a simple rendering omits the arduousness of the experience, the sense of an ordeal undertaken at great personal cost. Think about going to the Department of Motor Vehicles in the United States and you get the idea: a necessary, unavoidable bureaucratic hassle that you have to face if you want to function as a legal and legitimate member of society, but nonetheless an enormous drain on your time, energy, and resources.[1] On the urban periphery of Cochabamba, even the most simple engagement with the state is a trámite of this order. As the federal and municipal bureaucracies traditionally have been centralized in large downtown offices, transacting any kind of official business often means a long and costly trip to the city center from the margins. If you want to enroll your child in school, you have to stand in line for the better part of a day at the Ministry of Education with hundreds of other nervous parents, to hand in your application, pay your fee, and demonstrate proof of your offspring's age and residence. Paying your taxes involves a similar wait at the offices of the Finance Ministry. More complex procedures such as the regularization of a land title or acquisition of a building permit entail even more time and money, typically involving multiple trips downtown to visit several different offices, each visit requiring a disbursal of funds and the acquisition of stamps, permits, and other forms of official license. For such complicated transactions, the middle-class citizen might send an *empleada* (servant) to make the rounds of the bureaucracy in his stead or hire a professional *tramitista* skilled in the intricacies of the procedural requirements. But for the majority of urban residents, particularly for the residents of the marginal barrios, such options are not available, and people must contend with the bureaucracy on their own, lacking the material and cultural capital to expedite success. The instructions offered by service providers are typically unclear, the attitudes of the bureaucrats toward their indigenous or cholo clientele are generally frosty, and mistakes are commonly made, requiring even more trips downtown and even greater disbursal of funds (see Luykx 1999: 11). The process can become particularly thorny when the transaction in question is something like a land claim, as a rural migrant attempts to achieve official recognition of his or her right to be in the city.

A SPECTACULAR GENEALOGY

The arrival of the Casa Comunal into the marginal barrios of Cochabamba's southern zone in the 1990s altered the procedural dimensions of this microphysics of power by decentralizing state authority and repackaging it in a seemingly more user-friendly mode. With the Casa Comunal in place, clients of the state no longer had to travel to the city center to process their trámites, a remarkably important savings of time and money for people who lack the luxury of either.[2] Instead of dealing with hostile, unfamiliar faces, petitioners coming to the Casa Comunal could meet with municipal employees with whom they had established relationships: the architect who processed their paperwork for a land legalization claim was the same individual who had surveyed their lot and instructed them on changes that would need to be made to bring their dwelling up to code, who advised them on tax payment and made sure their permits were in order. In the case of Villa Pagador, these architects were highly trained and, for the most part, caring, sympathetic people who took a genuine interest in the plight of their clients, for whom lack of a legal title meant a host of financial burdens. In their homely one-room office in the corner of the barrio marketplace, the architects met with barrio residents to dispense advice and offer help in navigating the intricacies of the municipal bureaucracy, interpreting for their often illiterate and sometimes monolingual Quechua- or Aymara-speaking clientele the state norms and regulations that governed property ownership, house construction, and tax payment in the city. During the time of my fieldwork, these architects and bureaucrats were even engaged in the cultural life of the community, marching at the head of the barrio's anniversary parade on 10 February, carrying the banner of the Casa Comunal and waving to the crowds, or serving as judges of the dance competition in the San Miguel fiesta (see chapter 4). For the people of Villa Pagador, the Casa Comunal personnel and the services they offered were a distinct change for the better from the former system of centralized bureaucracy in the old downtown. It is perhaps not surprising, then, that pagadoreños today seem to regard the Casa Comunal as something like a friend in the land legalization and citizen-making process, despite the obvious irony that the Casa Comunal itself is a direct extension of the municipality, whose long period of neglect and subsequent labyrinthine requirements for legalization have imposed these hardships on barrio residents in the first place.

Another reason for pagadoreños' warm welcome of and proprietary interest in the Casa Comunal lies in the peculiarities of the community's own local history vis-à-vis the city's famously centralized administrative authority. Pushed to the very fringes of the city in their search for a space to create a community, the group of settlers who founded Villa Pagador was forced to locate the new barrio on the outskirts of town, at a distance of five kilometers beyond the city's southern limit. But this distance had the consequence, intended or not, of providing a kind of buffer between the barrio and the downtown municipal authorities. Far from the everyday scrutiny of the municipal government and the state (whose attention was firmly fixed on the problems of the old city center and its wealthier suburbs), Villa Pagador was left to go its own way in relative autonomy. This created a space in which the founders and leaders of the community could pursue their own agenda for community formation and development, producing through their active leadership an infrastructure and a public identity for the new barrio. But, as this chapter details, this autonomous space of community leadership soon led to problems in Villa Pagador, as the barrio continued to grow with the arrival of new migrants to the area. As the original founders and leaders of the barrio took for themselves increasing levels of power in the community, and as growth of the barrio produced socioeconomic diversity within the community itself, tensions arose around the emerging inequalities and the concentrated political power of the barrio leadership. To counter this, barrio residents dissatisfied with the domination of the local leadership began to look to the municipal and state authorities for assistance in breaking these leaders' hold on the community. The arrival of the Casa Comunal in Villa Pagador thus produced disruptions in the barrio's political status quo by extending formal municipal authority into the community and providing an alternative to the networks of obligation and indebtedness through which the local leaders secured their authority.

The previous chapter told the story of city-community relations through the lens of urban Cochabamba, looking from the downtown out to the margins; the present chapter inverts this perspective by situating the narrative gaze in the marginal barrio, looking back toward the city. Telling the story of urbanization from the barrio perspective recenters the story around Villa Pagador itself, thereby demarginalizing the margins by giving them center stage in the narrative of urban history.[3] And this history, in a sense, can be read as a kind of spectacular genealogy (Albro 2002), in which long periods of conflict and consensus building, unfolding continuously behind the scenes of local life, are punctuated by moments of elaborate, choreographed public display. These moments are what stand out in people's memories and constitute the stories they tell on reflection: the petitioning of the mayor for the barrio's original land grant, the creation of the barrio school, the negotiations with the World Bank to help the barrio establish its own water system. These events and others represent points of communal engagement for barrio residents, who, despite their many differences and conflicts with one another over the years, remember with pride and bitterness, anger and amusement, the spectacular moments of their collective experience. Understanding this spectacular genealogy provides us a position from which to view the complex and meaning-laden collective displays described in subsequent chapters.

The Politics of Community
In the account that follows, the idea of community emerges as a central trope in local people's discourse about what Villa Pagador has been in the past and should become in the future. People who participated in the founding and initial settlement of Villa Pagador remember the barrio as a face-to-face community in the classic ethnological sense, with individuals unified by their shared altiplano (and specifically Oruro) origins, capable of working collectively to achieve common goals. Particularly important is the extent to which barrio leaders and residents deployed the rhetoric of community to create change in the barrio itself: by organizing collective solidarity, barrio leaders were able not only to harness this solidarity as a force for achieving self-help development initiatives in the barrio itself, but they were also able to use the reputation of Villa Pagador as an organized community to encourage municipal and NGO investment in the barrio. The effectiveness of this approach is evidenced by the fact that even as Villa Pagador continued to grow in area and population over the twenty years after its initial founding, resulting in an increasing diversity in the barrio in terms of both place of origin and socioeconomic status, the language of community continued to be the dominant discourse for publicly expressing barrio identity. In other words, as the barrio became increasingly diverse and politically fragmented, making a sense of community increasingly difficult to sustain in daily life, the *idea* of community nevertheless continued to be a hallmark of barrio identity, particularly in spectacular public events like those described in chapters 4 and 5.

Community, then, emerges in this discussion not as some authentic product that springs fully formed from a group of people who share a cultural essence (though it is to their similarity of origins that barrio residents themselves attribute the nature of their collective solidarity). Rather, community here is a political tool, an ideology, and a rhetoric that pagadoreños use to foster change in a context of urban marginality and municipal neglect. This is a strategy with an established history in the Andean context. Anthropologists studying the rural Andes have long been fascinated by the collective forms of social organization and labor found there (see, e.g., Isbell 1985; Stern 1982: 4–9; Zuidema and Quispe 1973), their attention drawn to rural institutions based on a sense of unity derived from a cultural homogeneity that was thought to disappear on urbanization (Brush 1977: 7). The idea of indigenous communalism as an essential feature of precapitalist Andean life was a bul-

7. Residents of Villa Pagador march in celebration of the barrio's anniversary, 10 de febrero. Photo by the author

wark of early twentieth-century *indigenismo* (Starn 1991), as influential writers like Hildebrando Castro Pozo and José Carlos Mariategui marveled at the collective aspects of work and production in the rural Andean village, finding that even in contexts of abrupt social transformation such as the imposition of "feudal" relations of production in the countryside, an inherent "communist spirit" persisted (Mariategui [1928] 1985: 58). The corporate nature of these communities was supposedly observable in their ability to close themselves off to the outside world, to prevent outside interference in internal matters, and to protect community members from external threats (R. Adams 1962: 427–428; Van den Berghe 1974). Other so-called community studies focused on "open" communities, those more integrated to national culture and therefore more culturally "mestizo" than "Indian" but nevertheless maintaining corporate control of land, which were seen as points along a continuum between "ideal" closed communities and those fully incorporated into national political and economic structures and flows (Isbell 1985: 33; see R. Adams 1959; Dobyns 1964; Doughty 1968; Keatinge 1973; Wolf 1955, 1957).

More recent commentators have pointed out that community, consisting of ideas about solidarity and a language of collectivity to express it, is something that indigenous Andeans have long understood and consciously manipulated.[4] This pertains not only to ideological programs of indigenismo (de la Cadena 2000; Ferrufino Llach 1987; Francovich 1956; Tamayo 1975) and organized political movements like Bolivian *katarismo* (Albó 1987a), which exalt an imagined Andean essence of collectivism and primitive communism (see Flores Galindo 1988), but to everyday groups of people in both rural and urban settings as well (e.g., Lagos 1994; Mallon 1983).

Though the concept of community remains problematic for anthropologists, its usage implying homogeneity, boundedness, and lack of cultural and historical complexity (Brow 1990; Rouse 1991), it is precisely these features of the concept that most appeal to the people of Villa Pagador. For pagadoreños, a community is a group of people who are organized and active in their own development, working from a set of shared cultural principles, unified in their pursuit of collective advancement.[5] Questions of heterogeneity, of conflict and disarticulation, though necessary to a more complex understanding of the community concept, are inimical to community members themselves, who rely on ideas of their own homogeneity and unflinching solidarity to be able to mobilize *as* a community. Efforts to construct community in Villa Pagador have been fundamentally political, techniques for organizing and mobilizing a group of people in pursuit of a particular agenda. These efforts have been enacted against other forms of community imposed by outside authorities in their attempts to restructure political and social relations within the barrio itself (see Suttles 1972). Gregory's (1998: 11) understanding of community nicely captures the complexity of this intensely conflicted, contested terrain, which anthropologists neglect at their peril:

> For communities *do* exist. People move into them and are excluded from them. Public authorities chart their borders and "develop" them. Financial institutions invest and disinvest in them. Politicians represent and appeal to them. And those who inhabit these bewilderingly complex fields of political and socioeconomic relations struggle to define their needs, interests, and identities by constructing and mobilizing their own often oppositional versions of "community." From my perspective, community describes not a static, place-based social collective but a power-laden field of social relations whose meanings, structures, and frontiers are continually produced, contested, and reworked in relation to a complex range of sociopolitical attachments and antagonisms.

As the previous chapter explored, the municipal government's initial response to the urbanization of Cochabamba was to criminalize the settlement process and demonize the migrant settler, resulting in a policy of exclusion that led to the creation of "frozen," illegal communities on the periphery of the city. It was in this context that a group of migrants from the altiplano department of Oruro came together to create a new barrio on the city's outskirts. These migrants arrived in Cochabamba in 1974 and 1975 and were living in rental properties in some of the newer barrios of the city, concentrated in Cerro Verde and Huayrakhasa in the southern zone. Many of them were from the same province of Oruro, Sur Carangas (Andamarca), but it was through their work as tradespeople or small-scale ambulant vendors (*comerciantes menoristas*) in the Cancha that they remained in contact with one another and commiserated about the expense, difficulty, and shame of living as renters, lacking the dignity of being landowners. In a series of meetings in late 1975 and early 1976, these Oruro migrants came together under the coordination of a group of self-appointed leaders who began organizing the group into a movement to found their own community. These leaders—men like Eleuterio Mayta, Domingo Mollo, Ausencio Lopez, and Bonifacio Villca, urban tradesmen with savvy political instincts and an eye for economic opportunity—would continue to play an important role in the history of the community that would come to be Villa Sebastián Pagador. It was in the house of Bonifacio Villca that the group met at one o'clock in the afternoon on 22 January 1977 to create the *junta vecinal* (neighborhood council) that would organize and lead the new barrio.

The first task facing the group was to identify a territory suitable for settlement. Rather than proceeding through the usual methods of land invasion or irregular purchase of land, in early 1976 the group, consisting of 156 people, presented a petition directly to the mayor of Cochabamba, Humberto Coronil Rivas. Offered in the name of the entire group, which marched en masse to the very chambers of the alcaldía to deliver it, the petition asked for the mayor's help in identifying an area where they could settle to establish themselves as landowners and good citizens of Cochabamba. This petition described the members of this settlers' group as honest and hardworking people who wanted nothing more than to found their own community and to live within the law on

8. Villa Pagador, seen from across Valle Hermoso. Photo by the author

their own land, as they had been accustomed to doing in their places of origin in Oruro.

It is unclear why this petition met with favor from the mayor. Perhaps it was because, faced with so much illegal settlement that he could not control, the mayor was pleased to be given the opportunity to help found a legal settlement in the city. The group of Oruro migrants that now approached him was organized in the manner of a renters union; but rather than illegally invading land, as was the norm for that kind of organization, the group was petitioning the mayor for help, and he responded. Additionally, some people today claim that key public officials were bribed by group leaders (with money raised from among the petitioners) to have their proposal recognized. In any event, the group formed a committee (identified in the junta vecinal's first *libro de actas* as the Cooperativa de Viviendas, or Housing Cooperative, and consisting of the same men who made up the directory of the junta vecinal), whose task it was to identify land for purchase and settlement. This Cooperative was told by the municipal administration to look for a spot south of the Cancha, in the area of Villa Méjico, a barrio comprising mostly migrants from the Cochabamba valley. But this site was too expensive, and the *orureños* did not like the idea of settling in the midst of so many cochabambinos, whom they had come to realize had little love for altiplano migrants. So the mayor directed them to Lacma, an area of farmland near what is today the Wilstermann Airport. This area seemed acceptable to the migrants, but before they could formalize the arrangements, the alcaldía decided to cede that land as the site of a new hospital. Thus, the Cooperative turned its attention further south, to the area known as Valle Hermoso Norte. Though a full five kilometers from the southern edge of town, with poor roads, no public services, and a precipitous location at the base of an erosion-prone hillside, the site seemed perfect to the commission. The distance from town would be a problem for the vendors who needed to be at work in the Cancha early in the morning, but countering this was the recognition that the distance provided a buffer between the barrio and the rest of the city, which the migrants viewed as hostile and unwelcoming. On the periphery of the city, the migrants (particularly those men who had set themselves up as the group's leaders) hoped to be allowed to form their own community with their own internal leadership and so to be able to control their own destiny at a distance from municipal authority.

Prior to 1953, the entire area of Valle Hermoso (including Valle Hermoso Norte) was owned by the Tardío family and worked as one large hacienda. Following the 1952 national revolution and the subsequent agrarian reform, large estates were broken up and distributed as small-holdings to the peasants who lived on and worked the land. As was typical of this period, however, the peasant beneficiaries of the agrarian reform did not hold onto their real estate for very long (Klein 1992). For centuries the area of Valle Hermoso had been devoted to agricultural production, but as the city of Cochabamba began to expand south in the 1960s and 1970s, the peasants occupying these lands saw their property values rise and many of them began to sell and move closer in to the city. These sales were distressing to the downtown-based city planners of that time: the Plan Regional, designed to coordinate regional development outside the city proper, had stipulated that the Valle Hermoso area was eventually to become an orderly and self-sufficient "satellite city" to the main city center, and the areas around it were to remain permanently in agriculture as part of the greenbelt dividing the city from the surrounding countryside. However, there was little that municipal authorities could do to resist the profiteering impulse that circumstances afforded, and city officials watched helplessly as the division and sale of land in this region proceeded unchecked.

The parcel of land identified as the future site of Villa Pagador had been held briefly by a series of peasant families before being bought up by a land-owning cooperative known as the Cooperativa Agraria Alalay, based in Valle Hermoso. This cooperative had been purchasing chunks of farmland in and around Valle Hermoso, consolidating these smaller parcels into larger holdings, which it then sold to speculators who again divided them up into lots to sell to new settlers. From the perspective of the municipality, these land sales were all illegal: as the lands themselves had been designated to remain in agriculture and were located outside of the city's Radio Urbano, they could not be sold legally for residential construction, and the sales ignored the alcaldía's basic requirements of a tax payment, inspection, and cession of a portion of the land to the state for public use (the área verde). The land in Valle Hermoso was thus shifting out of agriculture and becoming residential land, the site of new marginal barrios on the far southeastern fringe of Cochabamba, despite the fact that such transformation was expressly forbidden by the terms of the Plano Regulador and Plan Regional.

Nevertheless, having been assured of the alcaldía's support and its promise to recognize the founding of the community, the leaders of the Oruro migrants' group, organized as the Housing Cooperative, contracted with the Cooperativa Agraria Alalay to buy a large plot of land (measuring an area of seven hectares and owned officially by a group of brothers named Peredo) at the base of the hills in Valle Hermoso Norte. The leaders of the Housing Cooperative themselves served as the loteadores, drawing up plans for the subdivision of this area into individual lots, which in early 1977 they resold to members of their own migrants' group. Functioning simultaneously as leaders of the community (through their positions in the directory of the junta vecinal) and as loteadores as the heads of the Cooperative, these men had positioned themselves to make a handsome profit from the settlement process, while at the same time creating a community that they themselves would control.

By this time, however, the mayor of Cochabamba, under pressure from within his administration not to legalize more settlements outside of the Radio Urbano, now seemed to be wavering in his support of the new community. To ensure that the alcaldía would not back down from its promise to grant legal recognition to the new barrio, the leaders instructed the settlers to set to work immediately on constructing their dwellings.[6] Believing that the mayor would have a much harder time backing out of the deal if it was already a fait accompli, barrio leaders and residents raced to construct homes on the recently purchased land in an effort to force the inconsistent mayor to provide legal recognition of their land claims. Doña Elena de Ramirez, one of the original members of the migrants' group, fondly remembers the process as the first of many clever ploys the barrio residents and leaders would use on the alcaldía:

> When the leaders divided the lots among us, they gave us just thirty days to build our houses! We all had to make adobe bricks, working until it was dark. I had to quickly send out an order to buy adobe. This little room [in which we are sitting] was all there was of this house! . . . The leaders told us that if we don't build anything, the authorities are going to kick us out. They are going to say to us, "Why did you divide up lots if you're not going to do anything with them?" . . . Afterwards, we did it like so, one little room, two little rooms, each of us according to what we could do, you see? Afterwards the mayor came, they invited the mayor one Sunday. . . . He came, and he said, "But you have built all these houses clandestinely, without authorization!" (Laughs) "But, now we can't do anything about it, we will approve it." Yes, that's how it was. (Laughs)

The barrio and its individual lots were thus legally recognized by the alcaldía (through an agency set up for this purpose, the Ministerio del Plan Sociourbano), which sent in a technical team to draw up plans of the community and map out the individual landholdings. In this one exceptional case, the alcaldía extended the Radio Urbano (something it had not done since declaring the southern zone of the city frozen in the mid-1970s) to include the new settlement as a legal community and hence part of Cochabamba proper. Questions about the legality of this recognition were erased by the cession of a large chunk of land, a space of several hundred square meters in the center of the settlement that the loteadores gave to the city to secure the legalization of the barrio's component landholdings. This space was to serve for public meetings and recreation and would later become the main plaza of the barrio, with a basketball court and large open areas for holding rallies. The initial group of settlers, consisting of 156 individuals from some twenty to thirty families, were given lots in a section of land known as Primer Grupo (First Group), situated in a grid-like pattern around the central plaza. Adding to this initial group were an additional two hundred or so people who had heard of the formation of the new barrio and quickly signed on as settlers; these people bought lots from the Cooperative on a section of land immediately to the south of and adjacent to Primer Grupo, in an area designated Segundo Grupo (Second Group). The residents of both Primer and Segundo Grupo were able to legalize their land claims under this first wave of approved settlement and were obligated to the members of the cooperative for this opportunity to acquire land legally in Cochabamba. Domingo Mollo, one of the community leaders and loteadores, remembers 22 May 1977, the day of the barrio's founding, as one of the proudest of his life.

According to those who were there, the first few years of the barrio's history were marked by a high level of unity and readiness among the local population. The local leaders had direct involvement in and authority over every aspect of collective life. The Housing Cooperative was reformulated as the Cooperativa Multiactiva Sebastián Pagador (the Multipurpose Cooperative), which, under the control of the same loteadores, would supervise all manner of activities and enterprises at the community level, including housing, education, social activities, and expansion of the barrio. Community meetings were held every Sunday in the main plaza, and every barrio resident was compelled to show up under threat of a fine for poor attendance. At these meetings the leaders held court, resolving local disputes and making decisions about community priorities and projects. They organized communal labor groups to perform local infrastructural improvements, such as paving roads with stones, building bridges across the irrigation canal that separated Villa Pagador from Valle Hermoso to the west, and constructing public buildings. Groups of residents patrolled the barrio at night, keeping watch for strangers who might be thieves preying on the unpoliced residences in the barrio. At the first sign of danger, a bell was rung and barrio residents would pour into the streets to apprehend suspected criminals. These suspects would be tied to a post in the barrio plaza, verbally chastised and whipped with stinging nettles collected from the hillside, before being released with a warning never to return to Villa Pagador.

The leaders, organized as the Cooperativa Multiactiva, orchestrated all of these activities, managing every aspect of the collective life of the barrio. Benefiting from their remove of five kilometers from the city and its centralized political authority, the leaders were able to act with impunity in directing the growth and development of the barrio. Much of the authority that they were able to command stemmed from the obligations created between themselves and the barrio residents under their

9. Parents of children at a school in Villa Pagador labor collectively to construct a new basketball court. Photo by the author

leadership. The barrio leaders, it should be remembered, were the men who contracted to purchase the land that they then subdivided into lots and resold to individual families. Having facilitated the land distribution that provided people with their landholdings (often at great profit to themselves), the loteadores consolidated relationships with barrio residents based on reciprocity and indebtedness, a common means of forging relations of patronage and clientage in the Andean context (e.g., Dandler 1971). Many barrio residents felt obligated to the men who had helped them to become legally landed in the city, pledging their loyalty and political support to these men in subsequent endeavors. These exchanges extended preexisting linkages between the barrio leaders and members of the original settlers' group; even before the founding of Villa Pagador, many individuals in the group had ties of *compadrazgo* (ritual coparenthood) with certain of the leaders (some of which even predated migration to Cochabamba[7]), and leaders like Mollo and Villca used these connections to recruit settlers into the new barrio and to consolidate their following. Additionally, as the wealthiest and most socially prestigious individuals in the community, the loteadores often were asked to serve as ritual kinsmen in various important social rites in the lives of community members. Thus, the loteadores became compadres with many barrio residents by serving as sponsors of wedding banquets, by supervising at first haircutting ceremonies (*rutuchis*), or by agreeing to serve as godparents (*padrinos*) to children at their baptisms. When these loteadores later needed support, they could count on a loyal group of fictive kinsmen to back them with a vote or a voice or with physical labor or cash donations when required. Furthermore, the loteadores used their wealth to sponsor important community activities, principally the barrio's patron saint festival, the annual fiesta de San Miguel. As the founders and first sponsors of the community's most important social event of the year, the loteadores established themselves as not only the political but the cultural leaders of the community.

The leaders themselves remembered their leadership as being in the interest of forging unity and progress in the barrio, deriving their legitimacy from what they called their "traditional" authority. They described themselves as "traditional leaders" (*dirigentes tradicionales*, to use their own term) or *jilaqatas*, a term used in both Aymara and Quechua for a leader of a rural community. In some rural Andean contexts, the jilaqata is a low-order rank in a hierarchical *cargo* system, through which men advance in the course of a political career (Rasnake 1989: 72). By referring to themselves in these terms, though, the leaders of Villa Pagador were calling on a more generalized discourse of rural communalism to cast their own leadership roles in this traditional light. Eleuterio Mayta, comparing the leaders of the early days with their contemporary counterparts, observed: "Today there are no traditional leaders like before. Leaders that wanted to drive the barrio toward unity. . . . We were traditional leaders because we founded the barrio in the spirit of progress, in the spirit that it should be something special."

Barrio leaders also gained wealth, status, and power by operating as something like local *caudillos*, brokering key relationships between barrio residents and powerful outside agents (see Albro 2001). Unlike the majority of barrio residents, who had come to Cochabamba from the countryside, the barrio leaders were of urban origin, mostly from the city of Oruro or nearby mining centers. Urban tradesmen by profession (Eleuterio Mayta was a tailor, Domingo Mollo a carpenter, Ausencio Lopez an upholsterer, and Bonifacio Villca a hat maker), they had grown up in the heyday of unionist politics in and around Oruro and had acquired a certain acumen in dealing with politicians and other authority figures. Additionally, they had gained a degree of sophistication from their experience in the real estate business and understood the ins and outs of the land legalization requirements in the city, which rural migrants poorly comprehended. The barrio leaders were thus able to navigate the bureaucracies and systems external to the barrio itself, helping their clients within the barrio to legalize their land claims, acquire loans, or get jobs in the city. By establishing their own clientage relationships with other, more powerful politicians in Cochabamba city, barrio leaders were at times able to use their connections to bring needed services into the barrio (see below). Additionally, some barrio leaders sought out and established ties with national-level political parties, pledging blocs of votes from their constituents to major party figures in municipal elections in exchange for the provision of needed infrastructure or social services.

It is important to note that in this first phase of barrio history, the number of people engaged in the barrio-founding project was fairly small (under four hundred), mostly from Oruro (countryside or city), and largely unified behind the barrio leaders in their goal of creating Villa Pagador. In addition to the reasons suggested above, this support derived from the fact that many people living in the new settlement had begun to do quite well for themselves economically. Attaining legal land title gave them the capital to borrow and invest resources elsewhere, and many barrio residents became small business owners in the city center or the Cancha, purchased trucks or minibuses and entered the lucrative transportation industry, or acquired land in the Chapare, the fertile agricultural (particularly coca-growing) lowland region of Cochabamba department. Resources began coming into the new barrio, portions of which were donated by individual families to barrio development projects. It is not surprising, then, that participants in this original settlement remembered the early days of the barrio as a time of unity, prosperity, and hope, especially in contrast to more recent times.

Despite this professed unity, however, even in this early period the barrio was showing some signs of the problems that would later come to divide the community. For one thing, not all in Villa Pagador were happy with the loteadores' leadership. Though the problems would later escalate much further, in this early period some barrio residents already resented the loteadores' power, describing them as lording it over Pagador as though they were "fathers of the place." Among the small group of settlers were a large number of evangelical Christians, who did not see eye to eye with Catholics on such matters as fiesta practice, a problem that would escalate with the founding of the San Miguel fiesta a few years later (Goldstein 2003a). And despite public professions of homogeneity, a number of the original settlers were in fact from the Cochabamba valley rather than the altiplano, and some questioned the articulation of local identity as rooted in the highlands. Some of these people today reject the idea that Pagador was ever a unified community, even in the good old days. These issues, plus the increasing economic differences among barrio residents that would soon emerge, would come to jeopardize community solidarity in Villa Pagador.

"WE HAD TO INVENT OURSELVES": COMMUNITY FORMATION AND COLLECTIVE ACTION (1977–1983)

We had absolutely nothing. This was a desolate land, very dry. But somehow the people became organized, and we worked together in unity. And in that way, we were able to shape it out of nothing, that is, we were able to create the reality of the barrio.—Fausto Huanca

Having created the barrio "out of nothing" through land distribution and home construction, the leaders of the junta vecinal now faced the daunting task of developing a working infrastructure for Villa Pagador. In setting about this task, they very quickly encountered the indifference of the alcaldía to the needs of its newest residents. Though the municipality had initially taken a paternalist interest in the founding of the new barrio, Villa Pagador quickly diminished in importance in the alcaldía's agenda: it was willing to extend legal recognition to the barrio's land claims, but the municipality was not prepared to back up this recognition with a large-scale material investment. Villa Pagador was on its own.

This period of barrio history is recalled by many of the original settlers as a time of difficulty, danger, and hard work. The land was barren and sere and offered little in the way of resources to the arriving migrants. In their reflections today, people emphasize the dryness and ruggedness of the land: "It was a complete desert here," recalled Arturo Ayma, an early founder of the community.[8] "The land was full of sharp thorns, and we had to work hard, hard, hard to clear it. There was no shelter from the sun or the rain, and when it rained the whole place turned to mud." Don Arturo, an evangelical Christian, beseeched God to grant him a plot of land that he could settle, "and God provided." He recalled that he bought the land sight unseen from Ausencio Lopez, a loteador of the barrio, and when he went to look for it he had to travel on foot from the city center, wandering further and further south in search of the lot ("I almost ended up in Tarata!" Don Arturo laughed). The emptiness of the land offered no distinguishing features by which he could recognize his property. This emptiness and barren aridity reinforced the sense of isolation and self-determination that settlers of the new community remembered themselves as possessing. Today they call themselves pioneers (*pioneros*), men and women who settled an untamed frontier without any help from anyone. Recalled Don Arturo: "The alcaldía never gave us any assistance! Absolutely nothing. The work always was done entirely by the people [*el pueblo*], by the community [*comunidad*]. And if one time we went to the alcaldía for something, the alcaldía would say to us, 'You'll get nothing from us, because to us you don't exist.'"

Recognizing that any improvements in local services and infrastructure would have to come either through self-help development initiatives or through active political lobbying of external sources of assistance, barrio leaders began a campaign of community formation designed to produce a coherent, unified, and mobilized collectivity out of the assortment of barrio residents and to enlist this community in the pursuit of a developmentalist agenda. By joining the barrio populace as a community of migrants from the department of Oruro, barrio leaders hoped to create a public reputation for the barrio as unified, organized, and active in its own development, both to create internal improvements in barrio infrastructure and to use this reputation to generate assistance from outside the barrio itself. Community formation in Villa Pagador was thus, from the very beginnings of the barrio, an explicit ideological project of the barrio's founders, a project with practical, material objectives. By organizing the barrio specifically as a community of migrants from Oruro, people who had left the altiplano but had not abandoned their original cultural commitments and essential identity, leaders hoped to create a unified local constituency that could be mobilized to create needed improvements in the barrio.[9]

The community-formation project of the barrio's leaders and residents can be understood as consisting of two complementary components. On the one hand, barrio leaders had to forge unity and collective solidarity among their constituents, and to do this they utilized the predominantly Oruro origins of the barrio settlers as a rallying point to generate a sense of shared identity and mission of self-help local development. On the other hand, barrio leaders accurately perceived the limitations of this kind of self-help activity in achieving their goals for the barrio, realizing that outside resources and services would be required. Thus, the second component of the community-formation project was to disseminate awareness of the collective nature of the barrio to the outside world and to assert their willingness to collaborate with the authorities in creating improvements in the barrio. By constructing a reputation for Villa Pagador as an organized community of Oruro migrants, unified in pursuit of their own development but willing to work with municipal authorities as cooperative citizens, barrio leaders could then project this reputation to the municipal government, NGOS, and other institutions and individuals with the resources to help the barrio achieve its development goals. Community formation within the barrio thus had to go hand-in-hand with reputation dissemination outside of the barrio. As the examples below indicate (and as the discussion of folkloric performance in chapter 4 demonstrates even more clearly), part of this calculus lay in the migrants' recognition of the symbolic capital of Oruro in the national cultural imaginary and mobilization of this symbolic capital in performances of collective identity in the barrio (see Goldstein 2000). Nationally prominent as a mining center (and thus for centuries a mainstay of the Bolivian national economy) and as the site of Bolivia's annual Carnaval celebration (and hence the heart of Bolivian national culture), Oruro holds a prominent place in Bolivian national geography. To be migrants from Oruro who had maintained ties to their place of origin would be a powerful identity for these displaced marginal settlers to adopt. Additionally, although sentiment in Cochabamba was strongly against migrants at that time, the leaders of the new barrio recognized that this antagonism could work in the interests of the barrio. By organizing as migrants, specifically as migrants from Oruro, the barrio residents could form themselves into a community with a shared sense of origin and destiny, surrounded by enemies but strong through their internal coherence.

An example of the dual strategy of community formation/reputation dissemination was the decision to name the barrio in honor of Oruro's most legendary hero, Sebastián Pagador. Like the expeditious construction of the houses, the choice of a name for the barrio indicates the political acumen of the local leaders. They had presented their original petition to the alcaldía on behalf of a group of migrants attempting to assimilate in an orderly fashion to the mainstream of Cochabamba;

now, by contrast, the leaders chose to emphasize their altiplano origins. Sebastián Pagador, hero of an early struggle by the people of Oruro against the Spanish, is a name strongly associated with Oruro: the city of Oruro is replete with references to Pagador, on street signs, plazas, and private businesses. In addition, the name Sebastián Pagador ("the Titan of the Andes," as he is known; Murillo Vacareza 1987) has important resonance in nationalist historiography, in which he is conceptualized as an early forefather of the later, more successful overthrow of colonial rule. Sebastián Pagador, a member of the Creole (white but American-born) elite, is perhaps most famous for his "harangue," a call to arms that he issued to the people of Oruro in 1781 to inspire them to revolt against the *chapetones* (Spaniards of the continental variety) who dominated colonial society (Cornblit 1995: 147). Pagador is thus regarded today as a symbolic progenitor of the Bolivian nation. One nationalist account acknowledges that little else is known of him: "But one can infer that he was a man of action, full of energy and decisiveness, and that he conducted himself with the greatest courage in the midst of the violence of those days and the dangers that confronted him. The portrait painted by his words would seem to embody that which materially and spiritually best represents the orureño; and therefore the figure [of Sebastián Pagador] also should stand everywhere as a symbol, so that its eponymous valor may inspire a permanent and unfailing struggle for the most noble and humane of ideals" (Murillo Vacareza 1987: 58–59).

By naming the barrio for this national (though specifically orureño) hero, the leaders of Villa Pagador constructed their community in his image, attempting to attach the "eponymous valor" of Sebastián Pagador to their own barrio. The masculine strength, courage, and determination of Pagador were asserted by the barrio leaders as attributes of the new community itself, founded in the image of Oruro and its historical claim to defiance in the face of exploitive and illegitimate power. The name Sebastián Pagador, iconic of Oruro and the altiplano more generally, also served to establish that the residents of this new community had not severed their ties to their place of origin, but would draw on the resources (both material and cultural) of Oruro in organizing their lives and their community in Cochabamba. At the same time, Pagador, himself an embodiment of all that is best about the orureño, would serve as a reminder to outside observers that orureños (and, by extension, the people of Villa Pagador) are valorous, unfailing in their determination, and willing to struggle against adversity in the pursuit of "the most

10. Manfred Reyes Villa, alcalde of Cochabamba, participates in the unveiling of a bust honoring Sebastián Pagador, the barrio's namesake, on 10 February 1995. Photo by the author

noble and humane of ideals." Pagador's association with incipient forms of nationalism also spoke to the significance of Pagador and Oruro to the Bolivian nation and the centrality of orureños to Bolivian national history and culture.

Oruro would continue to be a central trope in the collective identity of Villa Pagador. Oruro flags and emblems are today featured prominently in any symbolic representation of the barrio; the *himno de Oruro* (the department's anthem) is played by a brass band at every public gathering in the barrio, and Oruro is mentioned prominently in every public speech. The barrio celebrates its anniversary on 10 de febrero, which is also the anniversary of Oruro department. In public speeches at these anniversary celebrations, the idea is consistently put forth that orureños form something like a natural community, owing to their powerful inner qualities. The barrio's libro de actas records that at the very first 10 de febrero celebration in 1979 (an event attended by representatives of the alcaldía, the city school district, and the municipality's Ministerio del Plan Sociourbano), after the playing of the himno de Oruro, leaders gave speeches in which they reiterated the Oruro origins of the majority of barrio residents and asserted the Oruro identity of Villa Pagador. Interestingly, this theme was echoed in the discourse of the dignitaries invited to attend the anniversary celebration. In his speech to the assembled barrio residents and leaders, the representative of the Honorable Alcaldía Municipal spoke glowingly of orureños, who he said are characterized by their "unity" and propensity for hard work. In this same speech, not coincidentally, the representative promised that the alcaldía "would cooperate in resolving all the urgent problems of the Villa." That the Oruro theme had infected the discourse of the municipal authorities themselves speaks to the apparent early success of the reputation-dissemination strategies adopted by barrio leaders at this time.

Local Improvements

Despite the recognition that the barrio was beginning to receive, however, any improvements in barrio conditions were the result of local self-help initiatives. The barrio suffered from a lack of basic services, including water, sewers, electricity, and, critically, transportation. At a remove of five kilometers the barrio was extremely isolated from the city proper, a difficult situation for the many residents who worked in the Cancha as small-scale merchants. The existing bus lines had no interest in extending their services to the margins of the city, particularly because the poor roads connecting the barrio to the main avenues were unpaved and rutted and impassable during the summer rains. To get to work in the city center, barrio residents had to walk several kilometers to the one dirt track that ran into the southeastern sector of the city, and from there catch rides on mopeds or in the backs of privately owned pickup trucks. Children headed for school downtown (the only option, as the barrio lacked its own school at this time) had to make a similar journey each day. The situation seemed difficult to remedy: as all transportation within the Radio Urbano was controlled by a single transport owner/operators union with sole authority to determine where new bus lines could be created, the decision to extend bus service to Villa Pagador was out of local control.

In 1981, a small group of local operators began offering transportation to barrio residents in pickup trucks, taking vendors in to the Cancha early in the morning and bringing them back again at night. Soon these *transportistas* and their supporters in the community began to solicit the transportation syndicate for membership, which was granted that same year. As syndicate members, the transportistas of Villa Pagador were able to operate buses giving service directly into the barrio. The price of syndicate membership was high, though: barrio transportistas had to pay 500 to 1,000 bolivianos a month to the syndicate just for the privilege of being allowed to operate. It wasn't long before the transportistas organized a syndicate of their own under the authority of the Multipurpose Cooperative in Villa Pagador and began lobbying the government to grant them the right to operate outside of the control of the Radio Urbano syndicate. Supported by barrio residents, the transportistas began making vocal protests at the offices of the alcaldía and the prefectura of Cochabamba, decrying the syndicate's monopoly on transportation in the city and demanding to be allowed to operate free of this overarching authority. Finally they were granted legal recognition and permission to operate, securing the official *personería jurídica* in 1982, effectively breaking the syndicate's urban monopoly. The transport syndicate officially separated from the Multipurpose Cooperative (though it remained under the authority of the barrio leaders, who assumed command of the transport syndicate as well), and the "P" bus line was created, the P of course standing for Pagador. Today, Villa Pagador's transport syndicate is a constituent member of the city's larger urban syndicate but retains a degree of autonomy in directing its operations. "It is the light of the barrio," boasted one transportista of the bus line. "It is its splendor."

This achievement raised Villa Pagador's profile around the city. Recognized as the only barrio in all of Cochabamba to have its own dedicated bus service, operated by and for barrio residents, Villa Pagador was coming to be viewed as a force to be reckoned with in municipal politics, despite its marginal location and migrant population. The barrio's internal unity and Oruro identity were frequently named as causal factors in its ability to mobilize and act as a community. In contrast to the apparently chaotic heterogeneity that migration had produced in greater Cochabamba, the ethnic uniformity of Villa Pagador was viewed by outsiders and barrio insiders alike as their greatest strength, the source of their political will and their ability to act in concert. In the struggle[10] for transportation, for example, one transportista attributed the ultimate success of this endeavor to the shared Oruro nature of the barrio's residents: "It is certainly the case," he said, "that we understood one another, in one sense by language, in another sense by our character, by our constitution. We believed that we could trust one another, because everyone in this whole sector was from Oruro."

Community action at other times included deliberate manipulation and misrepresentation for the benefit of outside observers, particularly for those in the municipal government. For example, shortly after the barrio was established, the Pagador settlers began looking about for a school that their children could attend. This precipitated one of the pagadoreños' first encounters with the racism of the Cochabamba valley residents directed against altiplano migrants. Don Mario and Doña Elena remembered how the directors and parents of the nearby Fé y Alegría school[11] in Valle Hermoso refused to accept the children of the migrant settlers in their institution:

> DON MARIO: Those people down there at Fé y Alegría, they didn't want anything to do with the people from here. "Those are peasants, what do we want with them here?" They didn't want us for, for nothing...
> DOÑA ELENA: The nun from there didn't want us. She didn't want us, I don't know what her name was...
> DANIEL: That was how they treated you, the people from here?
> DOÑA ELENA: Yes, like that. Certain nuns are bad.
> DANIEL: Because you were immigrants, or orureños, or...
> DON MARIO: Yes, we all are migrants, yes. From the altiplano, from the Chapare...
> DOÑA ELENA: Look, the nun herself is an immigrant, right? She's not from here!
> DANIEL: She's from Spain! (Laughter)

Forced to send their children to school in the city center, barrio residents took the initiative to create their own school. Especially active in this regard was one Don Arsenio, who no longer resides in Villa Pagador but was an early settler of the barrio and a sponsor of the wedding (*padrino de matrimonio*) of Don Eleuterio Mayta, the junta vecinal's first vice president. At first, Don Arsenio organized classes in people's homes and went door-to-door enrolling children in his local school. Doña Elena remembered him at meetings, tears coursing down his cheeks as he beseeched the parents of the barrio to think of the future and send their children to classes. Everyone in the barrio recognized Don Arsenio's whistle, which he blew to announce the beginning of the school day; the children would run and hide at the sound of it.

But this kind of informal schooling was not sufficient to the barrio's needs nor to the community's public identity as a progressive and important barrio. The barrio, its leaders decided, deserved a real school, like any other neighborhood in the city. Leaders began conversations with municipal authorities to garner city support for the creation of a barrio school. At the same time, under the authority of the Multi-purpose Cooperative, barrio residents donated money to purchase a lot of 3,200 square meters in Primer Grupo for the site of a new school. On 14 October 1979, representatives of the alcaldía and the city school district visited the barrio to attend the ribbon-cutting ceremonies of the lot for the new school building. Speaking to the assembled crowd of dignitaries and parents, the representative of the alcaldía observed that Villa Pagador was an example of "urban progress" owing to the "enormous efforts displayed" by barrio residents in the formation of the school. More than that, though, the representative emphasized, was the willingness of barrio leaders to "cooperate" with the alcaldía's Ministerio del Plan Sociourbano in pursuit of their objectives. In the months that followed, each barrio resident was required by the leaders of the Cooperative to donate fifteen adobe bricks to the construction project, and members of the future Padres de Familia (parents organization) supplied skilled and unskilled labor on a voluntary basis to build the two-story structure.

Especially important in the formation of a barrio school, however, was that the school should be recognized and funded as an urban school (*colegio urbano*), with an urban teacher whose credentials and training, according to those in the know, were necessarily superior to those of a rural teacher. For a community of ex-peasant migrants, it was essential that the state recognize the barrio's existence as an urban community, another official acknowledgment of the transition from rural to urban that the migrants had undergone. But to be recognized as an urban school and to receive a state-funded contract for an urban teacher, the institution had to present itself to the state as having a large enough population to warrant an urban designation.[12] Don Arsenio continued his recruitment of students, which now had an even greater significance, as the creation of a school-age population was also an attempt to construct the community itself as urban, in need of an urban school to serve its large populace. With a population then of only about two hundred families, this required some creativity. Don Mario, in a conversation with me and my research assistant, Simón Lopez, remembered how this was achieved by artificially inflating the school's enrollment:

DON MARIO: Even women, young adults, he rounded up, no? In order to get the numbers up, for this to be urban. Because there weren't enough people.

DOÑA ELENA: It was . . .

DON MARIO: Rural is all, they said. But here they didn't want a rural teacher, he had to be urban, so, we had to stretch [the population], including young adults, young women, brought in by force.

SIMÓN: To study there?

DON MARIO: Yes, so that it could be opened like that, as an urban school.

Don Arsenio and his barrio committee signed up all sorts of people to fill out the school's roster, including children as young as three and women long past school age. In this way, the barrio was able to present a case to the Ministry of Education that it was an urban district in need of an urban teacher. After a lengthy trámite, in 1982 the state accepted the barrio's petition and granted it a contract to hire urban teachers. It was with great pride and a sense of accomplishment that people like Don Mario and Doña Elena spoke of these events. Proclaimed another friend, Fausto Huanca, proudly recalling the community's manipulation of its own image in such instances: "We had to invent ourselves [Teníamos que inventarnos]."

In its first years of existence (1977–83), then, Villa Pagador publicly exhibited a high level of unity and community action toward clearly identified goals and development initiatives. The successful struggles for a transportation system and an urban school are examples of what the barrio was able to achieve through these efforts. Not only did these struggles bring needed improvements to the barrio, enhancing the quality of life of its inhabitants, but they also served to establish a reputation for the barrio in greater Cochabamba as a highly effective and organized community. This reputation in turn contributed to further development initiatives: recognizing the political potential of the barrio, the alcaldía and NGOs were inclined to acquiesce to further demands of the community and its leaders. The key to success in their engagements with the alcaldía was the ability of barrio leaders to portray Villa Pagador as at once internally unified but respectful of municipal authority and willing to work in a collaborative fashion with the authorities to achieve their goals (recall the city representative's remarks on the willingness of barrio residents to "cooperate" with the alcaldía). In a context of urban migration and the migrants' apparent disregard for the city's laws and authorities, this seems to have been an effective strategy in both the effort to secure the mayor's permission to found a legal community outside the Radio Urbano and in the struggle to create a barrio school with city funding.

The unity the barrio residents exhibited during this period may be attributed to three sources. One was the orureño identity of the barrio residents. As self-identifying migrants from Oruro, the residents of Pagador were able to elaborate a collective identity as people who at their most fundamental level conceived of themselves as sharing a common origin and cultural heritage. Under the leadership of the loteadores, this collective identity was brought to the fore, mobilized and publicly represented to the city authorities as a force to be reckoned with. This, then, was the second source of barrio unity: the unchallenged authority of the local leaders, whose leadership compelled the cooperation of barrio residents in community-based projects. Operating in virtual autonomy from outside sources of authority and controlling all aspects of social, economic, and political life in the barrio, the leaders were able to compel unity within the barrio while building their own ties of political clientage to the administrative authorities in the city. Indeed, through their control of the junta vecinal, the Multipurpose Cooperative, and the transportation syndicate, barrio leaders by now had a virtual lock on the loyalty of barrio residents and could compel participation in collective labor regimes, political rallies, and other displays of community solidarity. Finally, it is important to note that for these original settlers of the barrio, unity under the leadership of the loteadores was in many ways in their own best interest. Through collective action under the auspices of these local leaders, who targeted community mobilization at particular audiences receptive to their requests for aid, barrio residents were experiencing a steady improvement in the quality of life in the barrio. But the tensions that this mobilization engendered were widening fault lines in the now expanding community.

GROWTH OF THE BARRIO:
ILLEGAL SETTLEMENT (1983–1991)

Villa Pagador had begun as a tightly knit, powerfully organized community. However, as the barrio began to grow with the continued arrival of new settlers, the initial unity and organization of the community began to weaken. The leaders who had founded and ruled over the barrio began to buy up areas of land adjacent to the existing barrio (i.e., further to the south and east beyond Segundo Grupo) and to subdivide these into lots to sell to newly arrived migrants. Though these areas were deemed part of Villa Pagador, they were not covered by the same legal recognition that those in the first sectors of the barrio enjoyed. The leaders, functioning again as loteadores, profited enormously from these illegal land sales, which began in the early 1980s, occurring even as these same men were actively engaged in forging community among the legal residents of Primer and Segundo Grupo. Other individuals arrived in the barrio and set themselves up as loteadores as well; some stayed only long enough to make some money through illegal land sales and then left town. At the same time as the original loteadores were profiting from the arrival of new settlers, the size of their domain was expanding greatly, as new sectors of Villa Pagador were subdivided, sold, and inhabited. From its original population of a few hundred people the barrio quickly grew to several thousand by the mid-1980s.

All along the base of the hills new sectors sprang into being, many of them perched precariously on the edge of eroded drainage canals or on the steep, rocky terrain of the hillside. The loteadores benefited from the fact that although their own land and that of their followers was legalized, the areas they were selling were outside of the Radio Urbano and so unregulated and unsupervised by the state. Eulogio Gordillo, a latter-day leader representing the people of one of these new sectors (a junta vecinal called Alto de la Alianza), remembered the subdivision and sale of land in this part of Villa Pagador as a story of unbridled avarice. The land speculators, Don Eulogio said, saw the lots in this area as "nice and juicy tidbits" that they could break into fragments and sell off. The altiplano people that bought and settled these lots came to the area like "innocent sheep," knowing nothing of the demands of the alcaldía regarding the necessary restrictions for urbanization and legalization of land claims. The land speculators, on the other hand, knew the story full well, but took advantage of the migrants' ignorance to boost their profits. They sold the areas of cession, which should have been donated to the alcaldía and dedicated to public use. They sold the same lot to more than one buyer and then skipped town. Worst of all, they charged people for basic services like electricity, water, and sewers, promising these while knowing full well that they would not be provided. (Quipped another friend: "No wonder they call this place Villa 'Pagador' [i.e., Payer Town]!") Some land speculators served as intermediaries on behalf of absentee owners, selling the land on the installment plan (*paulatinamente*) to people so poor they couldn't pay the

11. Illegal land sales and the unregulated construction of homes in Villa Pagador have left many barrio residents without formal title to their holdings. Photo by the author

whole selling price (often several thousand dollars) at one time. This selling of land by "quotas" was risky for the buyer, however, because if he failed to make a payment one month, the land could be taken from him and sold to someone else who was waiting in the wings to buy it. The first buyer and his family could be evicted from their home and left with nothing, the payments already made being nonrefundable.

In these newly created sectors, conflicts between settlers and loteadores were beginning to be expressed. Though originally grateful just to have had the opportunity to buy a plot of land in the city, the new settlers were coming to discover that what they had purchased was not, in legal terms, their own. In the eyes of the state they were not owners of their land but illegal squatters. Without a legal land title, the settlers were unable to borrow from banks or credit agencies; they were unable to sell or pawn their land, to transfer it to another, or to leave it as inheritance for their children. Furthermore, without the legal land title, people were not considered legitimate owners (*dueños legítimos* is the term people used) of their land, and so were not regarded (either by the state or in their own eyes) as full citizens or members of the municipality. Without state approval, their land was nothing more than a piece of ground that they could occupy until such time as the state saw fit to remove them.

Thus, tensions began to mount, and people's anger was directed at the men who had sold them this land. Today some say that these leaders treated the barrio like their own little kingdom: "They thought they were the only real owners" of the barrio, grumbled one man, remembering.

What was lacking, however, was a means to organize and challenge the loteadores' power within the community. Despite the abuses they committed in their role as land speculators, the original leaders of the community continued to maintain a good measure of their former authority.[13] Within their own original sectors, the loteadores continued to hold great influence, for people there had most directly benefited from their leadership, and this strong base of loyal followers served to maintain them in power even after the extent of their abuses came to be known. Some of their connections extended into the newer sections of the barrio as well, as people continued to feel a measure of indebtedness to the men who had helped them acquire a tract of land in the city, and sought them out as compadres on ceremonial occasions. At the same time, the loteadores were struggling to contain the growing criticism of their authority, afraid that if word of conflict got out, the barrio's reputation for unity and collective capacity would suffer a setback.

In spite of the conflicts they were now experiencing, barrio residents and leaders in the older parts of Villa Pagador were still able to articulate a coherent representation of their barrio as a unified and organized community. This reputation continued to lead to improvements in local infrastructure, exemplified by the struggle to bring a potable water system to the barrio. In 1990, a group of pagadoreños residing in these older sectors created the Association for the Production and Administration of Water and Sanitation (Asociación de Producción y Administración de Agua y Saneamiento, or APAAS) to try to resolve the chronic lack of water in the barrio. Villa Pagador, through APAAS, began a program of incessant lobbying of the city's water and sewers department, Saneamiento Ambiental, to induce the municipality to provide water to the barrio. Villa Pagador was a poor candidate for such attention, being so far from any existing water networks. Nevertheless, APAAS members continued to petition the water and sewers department for assistance. One of the engineers heading this department, a compadre of one of the barrio leaders and himself a migrant from Oruro, finally agreed to keep an eye open for possible funding sources.

Later that same year, the World Bank came to Bolivia to introduce a new pilot project to bring a water system to an urban community (previously, most of the Bank's development activities had focused on rural areas). The Bank's La Paz–based representatives contacted various municipalities in Bolivia seeking a suitable site for this project. The orureño engineer at water and sewers quickly recommended Villa Pagador, suggesting that the barrio's strong level of local organization and cooperation would make it a good collaborator in the project. The World Bank agreed to take a look, and in early 1991 a representative from the Bank arrived in the barrio by helicopter to meet the community, a spectacular display recalled years later by many in the barrio.[14] This representative, a North American engineer, was so impressed with the high level of unity and organization that she claimed to observe in the community that she immediately recommended Villa Pagador as the site of the program. Local leaders of APAAS remembered how they went to great lengths to impress the World Bank official that their barrio was a good choice for the water project, emphasizing that of all the marginal barrios in Cochabamba only Villa Pagador was a "community," with the organizational resources for managing such a project. Formal speeches were made, and barrio residents presented the North American visitors with folkloric handicrafts typical of Oruro, including a set of panpipes (*zampoñas*) purchased in the tourist section of the Cancha: "the kinds of things that gringos like," remembered Don Anacleto, the first vice president of APAAS. "Our first goal was to give her something," he said, "a small gift, but something that signified Sebastián Pagador. Then, the engineer's heart opened, though she was not Bolivian herself, and she promised us that this project was going to happen." Of course, no mention was made in all of this of the internal conflicts over illegal land sales that the barrio was then experiencing.

Ultimately the barrio's petitions were successful, and the World Bank began construction to install the water system in Villa Pagador. Pipelines were built to bring the water in from a well dug in the area of Quintanilla, near the town of Sacaba, a full seven kilometers from Villa Pagador on the other side of the San Pedro hills. Rather than reinforcing barrio unity, however, the water project quickly became divisive. Although theoretically anyone in the barrio was eligible to receive the water, in fact only those barrio residents who had been part of the formation of APAAS—some 385 people, all of whom resided in Primer or Segundo Grupo—were able to participate in the program. Each water recipient had to contribute US$347 to the project, which included the cost of thirty-three days of manual labor per family; individuals could contribute less money by doing the labor themselves. An original plan to install public water spigots on street corners was scrapped in the face of objections by APAAS members, who feared that this plan would make it impossible for them to limit access to the water to APAAS investors only. The World Bank agreed to install water spigots in individual homes.

Today, Villa Pagador is one of the only barrios in the zona sur to have its own water system, independent of the city. The water system itself is a distinguishing feature of the barrio, regarded by longtime barrio residents as a testament to their unity and the communal nature of the struggle that enabled them to receive what amounts to international development attention. This would seem an accurate assessment: according to one city official familiar with the water project and other activities by NGOs in the marginal barrios, Villa Pagador was chosen as the site of this and other projects because NGOs believe it to have a high level of poverty as well as a strong collective organization ("Creen que allá, realmente, hay pobres y que están mas organizados, creen que"). But the water system is also one of the more visible symbols that distinguish established residents of the barrio from newcomers living in far worse conditions on the barrio's periphery. These more recent arrivals to the community, excluded from membership in APAAS and hence from participation in the project, do not have water in their homes and so must purchase it from cistern trucks that make infrequent deliveries to the margins, or else collect it from the canal that borders the barrio and flows only in season. Thus, the newer fringes of Villa Pagador in a sense reproduced the problems that the older part of the barrio experienced in its earliest days.[15] Marginalized from the benefits available to those in the older sections of the barrio, living illegally on dearly purchased land with no political recourse to improve their situation, the residents of these sectors were increasingly becoming vocal in their denunciations not only of the loteadores who were the barrio's leaders, but of the municipality of Cochabamba for its refusal to do anything to help them improve their situation.

COMMUNITY, INTERRUPTED: LAND SPECULATORS
AND THE CASA COMUNAL (1991–2001)

At their basis, the emerging conflicts in Villa Pagador related fundamentally to land. Many of these conflicts stemmed from the land legalization requirements imposed by the city. As discussed in the previous chapter, the municipal authorities, after decades of abandonment, determined in the early 1990s that the time had come to assert municipal control over the unregulated and "chaotic" settlements of the urban periphery. The point at which the municipality's interests intersected with those of the migrant settlers was on the question of land legalization. Without the plano aprobado (the approved plan, representing the alcaldía's acknowledgment of one's rights as legal landowner in the city), barrio residents could not be considered citizens, full members of the municipality entitled to all the benefits due them, including basic city services, the right to vote, and the status of being a *propietario*, owner of one's own land. Citizenship, administered through the bureaucratic instrument of the plano aprobado, thus became a central technique by which the municipality could insert itself into the barrios that had heretofore escaped its control. And key to implementing that technique was decentralization of municipal authority through the Taller Zonal (and its successor, the Casa Comunal) system.

As the previous chapter explained, the Talleres Zonales began as an experimental program within the alcaldía to decentralize municipal authority by locating administrative centers in the communities that the municipality was trying to reach. Through an odd mixture of socially progressive discourse and a technical-bureaucratic function, the Talleres Zonales were intended to transform barrio life by raising the social consciousness of the supposedly alienated migrants of the urban margins and mobilizing them to improve the quality of their lives. At the same time, the property claims of these illegal settlers could be made to fit with the norms and requirements of urban land law, so that the squatters could become legal landowners in the eyes of the municipality. Thus, there was much initial enthusiasm in the barrios when the Talleres were installed. For many in Villa Pagador, particularly the most marginal of the settlers, the Taller Zonal also represented the arrival of a new form of authority in the barrio, one that could provide an alternative to the monopoly on power held by the loteadores of the old barrio.

In 1990, the first of the experimental Talleres Zonales was installed in an unused office adjacent to the central marketplace in Villa Pagador. According to some of the first architects to work in the Taller, Villa Pagador was chosen as the site of this experiment for two reasons. On the one hand, the barrio's reputation for strong community organization was thought to be an advantage in the Taller's efforts to train barrio residents to participate in their own development. On the other hand,

Villa Pagador also had a very high level of illegal settlement. Though the first sector to be occupied was fully legalized, the rest of the barrio (which by this time represented the great majority of both population and land area in the barrio) was clandestine and rife with conflict as a result of the land distribution process. Together, these two inherently contradictory barrio characteristics (i.e., unity and discord) oddly corresponded to the Taller's own contradictory agenda: whereas the idealistic architects of the Taller Zonal wanted to create an empowered and politicized citizenry that would be active in demanding its rights from the state, the bureaucratic functions of the Taller aimed to create an orderly and passive citizenry on the urban margins.

One of the challenges facing the architects of the Taller Zonal (and later, following a hiatus, the Casa Comunal) was to confront the loteadores, who still functioned in some sectors of the barrio as local leaders. In practical terms, the loteadores were the most significant obstacle to legalization, having failed to cede the green areas that the state required to legalize the land claims of barrio residents. The Taller Zonal's mission was to try to compel the loteadores to make these cessions so that the legalization process could proceed. This was made extremely difficult by the fact that this land no longer existed in Villa Pagador, having been sold by the loteadores and occupied by land-hungry migrants. The fact that some nonresident loteadores had illegally sold the green areas and then skipped town after making a quick fortune made it that much more impossible to reconcile the situation equitably. The only solution the Taller Zonal could suggest was for residents themselves to pay the alcaldía to make up for the lack of an area of cession. With this money, the alcaldía theoretically could purchase another patch of land in another part of the city, which, although it would provide no benefit whatsoever to the pagadoreños, would at least fulfill their obligation of ceding land to the state.

This plan had the unintended consequence of accelerating the fragmentation of barrio unity. With the municipality's urging, the residents of particular sectors within Villa Pagador pooled their resources to purchase areas of land to cede to the alcaldía to compensate for the lack of a green area. The result was an increase in *sectorismo*, as some leaders accused others of not thinking of the barrio as a whole: "Everyone pulls for his own side [Cada uno jala por su lado]" became a common complaint about the barrio leadership and the fragmenting of barrio unity. As new subsectors of the barrio were created through division, sale, and settlement of lots, these sectors, too, became organized under the authority of individual sector leaders who pushed for the legalization and provision of services to their own individual sectors. Older but unregularized sectors of the barrio also began to organize individually to lobby the state for the delivery of infrastructural improvements to their own sectors. Following established patterns of clientelism within and without the barrio itself, some new leaders pursued or extended local connections with city- or national-level political parties to bring needed services into their sectors. One sector in particular, 12 de octubre, was often accused of being egotistical and *sectorista*, putting the interests of its own sector ahead of those of the barrio as a whole, because its leaders used their connections with the Unión Cívica Solidaridad (ucs) political party to install public lighting and to pave the streets of their sector alone.

Another change introduced by the architects of the Taller Zonal was the reorganization of barrio political leadership along nominally democratic lines. The Taller implemented a Zonal Council (Consejo Zonal) composed of representatives of each of the barrio's officially recognized sectors (those named subdivisions of the barrio organized with their own internal junta vecinal). These representatives were elected by their constituents within their sector and met every Sunday in the main office of the Taller Zonal to decide issues of importance to the local community. In this Zonal Council the loteadores were but one voice representing Primer Grupo, and their power was greatly offset by the representatives of other districts. The head architect of the Taller Zonal also participated in this leadership council, representing the voice of the alcaldía. Through the council, barrio input was included in the workings of the five commissions (legal issues, infrastructure, health and human services, education, and ecology) of the Taller.

The Taller Zonal encountered much resistance from the original leaders of the barrio, who resented the intrusion of the municipality into a domain that for years had been under their personal authority. According to Don Eulogio, president of the junta vecinal Alto de la Alianza, the men who had served as land speculators and leaders of the original settlement wanted the Taller Zonal to fail from the outset, because its presence meant that city officials might force the loteadores to pay for the crime of selling land illegally. These older leaders also were critical of the fragmentation of authority and unity in the barrio, which to them represented the undoing of years of hard ideological and collective labor to produce a coherent and organized community in the barrio. Although this fragmentation had been developing over time with the growth of the barrio, the original leaders attributed the disunity to the arrival of the Taller Zonal in Villa Pagador. A number of these early leaders today describe the municipality's belated arrival in the community as a deliberate attempt to subvert collective identity and unity, which gave the barrio too much independence from the municipal authorities. Eleuterio Mayta, one of the barrio's founders, remarked on the political motive for undermining barrio unity that he perceived at the root of the alcaldía's intervention in barrio life: "At the beginning, the authorities were not around. Because the Oruro people worked for themselves, they made their own way. All of them did so. Now all of a sudden the alcaldía comes in with its Casa Comunal, intervening, offering some of the projects that people want done, but more than anything the alcaldía is putting the brakes on our self-progress [*autoprogreso*]."

The first architect to staff the Taller Zonal in Villa Pagador, María Hernandez, agreed with many in the barrio who claimed that before the Taller Zonal came to Villa Pagador the barrio was unified behind the original leaders. But she described this unity as an artifice, the product of the manipulations of the loteadores, who compelled barrio residents to collaborate in their schemes at the risk of being disbarred from the community. The Taller Zonal, she said, was a way to rationalize and democratize the community by establishing the municipality as the supreme authority over these assorted forms of local, autocratic rule. Through the Zonal Council, barrio residents for the first time could elect their own local representatives, rather than submitting to the rule of the loteadores. After the Taller began to instruct people on their rights as citizens, this architect suggested, the organization and unity of the barrio populace began to break down, but so did their passivity in confronting their problems and their dependence on the loteadores for leadership. From her perspective, it was the Taller that served to break the authority of the so-called traditional leaders in the community and the driving force behind the mobilization of the barrio population in demanding attention from the municipality. However, on reflection, she felt ambivalent about what the Taller had accomplished:

HERNANDEZ: I have done them much harm, do you know why? Because I opened (pause) spaces (pause) of reflection in them that previously, perhaps, no professional had done for them.

DANIEL: Like what?

HERNANDEZ: For example, prior to my arrival they never realized how the land speculators had swindled them . . .

DANIEL: Ah.

HERNANDEZ: . . . so I, I pointed out to them that, that the swindle occurred when they purchased their lots.

DANIEL: Uh huh.

HERNANDEZ: For one thing, no? Another thing (pause), I opened for them another space of reflection about—a leader doesn't only have to limit himself to, to take what happens sitting down, no? But also to, to shout, to cry, to plead before the authorities, forcefully, their needs, and they have to be heard. . . . No? Because when we entered it was more a community, more a barrio where there was a series of needs, but (pause) they saw those needs as something normal and that there was nothing that could be done about them, that there was—if some time someone complained, fine he complained, but nothing more was achieved. But we taught them to open these channels, no? Where one could go to complain, where one could go to fight, or to ask for a, at least a brick in order to build something.

DANIEL: Yes.

HERNANDEZ: And that's it. I believe that we did them this harm (laughs), or maybe we did them this favor, I don't know which. (Laughs)

For this architect, it was the Taller Zonal that made people aware of the abuses of the loteadores, radicalizing them to come together and to work for change in the community. This is a fascinating suggestion, as it implies that the famed collective unity of Villa Pagador was actually the product of state intervention in the barrio, rather than an indigenous response to state neglect. An alternative interpretation of the impact of the Taller on the local community is that it provided a space within which the already brewing anger and resentment against the loteadores and the state (for its failure to defend the settlers against the predations of the loteadores) could find expression. Most barrio residents disagreed with the perspective offered by the architect, that it was through the Taller Zonal that they became self-conscious political actors, demanding redress of grievances from the alcaldía. Original settlers pointed to the high level of community organization and self-help development ongoing in the barrio prior to the arrival of the Taller Zonal as evidence of the local origins of their political consciousness and collective action. Later settlers, and those among the early group dissatisfied with the rule of the loteadores, concurred with the architect's assessment of Pagador's early unity as a product of the fear inspired by the loteadores; but these settlers also rejected the notion that the Taller Zonal was instrumental in raising their political consciousness. Pagadoreños did credit the Taller with being an important tool in helping them to contest the control of the loteadores, by providing them a means to select new leaders (through the formation of the Zonal Council) and to have these leaders recognized by the municipality as the official representatives of the barrio. And they credited the early functionaries of the Taller Zonal with providing them a friendly ear and unprecedented access to actual official representatives of the municipality.

Whatever the case, the installation of the Taller Zonal in Villa Pagador coincided with a rupture of the system of traditional leadership in the barrio and its replacement with an ostensibly more democratic form of local political participation. For the majority of residents, eager for a means to organize and break the domination of the loteadores, the Taller Zonal (and then the Casa Comunal) offered a space within which the barrio's elected leaders could meet and propose solutions to their problems, supplanting the patronage-based authority of the loteadores. The politicization of the populace also resulted in increasingly strong demands being made on the alcaldía to provide services to the barrio. The barrio population, behind the new leadership of the Zonal Council, became active in demanding redress of their grievances, not only from the loteadores but also from the alcaldía itself, which had provided the space for this organizing in the first place. According to the architect María Hernandez, this was precisely the intent of the project: "We went to work on the resident's most basic level of thought. . . . The resident will never again be the same as he was before the arrival of the Taller. Never again will he be like that! . . . That is the greatness of the Talleres Zonales. That after that project, the community began to demand its right to participate more democratically in municipal life, in the life of the government, in whatever they wanted to participate."

The task of organizing and mobilizing the population became more difficult as the Talleres Zonales were transformed by the alcaldía into the Casas Comunales in 1993. Not pleased with the apparent success of the Talleres Zonales in raising the consciousness of the barrio population, which was becoming increasingly irritating in its demands on the municipality, the alcaldía diminished the social service function of the office as it transitioned into the Casa Comunal, emphasizing instead its bureaucratic role in the land legalization process. This shift in emphasis was not lost on the pagadoreños; one friend, Celestino Loayza, commented on the problems a unified community poses to the authorities: "Every person that takes the job of mayor . . . always is going to want to see a more fragmented population. Why? Because when a people is united, it is a problem for the authorities. Because those people are going to make demands, according to their rights. But when a people is fragmented, one person demands from there, another demands from here, from another side come other demands. . . . 'But to whom am I going to attend? Who is the leader here?' It is for that reason that he [the mayor] wants things to be fragmented here."

Don Celestino's comment also seems to recognize the difficulty authorities have in dealing with subject populations that are not organized according to a model imposed from above by the state. By 1995, this problem began to be addressed by the requirements of the Law of Popular Participation, which called for the reorganization of local communities along lines established by the national government. This reorganization further contributed to the fragmenting of Villa Pagador and other similarly large urban communities: by recognizing local political units only at the level of the OTB (rather than as juntas vecinales, barrios, or other preexisting forms of local organization), the state further promoted the kind of sectorismo that had become so troublesome to broader, barrio-wide forms of organization. As people's loyalties shifted from Villa Pagador as a whole to their own local OTB (source, after all, of development money and political recognition), the sense of a single community called Villa Pagador was further weakened. Additionally, different OTBs and their leadership tended to affiliate with different national political parties, a process that further differentiated groups from one another.

Despite the Casa Comunal's role in destabilizing the community, most barrio residents warmly embraced its bureaucratic function, grateful that its location in the barrio saved them the bus fare and hassle of processing their land legalization paperwork downtown. In the residents' struggle to become full citizens and legitimate landholders in the eyes of the state, the Casa Comunal by the mid-1990s had come to be regarded as a faithful friend of the barrio. Though largely unsuccessful in its efforts to bring the land speculators to account for their crimes against the population (despite bold proclamations like the newspaper headline "Municipal Government Declares Struggle to the Death with Loteadores" ["Gobierno municipal declara lucha a muerte a loteadores" 1993]), the Casa Comunal was locally regarded as having broken the hold of the loteadores over Villa Pagador. Barrio residents expressed a proprietary sentiment toward "their" Casa Comunal, which was locally viewed as an indication of the importance of the barrio in the eyes of the alcaldía, giving them a direct line to the municipality. At the same time, the Casa Comunal proved an effective instrument in regulating and incorporating the marginal barrios, which had been the source of so much trouble to the municipality in the past.

The importance of the Casa Comunal to communities like Villa Pagador was likewise recognized by the alcaldía, whose representatives frequently pointed to these branch offices as evidence of the municipality's commitment to the marginal barrios. The city's former mayor, Manfred Reyes Villa, frequently touted the Casa Comunal system as one of his greatest achievements and used it to generate support for his administration in the barrios. During a visit to Villa Pagador during his campaign for reelection in 1996, Manfred named his support for the Casas Comunales as his greatest contribution to the marginal barrios of Cochabamba: "We believe that right now, the moment of work has arrived, the moment of unity has arrived, among all cochabambinos. . . . Our municipal government will be characterized by the participation of all of you, of the barrio residents, of the leaders, in all the work that we are going to do. We are going to strengthen our Casas Comunales [applause] in order to have the support of all of you [applause]."

CONCLUSION

Los Tiempos, 7 June 1994. Sebastián Pagador: On 5 June the mayor Cap. Manfred Reyes Villa visited at the invitation of the residents, and in his most excellent speech he said that "the moment has arrived to pay the social debt and for the periphery to begin to move closer to the center. Because there is plenty of money. What is missing is the capacity for dialogue and the willingness to work."

The speech was interrupted by a resident of Alto Pagador, who asked the mayor to fulfill the promises made during the last election.

Another resident asked the mayor to force the loteadores to respect the áreas verdes that are rapidly disappearing.

The mayor promised to pave the main avenue of the barrio, which would bear his name, and concluded by saying that we was going to talk less and work more. (Luján 1994)

One key to the effectiveness of the Casa Comunal in displacing the loteadores' hold over the community in Villa Pagador was the introduction of a rationalizing discourse of citizenship. As the discussion in chapter 2 indicates, one goal of the Casa Comunal ideologues was that the institution (particularly in its first incarnation as the Taller Zonal) should work to raise the consciousness of the urban migrant population to recognize and fight for their rights as national and urban citizens. To the extent that it helped barrio residents to establish a new political identity as citizens and provided them with political connections outside of the barrio itself, the Taller Zonal would seem to have fulfilled the goal envisioned by its idealistic authors. Helping barrio residents to conceptualize the lack of infrastructure in their neighborhood as a denial of citizenship also provided them with a new discourse for making petitions to the authorities for provision of services previously unavailable to them. The introduction of this discourse of democracy, citizenship, and rights correlates with the movement, introduced through the Law of Popular Participation in the mid-1990s, to increase "citizen participation" in the workings of government, as well as with larger, continentwide movements toward democratization and expanded citizenship at multiple levels of society.

The hook, so to speak, that the municipality has used to recruit the residents of the marginal barrios to citizenship is the land legalization process, leading to the plano aprobado. Pagadoreños believe that only as holders of a registered deed from the alcaldía will they be seen as citizens of the municipality and of the Bolivian nation; only as "legitimate citizens" can they ever hope to gain state services and attention for their barrio. By securing land titles, people hope to overcome their marginalization, removing the obstacle to recognition as legitimate and deserving citizens. In the words of barrio resident Raúl Flores, "It is necessary that we have that, that paper of approval . . . to have the individual plan, where the mayor has to sign and to place his seal. With that our land is urbanized. With that—maybe it's going to cost us a little more to pay our taxes, maybe they will charge us a little more annual tax. But our papers will be up to date, they will be recognized. Right now we are—how can I put it? Like a natural son that is not recognized by his father as natural, you see? When he is recognized, then he is the legitimate son. So our documents are sort of like that, no? They make us legitimate."

It is perhaps ironic that the institution of the Casa Comunal, primary instrument in state incorporation of marginal barrios to the city, should be so embraced by the residents of these barrios. The Casa Comunal's main function, after all, is to create local legibility by imposing its own definition of order in and asserting municipal authority over the barrios, thus extending state control to those areas of the city that previously had escaped its jurisdiction. It is indeed the case that by accepting the state's terms for citizenship, barrio residents have thereby accepted the alcaldía's claim to legitimate authority over and regulation of Villa Pagador. Such an acceptance would seem to legitimate state domination, implying that the people have exchanged one master for another as the alcaldía has replaced the loteadores as ruler of the barrio, that now it is the municipality to whom barrio residents must pledge loyalty in exchange for needed attention and services. To the extent that state patronage replaced the personalistic relations that characterized barrio politics in an earlier period, this is indeed the case.

From another perspective, however, submission to the state and incorporation in the municipality as citizens is a reasonable political strategy for barrio residents and the new generation of barrio leaders to pursue. For these leaders, elected by the residents of the barrio to serve in the Zonal Council, the alcaldía is welcomed as a provider of services and a means of breaking down the loteadores' authoritarian dominion. The stigma of being classified as illegal, their inability to get credit or to be full owners of their land, their limitations as a barrio in competing with other, legal barrios for state resources and services: all of these figure into people's evaluations of what the state has to offer them. The Casa Comunal from this perspective represents an avenue to achieving the goal of integration into the municipality, providing a means to put one's affairs in order, to receive one's approved plan from the state, and to thus be able to represent oneself to the state as a citizen, deserving of equal rights before the law. In addition, the state as a rational, legal system of domination can offer barrio residents a modicum of protection from the unregulated and arbitrary authority of the land speculators. State authority is judged to be preferable to the rule of the loteadores, constructed through ties of ritual kinship and indebtedness rather than an ostensibly democratic form of governance.

However, acceptance by barrio residents of the state's authority to regulate land sales and determine citizenship does not mean that the residents of Pagador are uncritical of the municipal authorities or ignorant of their own subordinate position. To the contrary, the people of Villa Pagador are extremely critical of the state and engage in multiple struggles for recognition and improved quality of life in their barrio. But people in the barrio recognize that it is only as citizens and full members of the municipality that they can successfully petition the state for services and hope that the state will recognize their demands as legitimate. Long defined as illegal, people in Villa Pagador don the mantle of citizenship to more effectively lobby the municipality for the services they feel they deserve. As shown in the newspaper report of a public meeting quoted above, barrio residents are not afraid to talk back to even the highest-ranking authorities, to express grievances and demand accountability from their elected officials.

Accepting the identity of citizens of the municipality thus does not necessarily imply an abandonment of community or the complete subjection of the barrio to state domination. Indeed, despite the multiple internal conflicts in Villa Pagador, it is remarkable that people of the barrio today continue to elaborate a strong reputation for community, emphasizing in conversations with outsiders their shared origins, strong local unity, and high level of organization. The displacement of the loteadores by the Casa Comunal effectively ruptured the original system of organization within the barrio, resulting in a more fragmented political process; this has been compounded by the individualizing effects of land legalization and the fractioning of community cohesion by the organizational requirements of Participación Popular. Publicly, however, Villa Pagador maintains its character and reputation for unity and organization. The present cadre of leaders, organized through the Zonal Council (which, somewhat confusingly, is today called the Casa Comunal, having named itself after the municipal office of the same name), elaborates a coherent discourse of community that is mobilized in the ongoing struggle to bring infrastructure and other improvements to the barrio. People in the barrio continue to describe Villa Pagador as "the most progressive barrio in the southern zone," a model of organization for all other marginal barrios in Cochabamba, which continues to make progress through the unity and communal labor of its inhabitants.

Nor should it be assumed that the municipality today regards Villa Pagador as its loyal constituency. Municipal authorities are ever vigilant to maintain a presence in the barrio, having learned from historical experience that neglect of the marginal barrios leads to chaos and the emergence of forms of authority that escape municipal control. The alcaldía's willingness to collaborate in barrio projects, to provide infrastructural improvements to barrio residents, may also stem from a certain degree of trepidation regarding the barrio's potential for independence, even for political violence. Believing that its own interventions into barrio life radicalized a now active citizenry in Villa Pagador, the alcaldía fears that it may have created a monster. The willingness of barrio residents to participate in large-scale spectacular displays like those described in the next two chapters only serves to confirm these official fears about the dangerous activities and revolutionary potential of the people of the margins. The architect María Hernandez says that despite its fragmentation today, Villa Pagador continues to be viewed by the authorities as a cohesive unit (*una masa compacta*), united in its political goals as a single community: "They [the authorities] believe that . . . really, if one of them rises up, all of Sebastián Pagador is going to rise up."

4

Performing National Culture
in the Fiesta de San Miguel

In 2001, the United Nations Educational, Scientific and Cultural Organization (UNESCO) announced a campaign to protect and preserve varieties of cultural performance around the world by creating a list of "Masterpieces of the Oral and Intangible Heritage of Humanity." This heritage was defined by UNESCO (2001) as "the totality of tradition-based creations of a cultural community" and included a variety of expressive genres, such as "language, literature, music, dance, games, mythology, rituals, customs, handicrafts, architecture and other arts." For a people's cultural product to be given the grandiose title of "Masterpiece of the Oral and Intangible Heritage of Humanity," it would have to possess "outstanding value" to the society of which it is a part and to be at "clear risk of disappearance." Additionally, UNESCO would require the national state to have compiled an inventory of its intangible heritage and to have adopted strategies for its preservation: "The greater their [the state's] awareness of these treasures, the more attentive they are sure to be to their protection and to that of the local actors who sustain them." UNESCO's intention was thus principally salvage-oriented: "The UNESCO program is based on the conviction that urbanization, modernization, and globalization constitute a great danger for the variety of human culture" (Nas 2002: 142). On 18 May 2001, UNESCO named Bolivia's folkloric Oruro Carnaval, along with eighteen other "traditional cultural expressions," to its World Heritage List.

The UNESCO project, though noble in intent and unprecedented in its effort to preserve "intangible" culture, nevertheless contains some striking contradictions. Most obviously, while decrying globalization as a threat to the persistence of intangible traditional culture, the UNESCO project itself is a globalizing movement, enlisting local cultural manifestations in the service of the development of all humankind, alienating them from their "folk source" and making their continued existence the responsibility of national and international agencies (Nas 2002: 142).[1] Additionally, in selecting the Oruro Carnaval as an aspect of folk culture worthy of preservation, UNESCO has conflated the local with the national, the folk with the elite—a problem inherent in the concept of folklore itself. The Oruro Carnaval is a national cultural event, as emblematic of the Bolivian nation as the Superbowl is of the United States. Carnaval serves an identity-building function (another criterion of UNESCO's selection process), but it is for the formation of a Bolivian national identity predicated on folklorized images of indigenousness, in a society in which those people categorized as indigenous are themselves relegated to the social periphery (Abercrombie 1991, 1992). Rather than an autochthonous expression of indigenous culture, Carnaval in Oruro is a spectacular display of what the Bolivian state identifies as "its" folklore.

The concept of folklore has its origins in mid-nineteenth-century Europe, when scholars of a romantic bent, anxious over the accelerating pace of technological change, industrialization, and urbanization, coined the term to designate the cultural traits of a predominantly rural society that was seen to be rapidly disappearing. The idea of folklore as the expressive culture of the "folk" or "people" connoted this sense of the retrospective, a longing for the cultural traditions of the past; where it referred to contemporary peoples, it implied the existence of survivals, as in the Tylorian conception of cultural elements from the past lingering on into new social states (Williams 1976). Folklore was closely linked to the idea of the premodern peasant community, whose intrinsic *Gemeinschaft* (community, communalism) joined its people in bonds of unshakable solidarity. Such people were viewed as essentially agrarian, communitarian, and somehow outside the flow of modern history, living examples of the nation's past (Rowe and Schelling 1991). Following Herder, folklore also referred to the authentic, uncorrupted, and essential elements of national cultures, the *Volksgeist* that represented the organic spirit of the nation and its people (Bendix 1997). National folklore is thus a repository of the cultural inheritance of the nation; it constitutes a patrimony that the state, identifying itself as guardian of the nation's essential property, can deploy to consolidate its own legitimacy, often in spectacular fashion (García Canclini 1995; Hill 1991).

These conceptions of the essentially rural, autochthonous, and timeless character of folklore and the folk who created it are evident in the application of this idea in contemporary Latin America, where the term simultaneously refers to the cultural practices of the indigenous peasant communities of the countryside and to those of the nation in which these people typically occupy the lowest position in the national socioeconomic and racial hierarchy. Folklore at once refers to the expressive culture of the Latin American peasantry, its origins lost in the ancient past, and to the cultural traditions of the modern nation, in which folklore "constitutes the essence of the identity and the cultural patrimony of each country" (as the Charter of American Folklore, created by the Organization of American States in 1970, asserts; quoted in García Canclini 1995: 152). Implicit in this dual definition is a particular understanding of history that views the rural producers of folklore themselves as trapped in the past, while rescuing folkloric objects and performances as fully emblematic of the modern nation-state. Folklore, then, is seen as something profoundly traditional, descended from the past, while simultaneously representative of the modern nation, or the continuity of the national essence through time (Alonso 1988). The fact that many significant folkloric events (including Bolivia's Carnaval de Oruro) are performed in urban settings further reinforces this dualism, the fact of urban performance serving to underline the modernity of "traditional" culture. In becoming urban, folklore sheds the antimodern associations derived from its purportedly indigenous rural origins and attaches to itself the essence of modernity that the city represents. As a counterpoint to modernity, folklore tends to evade interrogation as a site for the production and legitimization of state power. At the same time, it is folklore's hybridity, its careful blending of tradition and modernity, that enables it to stand as emblematic of the modern, progressive, urban nation that has not lost touch with its traditional, rural past.

Despite Carnaval's role in the production of a hegemonic national formation, the association of Bolivian folklore with the city of Oruro has facilitated the creation of collective identity in places far removed from Oruro itself, where local groups trade on the currency of national folklore to imagine publicly their collective selves through spectacular performance. The association of Bolivian national culture with Oruro

12. Members of a dance fraternity perform in the demostración, part of Villa Pagador's annual fiesta de San Miguel. Photo by the author

produces a contradiction whereby those who are natives of Oruro's countryside can claim to be masters and even progenitors of folklore (despite folkloric Carnaval's urban character), thereby depriving the state of exclusive ownership of national culture. In Villa Pagador, people recognize the potential utility of the national discourse of folklore to confer visibility and prestige on their neglected community. As self-identifying natives of Oruro, the so-called Folklore Capital of Bolivia, pagadoreños are uniquely positioned to manipulate the discourses of the Bolivian state, creatively reappropriating the nationalized meaning of folklore to characterize their own expressive culture.[2] By positioning themselves as the true bearers of the national cultural patrimony, the authentic owners and originators of what has become Bolivian national culture, the people of Villa Pagador can articulate with the national state and the local municipality, transforming their marginal barrio into a location with national folkloric significance, thereby contesting their own political, social, and economic marginalization from Bolivian national life. In public spectacles on the order of Oruro's Carnaval, pagadoreños as self-identifying orureños try to confer on their own community a measure of the prestige that Oruro enjoys at the national and (with the UNESCO announcement) global levels, repositioning themselves closer to the center of national identity (see Rogers 1999).[3]

Additionally, by adopting a distinctly extraregional identification for their community, pagadoreños attempt to distinguish themselves from the larger Cochabamba population that surrounds them.[4] In the Bolivian national imaginary, Cochabamba as both city and region has long been regarded as a site of *mestizaje*, or cultural blending, as opposed to the putatively more "authentic" and "indigenous" locations on the Bolivian altiplano (Albro 1997). As a supposedly hybrid region lacking what many regard as a "deeply Andean" history and culture (see Bouysse-Cassagne et al. 1987), Cochabamba has been described as also lacking its own distinct identity, its very population consisting of groups whose origins lie elsewhere (Albó 1987b). The association of Oruro with the authentically Andean intersects with its identification as a folkloric locality, the idea of folklore itself deriving its symbolic prestige from its unassailable authenticity and traditional status (Bigenho 2002). People in Villa Pagador recognize these large-scale cultural identifications and, in their quest to establish a local identity based on their enduring ties to the cultural traditions of the Bolivian altiplano and specifically Oruro, mine these regional reputations for their own community-building projects. By establishing historical and cultural affiliations between themselves and Oruro, pagadoreños are asserting a claim to authenticity as well, framing their own collective genealogy through a spectacle that demonstrates their connections to the origins of Bolivian national culture.

It is this process of spectacular demarginalization that this chapter explores. I examine the role of religious festivity in the construction and representation of community and collective identity in Villa Pagador and the relationship of the barrio fiesta de San Miguel to other, extralocal folkloric displays. This discussion further explores the theme of community begun in earlier chapters, for it is through performance of what pagadoreños call "our folklore" that local community is produced, reinforced, and performed, for both insiders and outsiders to the barrio. I suggest that the fiesta is best understood as a set of spectacular cultural performances, "important dramatizations that enable participants [and, I would add for Villa Pagador, spectators] to understand, criticize, and even change the worlds in which they live. . . . These public displays provide forums in which communities can reflect upon their own realities" (Guss 2000: 9; see also Bauman 1986; Cohen 1980, 1993; Poole 1990a; Singer 1959). They also enable fiesta practitioners to assert alternative versions of reality, creating new meanings through festive performance (Mendoza 2000; see also Desmond 1997; Goldstein 1998a, 1998b;

Guss 1993; Turino 1993). And significantly in this context of marginality and exclusion, the fiesta as spectacle serves to demonstrate the national belonging of the fiesta performers and provides a vehicle of publicity that calls attention to the barrio's unjust marginalization and potential for collective action.

The chapter is organized into two parts, proceeding from two different but conjoined perspectives, what I have labeled "from within" and "from without." Following a historical description of the fiesta in Villa Pagador, I present an ethnography of the fiesta as experienced on the ground ("the fiesta from within"), exploring the various social, cultural, and economic factors that make the fiesta a central institution in the lives of pagadoreños. This discussion includes a detailed ethnography of the practice of individual fiesta sponsorship and the role the fiesta has played in consolidating Villa Pagador as a unified community. The second part of the chapter ("the fiesta from without") examines the individual- and community-level interpretations of the meaning and significance of the San Miguel fiesta, considering the ways national ideas about Bolivian folklore are deployed in the construction of local identity in Villa Pagador. Especially important here is an understanding of how local ideas about community shape people's evaluations of the meaning of the fiesta. Through this analysis I hope to situate the preceding ethnographic description in the broader context of the local, national, and global meanings ascribed to fiesta practice by both pagadoreños and the Bolivian state.

COLONIZING SAN MIGUEL:
THE HISTORY OF THE PAGADOR FIESTA

Given the centrality of the event to barrio identity and social life, it is curious to note that the fiesta de San Miguel predates the founding of Villa Pagador by some fifty years.[5] Since the early 1920s, the people of neighboring Valle Hermoso, a formerly agrarian community that borders present-day Villa Pagador to the west, have observed the day devoted to their local patron saint, the archangel Michael. It is said that San Miguel appeared miraculously to a peasant in the form of a glowing stone on the hilltop where the chapel presently stands. This peasant, an old man with the family name of Costa, reported the miracle to the rest of the community. A temple was built in the saint's honor, and a painted image of San Miguel beating down the devil with his blazing sword was hung on the wall over the altar. The Costa family became the super-intendents (*dueños*) of the saint, charged with maintaining his image and protecting it. The granddaughter of this same old man later became custodian of the saint.

The origin of San Miguel in the Cochabamba valley is a fact freely acknowledged by pagadoreños, who value the fiesta's history in the region despite the fact that it predates their own. "The fiesta had always existed," acknowledged Don Fausto Huanca, a founder of the fiesta and one of its *pasantes* (sponsors) in 1996. "For the native cochabambinos, it had always existed." In the early days of the barrio, residents of Pagador would wander over to observe the San Miguel celebration next door in Valle Hermoso. People described the Valle Hermoso fiesta in those days as being small and loosely organized, with just a few small groups of dancers marching in a celebration that lasted only one day. In 1979, Eleuterio Mayta, president of the barrio at the time, received an invitation from an acquaintance in Valle Hermoso, asking him to be pasante of their Diablada fraternity for the coming year. Don Fausto explained that the pagadoreños' response to that invitation was to create their own local dance troupe:

> But anyway we [in Villa Pagador] were new here. But one day, maybe he was under the influence of alcohol, or just for fun more than anything else, one of the leaders then, who came after Don Villca, was Don Eleuterio Mayta. And he, at that time, the year was '79, he always had made visits to the dear Señor, and we were like his congregation, we knew what to do. But this man [from Valle Hermoso] took him by surprise, he said to him, "As a leader, you have to cooperate with us, to make the fiesta, to be a participant in our fiesta." So then in that way [Don Eleuterio] took on [the responsibility of being pasante] of the fiesta of the Diablada fraternity. The Diablada of Valle Hermoso. But he didn't take into account his own neighbors, didn't take into account those that lived around him, his countrymen, his friends. But anyway, being that here there were so many people, we got to-gether on one occasion, some time in May of that year. . . . We got together, we organized ourselves, and in other words we basically compelled [Don Eleuterio] to make a new fraternity that now is called the Morenada Central Pagador.

Don Fausto emphasized that it was the people of Villa Pagador who pressured their leader, Don Eleuterio, to reject the invitation to partici-

13. Men dancing the Morenada in the fiesta de San Miguel. Photo by the author

pate in the fiesta alongside the natives of Valle Hermoso. Having been offered the sponsorship of the Diablada fraternity that already existed in Valle Hermoso, Eleuterio was urged by the people of Pagador to form a separate dance troupe in the spirit of the altiplano, from whence the pagadoreños had migrated: "Basically, we forced him to change, no? To change the fraternity. That it shouldn't be a Diablada, but that it should be, something from the altiplano, a Morenada."[6]

The Morenada Central Pagador thus became the first fraternity in Villa Pagador. In that first year the Central danced with only seven morenos, accompanied by a band with seven players. With time, though, as more and more people settled in Pagador and sought to participate in the fiesta, other fraternities formed out of the Central. The Morenada Central is sometimes called the "mother" of the fiesta, for out of it were born all the other fraternities in the barrio. Anacleto Quispe, a local barber and longtime participant in another dance troupe, the Morenada Fronterizos, told the story of this reproduction-through-fission:

First our fraternity was created by the barrio residents, and then it separated from the Morenada Central. Our fraternity didn't have a name, it was also like "the Morenada Central." But then the young people joined in. They said, "Look, the Morenada should give itself a name. Maybe the name of our *llaqta* [Quechua: home, place of origin] or maybe of the province," you see? So they called it Morenada Unión Carangas. At first. But there were others, other sectors, so to speak, our province was adjacent to many others. "Why don't we make a Morenada of *fronterizos* [people from the border with Chile]?" Because many of them worked in transport, contraband for the most part, you know? Smugglers, they're called. "Let's do it." Good, and we agreed, "Do it." Because when there is money anything is possible. Because we were completely certain that the smugglers were going to make it the best fraternity. And they did it. They did it.

Following the introduction of these new Morenada groups, several other fraternities were formed in the barrio, comprising mostly young people and teenagers. These youths introduced new dances into the fiesta apart from the Morenada, whose heavy costumes and clumsy, plodding movements they found unappealing. As Don Anacleto put it, these young men and women were possessed of "an urge to move their bodies" and so formed the fraternity Tinkus Pagador. The Tinku, originally a form of ritualized combat from the north of Potosí, is a popular folklorized Carnaval dance and holds much appeal for young people due to its lively, almost violent movements. Later, in 1989, another group of young people founded the fraternity Valleymanta, which performs the Caporales dance, another familiar Carnaval theme popular among young people.

The changes that the fiesta de San Miguel experienced as a result of the participation of pagadoreños can be characterized as the transformation of a small, semirural, Cochabamba fiesta into a mini-Carnaval, on the model of Oruro's urban extravaganza. Beginning in 1979, when Don Eleuterio formed the first San Miguel dance troupe in Villa Pagador, pagadoreños began to take the local fiesta and recast it in an Oruro idiom, incorporating many distinctive features. Dance groups in the manner of Carnaval fraternities were organized, new Carnaval dances were introduced to the Saint's Day celebration, and other specifically Oruro features were incorporated into fiesta practice, including the ad-

dition of a judged competition on Sunday (the *demostración*) and the
Saturday morning salute to the sunrise (the *alba*). Special foods eaten
only during Carnaval were prepared for the San Miguel fiesta, and specific altiplano rites began to be practiced. From a small, agrarian affair,
then, the San Miguel fiesta was transformed by the Oruro migrants into
a miniature Carnaval in an explicit effort to introduce the traditions of
Oruro to their new valley home (though this process incurred the lasting ire of their Valle Hermoso neighbors, as the anecdote that begins the
book's introduction suggests). At the same time, by changing the local
Saint's Day festival into a Carnaval, pagadoreños could incorporate this
fiesta into their repertoire of strategies for constructing and performing
their community as specifically orureño, thereby tying in to the national
significance of Oruro as the Folklore Capital of Bolivia, a strategy discussed in more detail later in this chapter. First I turn to an examination
of the ethnographic details of the fiesta itself, as it has been practiced in
Villa Pagador.

THE FIESTA FROM WITHIN:
SAN MIGUEL AND VILLA PAGADOR

FIELDNOTES, 29 September 1995. *For much of the day it seemed like
nothing special was happening, people going about their business in much
the same way as they always do. I was reminded of the quiet before the 10 de
febrero anniversary celebration: all morning, nothing to indicate that
something big was about to go down. And then, the hour of the big entrada
comes, and . . . nothing.* Hora Boliviana *("Bolivian time") the people say,
laughing. And sometimes,* Hora Sebastiana, *which is even later and less
reliable than the Hora Boliviana. Then, just when you've begun to give up
hope, thinking it all a big hoax played on the anthropologist with his taste
for fiestas and large public displays, everyone suddenly gathers at the predetermined location, and within fifteen minutes what was a typical quiet
day on the main avenue of Villa Pagador is transformed into a huge, noisy,
colorful parade, unlike anything you'd expect to see suddenly materialize
on this dusty fringe of Cochabamba's periphery.*

For many of Villa Pagador's residents, the fiesta de San Miguel is the
highlight of the year. Especially among the young people in the barrio,
the passion for the fiesta is palpable: you can hear it in their voices when

they describe their plans for the event. Though in terms of sheer numbers most people don't actively dance in the fiesta, the fiesta touches nearly everyone who resides in the barrio. Many people turn out to view the entrada, lining the streets of the barrio to watch the parade pass by, or to watch the demostración, the competitive performance held on the football field on Sunday afternoon. Many people attend the parties hosted by the pasantes in the evenings following the day's dancing; many others attend the weddings that take place during the fiesta; and even the evangelicals in the barrio, who would prefer to avoid the event entirely, can't help but notice the constant music, the shouting in the streets, the normally staid barrio populace reeling drunkenly in the public square.[7] Hundreds of visitors pour into the barrio from the countryside, coming to visit their migrant relatives and friends and to participate in or observe the fiesta. For nearly a week in September the barrio is transformed, and the fiesta reigns over daily life.

The day devoted to San Miguel in the Catholic ritual calendar is 29 September, but in Villa Pagador the fiesta celebrating this devotion spans some five days before and after the official Saint's Day. Preparations for the fiesta begin long in advance of the actual day: an aspiring pasante, for example, may begin saving his money and incurring reciprocal obligations years ahead of the time of his actual sponsorship. Participants in the fiesta are grouped into dance troupes, called *comparsas* or *fraternidades*, the membership of which includes both men and women. Each fraternity names its pasantes, the man and woman (usually a married couple) who will sponsor the troupe, providing the band, the refreshments, and the party that all the participants will attend. Preparations and rehearsals for the fiesta are organized sporadically throughout the year but begin in earnest in June, when the fraternities meet in the evenings or on Sundays to learn their dance steps and to coordinate their routines. These rehearsals continue throughout the (South American) winter, culminating in the *convite*, the big dress rehearsal for the fiesta, which takes place on the Sunday before the entrada, the parade that marks the beginning of the fiesta weekend. In the convite, all of the different dance troupes that have been rehearsing separately convene for a run-through of the entrada, which culminates in a visit to the saint, where the pasantes ask for success in the fiesta.

The fiesta de San Miguel officially begins on a Friday with the entrada, when all of the dance troupes line up in a predetermined order and parade through the barrio, each group dancing its particular folkloric dance to the characteristic music of the brass bands that accompany them. For years people have danced the familiar Carnaval dances of the Morenada, Diablada, Tinku, and Caporales, and in recent years new fraternities have introduced the Tobas (a folklorized version of "savage" North American Indians) and the Sambos (kids in black face and ragged "slave" attire), both imported from the Oruro Carnaval. Along its route the parade winds through the streets of Villa Pagador, which are lined with spectators waving and cheering at the troupes as they dance by.[8] The parade crosses neighboring Valle Hermoso and ends up at the chapel that houses San Miguel, perched atop a small hill overlooking Valle Hermoso and Villa Pagador beyond it. Here the pasantes kneel before the saint, asking him to recognize their devotion and bestow his blessings upon them. Afterward, the fraternities go outside to dance and perform for one another, making a circuit around the church. Later, they return to the homes of the individual pasantes for food and drinks and a party that lasts all night.

At sunrise the next morning (Saturday) everyone returns to the chapel for the salute to the sunrise (the alba), which involves more dancing and drinking and the preparation of *q'alapari,* a cornmeal soup cooked by submerging a hot stone in the broth. This is followed by a mass said in the chapel and then more parties in the pasantes' homes. On Saturday night there are weddings, as those pasantes who have never been married in the church religiously formalize their civic vows. The wedding is followed by another party, which again lasts all night. On Sunday the partying continues into the afternoon, when the demostración is held. This is the formal competition of the fiesta, held on the main football field in the barrio. One by one the dance groups take their turns performing their steps on the field, dancing before a reviewing stand where a group of dignitaries sits to judge the performances. Barrio residents and visitors crowd the edges of the field, elbowing one another for a better view of the show. Later, prizes are awarded in several categories, including best band and best dancers. More parties follow the demostración. On Monday, the last official day of the fiesta, the pasantes of each fraternity pay a visit to the home of the couple who have been designated to serve as pasantes for next year's fiesta, and "deliver" the fiesta to them in a ritual called the *kacharpaya.* Parties follow this event and continue for a day or two afterward, essentially until all the beer and chicha have been finished.

This is the ideal itinerary of the fiesta. Analysis at this level of abstraction can say much about how the fiesta is *supposed* to look, accessing as it does the general model that serves as a kind of organizational tool for fiesta planners, helping to guide the unfolding of the actual fiesta on the ground. In the absence of an effective coordinating effort (the central Comité de Festejos was formed only in 1995 and performs a minor role in this regard), such a model is a necessary means of directing action so that people know generally where they are supposed to be and at what time and what they are supposed to do when they get there. But the ideal version of the fiesta rarely unfolds as it ought to in actual practice and reflects little of the way anyone actually experiences the fiesta. In the next section, I present an ethnography of one pasante and his efforts to host the fiesta, focusing on a description of the first day of the fiesta, the entrada. Through this description, I hope to illuminate many of the more general details important to an understanding of the fiesta de San Miguel in Villa Pagador, while maintaining the flavor of the experience of one pasante's fiesta seen from the inside, to evoke a sense of what it meant and how it felt for him (and for me) to be a part of the entrada in the fiesta de San Miguel. This ethnographic account will serve to ground the interpretations of the political and symbolic significance of the fiesta that follow.

Passing the Fiesta with Don Fausto

Don Fausto Huanca is a *paceño,* meaning that he is from La Paz, but he is from a rural pueblo in La Paz department, not far from the Oruro border, and he knows so much about folklore and how to host (*pasar*) a fiesta that people tend to forget that he is not himself an orureño. When I first made his acquaintance, following the fiesta de San Miguel in 1995, he had just received the office (*cargo*) of pasante of the fraternity Morenada Central Pagador for the fiesta in 1996. To be a pasante was a lifelong goal of Don Fausto; he had danced in fiestas as a kid in the countryside, had been one of the original organizers of the first dance troupe in Villa Pagador (the very same Morenada Central), had served as a guide (*guía*) who helped to instruct others in Pagador about how a fiesta should be run, and had been involved in the fiesta in various capacities ever since. Now he would have the chance to sponsor the show himself.

Don Fausto and his family were also among the first people to settle in Villa Pagador. He arrived in 1977, after his obligatory two years of military service. His parents were ambulatory vendors; they knew Eleuterio Mayta through their work in the Cancha and had bought a small lot in Villa Pagador during the very first sale of land, in the sector known as Primer Grupo. Don Fausto is a cop; he entered the police academy right out of military service, and in one year was trained and certified to be a member of the national police force. He was instrumental in the barrio effort, begun in the early 1990s, to lobby the municipality to station three police officers in Villa Pagador, though he himself is stationed in Temporal, on the far northwest side of the city. In 1996 he was thirty-eight years old. His wife, Doña María, is also from La Paz. She takes care of their seven children and sometimes works selling things in the Cancha when the family needs extra money.

On the morning of the entrada, Friday, 27 September 1996, Don Fausto was busy with last-minute preparations for his fiesta. With some compadres, relatives, and friends he stood in the street before his house, erecting a large metal divider to block off a section of street to be used as a party area. The men used strips of wire to lash tall, corrugated metal sheets to wooden planks, anchored at the bottom with adobe bricks. A huge pile of dirt sat in the street by this barrier, blocking access to Don Ramiro's vacant, roofless garage across the street, which also was to serve as a party area. A terrible argument ensued between Don Fausto, backed by several angry comadres, and a neighbor, the owner of the dirt pile, who claimed that as the street was public space he had every right to leave his dirt there. Eventually he was prevailed upon to move it, but only after Don Ramiro came out and threatened to call the architect down from the Casa Comunal, who would surely fine the man for dirtying the streets. Don Fausto, though obviously tense, retained his excitement and good humor throughout, only occasionally crying out "¡Qué macana! [What a mess!]" with a laugh, throwing his arms to the sky.

In the enclosed yard of Don Fausto's house, a group of about fifteen women, all of them relatives, friends, and comadres of the pasantes, sat beneath the metal awning that covered the outdoor kitchen, talking, preparing food, and sorting out the rented costumes for the entrada. Many of them were laughing, peeling carrots and potatoes, infants strapped across their backs, speculating about the upcoming fiesta and remembering past ones. The rented clothes lay on a sheet of plastic in a big pile beneath the awning. At a word from the comadre in charge of doling out the costumes, the women rose and stood around the pile, each with a glass of beer in her hand served by the comadre. Each woman poured an offering around the edges of the pile in the ritual act of the *ch'alla*.[9] As she poured the offering, each woman asked the *Pachamama* (Earth Mother) to provide a successful fiesta and good luck for Don Fausto's fraternity in the entrada. With a laugh, each woman finished the beer that remained in her glass. The comadre in charge of distributing the costumes then handed each woman her outfit: an elaborately decorated red and pink pollera, a white blouse with lace edges, and a *matraka* (noisemaker) to twirl as she danced. The women supplied their own brown derby hats.[10] In a small notebook the comadre kept a record of what each woman received, how much she had paid, and how much she still owed for the rental.

The fence out front now ready, Don Fausto came inside and washed his hands, and with Doña María and four of their kids we headed up to the house of Don Salvador, last year's pasante of the Morenada Central. As pasante of the previous year it was Salvador's job to accompany the present pasante in the entrada and demostración and to host a small party at his house after the alba on Saturday morning. He also would host the *kallayku*, the blessing of the men's costumes that marks the beginning of the fiesta. In Don Salvador's yard a number of male dancers had gathered to divvy up their costumes. These had been brought from the city of Oruro by a husband-and-wife team of professional costume makers. They had been coming to Pagador for ten years, bringing costumes for the dancers in the barrio fiesta. They explained that there is no good folkloric costuming in Cochabamba, and so for a really superior fiesta you have to import the costumes from Oruro, where these same outfits are used in Carnaval.

There are two kinds of male dancers in the Morenada: the Morenos, with large, tiered costumes that resemble wedding cakes, and the Achachis, similarly dressed but with big tails that protrude like a dragon's out of the back of the costume. I tried on one of the Achachis; they weigh 50 kilos, and I instantly broke out in a sweat, to the amusement of my friends. The dance of the Morenada is said to represent the exodus of the African slaves, who were held by the Spanish in the mountains of Potosí, where they worked the mines to extract silver for export to Spain. But the Africans (so the story goes) were physiologically ill-suited to the high altitudes of Potosí and so were marched across the mountains to the tropical lowlands of the Yungas, where the Afro-Bolivian populations of today reside (see Boero Rojo 1991). In Oruro, Morenada dancers wear huge, terrifying masks, grotesque caricatures of "black" (*negro* or *moreno*) faces, with big protruding eyes, pendulous lips, and slathering

14. Women dancers in a Morenada fraternity in Villa Pagador. Photo by the author

tongues, said to represent the exhaustion that the slaves felt as they marched across the high mountains. In Villa Pagador, however, the dancers don't wear masks, only brown or black fedoras on their heads. They say it is because of the climate in Cochabamba: in frigid Oruro it's not a problem to wear a big heavy mask, but in the heat of the valley it would be suffocating. The dancers crank matrakas as they dance, which are said to reproduce the sound of the slaves' chains as they dragged them along the trail. These matrakas often are shaped like icons of the groups that carry them; the dancers in the fraternity sponsored by the transportation syndicate in the barrio (the Morenada Transpagador), for example, carry noisemakers shaped like the buses they drive. The matrakas twirled by Don Fausto's dancers were simple in shape, red wooden rectangles with Taquiña beer stickers pasted across the front.[11] The costumed male dancers in the San Miguel Morenada are followed by groups of female dancers, dressed in identical shawls and multi-layered pollera skirts.

Though the entrada was slated to begin within the hour, Don Fausto still had errands to run in the Cancha, so together we left Don Salvador's and got on a bus for the city. Don Fausto was quiet and distracted—now, he admitted, I'm starting to get nervous. He had a bad cold and had not slept the night before, getting things ready for the party. Arriving at the

Cancha we headed for a tailor's stall, set among dozens of others like it, where Don Fausto stopped to pick up his new suit for the entrada. (He previously had purchased another new suit, which he would wear for his wedding on Saturday night.) We waited while the tailors sewed the final buttons on the brown polyester jacket. When the suit was ready we performed a few other errands, picking up some red gladiolas for Doña María and her comadres to carry in the entrada, a few bags of white confetti to rub in people's hair, and two boxes of bottle rockets that I paid for, Don Fausto by now being completely out of cash.

By the time we returned to the barrio it was past one o'clock, the scheduled hour for the departure of the entrada. Some men in Moreno costumes were milling about in Don Fausto's yard, and the women in charge of the kitchen were beginning to serve up bowls of noodle soup. The band arrived then, Juventud Nobles of Cochabamba, all of them dressed in identical light-brown suits with matching fedoras, white shirts open at the throat, and piled their shiny brass instruments in a big heap in one corner of the house compound. The band members took seats along the wall of the compound, where they were served bowls of soup by one of the comadres.

After they had eaten, the band members gathered in a loose circle around the pile of instruments for the q'owa, a blessing intended to bring success to the fiesta and its participants (Rocha 1990). On the altiplano the q'owa is traditionally performed on the first Friday of each month, as a ritual to purify homes and bring health and well-being to the occupants. It is also observed before important fiestas like Carnaval, when success in a particular endeavor is desired. The band members now passed from man to man a bag of coca leaves and a small bottle of clear grain alcohol. Each man sprinkled some of each of these substances over the instruments, mumbling a short benediction before taking for himself a small sip of the grain alcohol. They also passed around two brown eggs: when a man received an egg he passed it all over his body, muttering softly to himself, finally kissing the egg and blowing on it before passing it to the man next to him. It was explained to me that through this act all of the *maldición* (wickedness, evil) was drawn from the man's body and into the egg. When the eggs had made a complete circuit of all the band members they were flung far away from the house compound, taking their bad luck with them.

Meanwhile, a small fire had been lit in another corner of the compound and a *misa* was burned over it. The misa is a ritual offering consisting of a sheet of paper covered in various ingredients, including herbs and plants, food items, and small plaster images of desired objects, which are presented as a gift to ensure the blessing of supernatural beings (Bouysse-Cassagne et al. 1987; G. Martínez 1987; Van den Berg 1985). The misa is burned as part of the purifying ritual of the q'owa.[12] In urban Cochabamba misas are often purchased ready-made from vendors in the Cancha. The burning misa, laid atop a rusted metal sheet, was carried over to the pile of musical instruments, where its thick, fragrant smoke would purify the instruments so they would produce better music for the fiesta. Finally, a live chicken was brought over to the pile, where a man touched it to each of the instruments as other men sprinkled coca leaves and grain alcohol over the pile and onto the ground. The chicken would serve the same function for the instruments that the eggs had for the men, drawing the evil and bad luck into itself. After touching it to the instruments, one man held the chicken while another grabbed its head and hacked it off with a dull kitchen knife. The men cheered and sprayed beer over everything, and the man holding the chicken tossed it to one side, where it ran in circles for a few moments before collapsing lifeless to the floor. Some men chanted "Lengua! Lengua!" and one picked up the chicken's head and French-kissed it, rising bloodied and grinning to the cheers of his friends.

The entrada got going around two o'clock. Dressed in brown fedora and beaded poncho, I danced at the front of the Morenada Central with Don Fausto, Doña Maria, and their invited guests: Don Salvador and his wife, last-year's pasantes; Doña María's ancient mother; the ritual godparents (*padrinos religiosos*) of Fausto and María's upcoming church wedding; and Fausto's sister and her husband. We were followed by the dancers, who were organized into several subgroups or *bloques*. Each gender-segregated bloque consisted of a number of dancers who performed their choreographed steps in unison. By local estimation, the more bloques a dance troupe has the better, as size of the group is taken as a measure of its popularity and success. ("We had *seven* bloques this year!" bragged a friend from the Morenos Fronterizos, which took first prize for heavy costumes in the demostración.) Each bloque within the larger fraternity had a leader, who carried a whistle to coordinate the group's dance steps. The band followed in the rear of the troupe, so those of us at the very front had trouble hearing the music. The Morenada is a slow, rhythmic, plodding dance, whose side-to-side movements are said to parody the court dances of colonial Spain (a claim that either contradicts or complicates the description of the dance as a slave exodus; Morales 1992). Thus, the progress of the entrada through the barrio was slow, and I was surprised to find that it took great physical exertion to dance at such a deliberate pace. Don Fausto's fraternity had six bloques, each comprising twenty to thirty dancers, so all told, the group (including the band, the invited guests, and other participants such as food servers and chicha pourers who followed alongside like a mobile pit crew) numbered over two hundred people. Dancing at the front of the parade I could see the fraternity stretching along the street behind me, a moving, brightly colored ribbon against the monotonous brown of the barrio's streets and homes. Don Fausto beamed with pride at the size and organization of his group.

The parade wound through the barrio, ending at the small chapel where San Miguel is housed. Along the way people watching cheered as we passed by, occasionally running out to offer us a bottle of beer or a gourd cup (*tutuma*) of chicha. We arrived at the chapel and danced a circuit around it before going inside, where the pasantes knelt before the painted images of the saint and Jesus on the cross.[13] Fausto and Salvador had been carrying giant white candles in the entrada, and these they now set among others placed on the altar before the saint, lighting them with a prayer and a petition for his blessing. Afterward, we all filed out through a door in the back of the church, admitting a cold, late-afternoon wind that whipped in from outside and nearly extinguished most of the candles on the altar.

Outside, we watched other groups as they arrived and danced around the church. Don Salvador invited me to drink with him at a nearby storefront. When it was dark, the fraternities reassembled and danced down the backside of the hill we had earlier ascended, the dancers from the Central ending up at Don Fausto's house, where the comadres served a meal of thin, spicy soup. Everyone was drunk and happy and laughing. In the street in front of the house the dancers gathered for *vísperas*, the final event of the evening. The band played thunderously as the dancers went through their steps for the last time that day. The party continued through the night, with people gathered in small groups in Don Fausto's compound, singing, laughing, and drinking chicha till they could no longer keep themselves upright.

Paying for the Party

By local estimation, the pasantes' generosity and gross expenditure is one important measure of the quality of the fiesta. The expenses facing every pasante are enormous. A good band, for instance, one that has made the trip from Oruro, wears matching outfits, is composed of a large number of players, and plays with ability, can cost up to US$5,000, an astronomical figure in a country where the average per capita monthly income for urban residents in 1995 was about US$40 (Crespo 1995). In Don Fausto's case, he contracted with a Cochabamba band—a local band, but famous, Don Fausto apologized—called Juventud Nobles, composed of forty-five members, a medium-size group by all accounts. Hiring this band to play the entire three days of the fiesta cost him US$2,500. Providing food for all of the dancers, band members, and others associated with the fraternity or attending the party can cost another US$800–1,000. Don Fausto didn't even want to think about how much he was spending on alcohol for his party; he provided eight huge barrels of chicha and one hundred cases of beer, some 1,200 liter bottles. I would estimate Don Fausto's expenditure (totaling in the end about US$4,400) to be in the low to middle range of what is normally spent in sponsoring a fraternity, owing to certain efforts to economize. For instance, in hiring a local band, he spared himself the expense of housing the band members, an outlay facing those pasantes who hire the more expensive and prestigious Oruro bands. The only aspect of fiesta expense for which the pasantes are not responsible is the costuming of the dancers, who individually rent their outfits, which can cost up to US$50 for the heavy Moreno costumes. Although not prohibitively expensive, the cost of costume rental does require individuals to save their money to dance in the fiesta.

Don Fausto described the burden one assumes by accepting the economic obligations of fiesta sponsorship as like "throwing the house out through the window," that is, an insane distribution of wealth ("uno tiene que erogar demasiado dinero"). Critics of the fiesta, especially evangelical Christians, often cite the incredible "waste" (*derroche*) associated with fiesta sponsorship in their condemnation. Indeed, figuring out how individual pasantes manage to pay for their fiestas is one of the great topics of conversation during San Miguel, provoking much speculation among observers. Some from outside the barrio assert that trafficking in illegal drugs pays for the fiesta, and certainly some people in

15. A fiesta band. Photo by the author

Pagador are involved in the drug trade, as people are in many communities in nearly every corner of Bolivia. Narcotrafficking touches every aspect of Bolivian economic life, and to some extent it probably plays a role in funding San Miguel. But among the pasantes I know well, including Don Fausto, coca production and narcotrafficking are not income sources for fiesta sponsorship.[14]

Many pasantes are among the wealthiest residents of Villa Pagador, including land speculators and transport owner-operators; the sponsor of the Valleymanta fraternity in 1996, for example, was a well-known loteador, transportation syndicalist, and the owner of a lucrative beer distributorship. Others, like Don Fausto, have no such income sources. Don Fausto is a police officer, and in 1996 took home a monthly salary of about US$32. When asked how he paid for his fiesta that year, Don Fausto first answered philosophically, saying, "Where there is faith, anything is possible." He compared it to Jesus with the loaves and fishes, observing that when one honestly believes in the power of the saint a small amount of money can go a long way. He also rejected the criticism of some in the community who hint that as a police officer he paid for the fiesta with bribes solicited from criminals he had apprehended, in exchange for looking the other way or releasing them from custody after they had been captured. Don Fausto said that such comments reflect the jealousy of others who lack his true faith in the saint and can only imagine the worst in people. He is as honest in his professional practice as he is in his faith in San Miguel.

At a more practical level, Don Fausto called in some of his debts established through the *ayni* system to pay for the fiesta (see Albó 1985; Izko 1986). Historically in the Bolivian countryside, ayni is an institution of delayed reciprocity in which a fiesta sponsor receives gifts of money, beer, food, and the like from friends, relatives, and people who may want to sponsor their own fiesta sometime in the future (Isbell 1985; Yampara Huarachi 1992). The pasante is then obligated to return these contributions at a later time, through reciprocal exchange at a later fiesta. This system functions to a limited extent in Villa Pagador, perhaps less so than in other urban fiestas described in the literature (e.g., Buechler 1980; Crandon-Malamud 1993). Don Fausto, for example, asserted that ayni contributions to his fiesta were not extensive, and the people making ayni contributions did not form a special retinue of retainers around the pasante during the fiesta. Nevertheless, over the years he had contributed to the fiestas put on by other pasantes in his fraternity, the Morenada Central—a case of beer here, 100 pesos there— and these people reciprocated to help support his fiesta in 1996. More significant than ayni was the naming of ritual compadres (kinsmen) or padrinos (godparents) to help pay for the event. These people pay a specific amount or provide a designated item to the fiesta and are named padrino of that item. As Buechler (1980: 159) has indicated for La Paz, the naming of padrinos in a fiesta context is akin to naming cosponsors of the fiesta, and so does not incur the obligation to reciprocate that is associated with ayni. A number of these people did in fact dance at the front of the parade with Don Fausto, including myself as "padrino of the video" that I later shot of Fausto and María's church wedding.

The pasante's family and ritual kin play important roles in organizing the events and making sure things run smoothly. Each aspect of the party has a designated coordinator, usually a relative, a compadre, or a godchild (*ahijado*), who takes charge of certain activities. For example,

Don Fausto's sister organized the food, supervising its preparation and making sure each guest received a plate; his brother-in-law organized and doled out the alcohol; other kinspeople distributed the costumes to the dancers, organized the band, and so on. Don Fausto described himself as being like the general in charge of coordinating the activities of all of his officers. Most of the organizational work at the party seemed to fall to two lieutenants, Don Fausto's sister and one of Doña María's goddaughters, who were particularly active in serving food and managing the behavior of drunken revelers. In general, women are critical participants in the behind-the-scenes coordinating of the fiesta's many support systems.

When a wedding is involved, as it was for Don Fausto and Doña María, a series of people take on the responsibility of providing various elements of the wedding bash that supplements the regular San Miguel party. Each of these people is termed a padrino or madrina for that aspect of the party. For instance, there are *padrinos religiosos*, who pay for a good part of the wedding itself, such as hiring the church and the priest; a *padrino de amplificación*, who hires the speaker system for the music and narration at the party; a *padrino de la torta*, who buys the wedding cake; and a *padrino de la colita*, who provides the commemorative pins with ribbons bearing the names of the various padrinos. Especially important in terms of keeping tabs on future reciprocal obligations is the *padrino de conteo*, who is responsible for recording all gifts given or promised to the marrying couple, to facilitate later reciprocation. Furthermore, should a promised gift not be delivered, it is the padrino de conteo's responsibility to make up this loss to the couple out of his own pocket. As padrino de video, I provided a videotape and photo album of the wedding and the fiesta as a gift to the couple. Additionally, individual guests at the wedding reception make small contributions to the cost of the party through small monetary gifts, which they pin to the clothing of the bride and groom during the course of the reception. These small individual contributions, given as wedding gifts, can add up to significant amounts by the end of the evening (Crandon-Malamud 1993).

The fiesta de San Miguel in Villa Pagador, then, only vaguely approximates the rural fiesta in terms of the role of traditional systems of reciprocity in fiesta sponsorship (see Foster 1967; Vogt 1969). Although reciprocal fiesta sponsorship through ayni is recognized as a traditional aspect of the rural fiesta, it is only partially utilized in Villa Pagador, such

16. A fraternity parades before the Catholic church during the
fiesta de San Miguel. Fiesta sponsors often observe their religious
weddings in the church at fiesta time. Photo by the author

as in the small donations people make to a fiesta sponsor in the hope of
securing reciprocity from him in the future. These contributions are
nonetheless significant to fiesta sponsorship, as the small gifts do add
up, and an individual who has made many such gifts to fiestas over the
course of several years can later recall them in sponsoring his own fiesta.
This is one of the principal roles of the dance fraternity, in that it coordi-
nates a group of ayni participants among whom many small donations
are concentrated to produce a strong cumulative effect. However, sponsorship of the barrio fiesta is also highly individualized, with the naming
of padrinos being a form of cosponsorship that does not incur the
formal obligation to reciprocate. This type of cosponsorship reflects the
individualized nature of economic life in the barrio; economic collaboration by family and friends, such as it is, is not formally institu-

tionalized through ayni giving. At the same time, the description of certain forms of gift exchange as ayni implies a communalist agenda, an effort to establish symbolic ties to the forms of reciprocity that characterize the rural fiesta so as to bolster the "community-building" function of San Miguel (see below).

The burden of sponsorship that a man and his family assume can last for many years after the fiesta ends. When I saw Don Fausto in 2002, six years after his sponsorship of the Morenada Central, he complained that he was still paying off debts incurred in 1996. He had given up dancing in the fiesta himself, afraid of incurring new obligations which he did not expect would ever be repaid, as he had no intention of sponsoring the fiesta again. Some friends and relatives from his pueblo in rural La Paz had urged him to return and sponsor a Saint's Day celebration there, but he had refused; the specter of incurring a fresh round of debts and obligations was too much for him to even consider. Still, said Don Fausto, being the pasante of San Miguel was the great experience of his life, and well worth the expense.

A Pasante's Motivations

Don Fausto professed a strong faith in the Señor de San Miguel. His primary motivation for being a pasante was to express this faith, and through this expression to bring the blessing of the saint on himself and his family. Doña María claimed the same motivation, as did every fiesta participant with whom I spoke, from pasantes to the ordinary dancers in the fraternities. The more cynical accused the pasantes of wanting to sponsor the fiesta out of a desire for material gain, in the hope that the saint would bring them a new house, or a car, or some material good fortune, but Don Fausto insisted that those who make such accusations simply don't understand what it means to be a pasante. Fiesta sponsorship must come from a true faith in the saint. One young woman, a hairdresser with her own little salon in the barrio and a dancer in the Valleymanta fraternity, described a "good" fiesta sponsored by one Don Felipe, who was motivated not by material aspirations, but by faith alone:

> The following year they gave it [sponsorship of the fiesta] to Don Felipe. He passed the fiesta very well. Yes, it was a very good fiesta, he passed the fiesta with complete faith. And all the members of the fraternity, he always guided us with that faith. He always told us that to dance in this fiesta for the Señor, that it shouldn't be out of a

devotion to drinking or wanting to look for girls or guys or to get in a fight. None of that, no—it should be out of devotion to the Saint. To the Señor. Yes. He who dances out of devotion to the Señor, it's because he has faith, and He will help him and all will be well for him. One has the right then to ask for things that he desires, if he is dancing out of faith then this wish will be considered. But if he is not doing it [for faith], he won't get that wish, it won't be considered by the Señor.

A second motivation for Don Fausto to be a pasante was the desire to have a church wedding, to ratify in religious ceremony his civic union to Doña María. A number of pasantes expressed similar motivations, and every year during San Miguel three or four couples have a church wedding and a party afterward. This party, which by custom anyone marrying in the Catholic church is obligated to host, poses the obstacle to having a church wedding in the first place, for the expense of such a festivity forces many young, struggling couples to forgo a religious wedding and to observe only the civic vows.[15] Pasantes typically describe the church wedding during San Miguel as killing two birds with one stone ("matar dos pájaros con un solo tiro"): because they are already laying out the expense to host the fiesta, they can easily make the party into a wedding celebration and thereby satisfy the demands of custom. A church wedding is seen as the real ratification of the union between a man and a woman; prior to that, it is as though they are not really married, and men often take the opportunity to maintain other women, sometimes with children, on the side. This practice of "concubinage" is very common in Villa Pagador and elsewhere. Don Fausto said that many young men don't want to be "tied down" to one woman, and lacking the money for a church wedding, they feel little obligation to be faithful. This is a practice many women find intolerable and is a motivating force in driving some Catholic women to the evangelical church, where parties are prohibited and religious weddings are much more common (Brusco 1995; Gill 1994; Paerregaard 1994). Although Don Fausto does not have extramarital affairs, Doña María said that the desire for a church wedding was one of her primary motivations for being a pasante. For his part, Don Fausto regarded it as a sign of his maturity as a man, a husband, and a father to commit to a marriage in a church wedding.

A final motivation for becoming a pasante, sometimes hinted at but rarely stated openly, is what one pasante termed the *aspecto social*, the social dimension of fiesta sponsorship. In becoming pasantes, a couple garners a certain measure of social status or prestige in the eyes of the community. The acquisition of prestige is a feature commonly identified by anthropologists interested in fiesta-cargo systems throughout Latin America as an important motivation of fiesta sponsors, a means to redistribute wealth and tie individuals into a collectivity through office holding (Buechler 1970; Cancian 1965; M. Harris 1964). Becoming a fiesta sponsor in Villa Pagador is not part of a hierarchical or integrated system of offices, although it is seen as another role that a community-minded individual will take on in the barrio. Being a fiesta sponsor can open the door for a man to other, elected offices in the community, for in sponsoring the fiesta he demonstrates his commitment to and willingness to serve the barrio. Assuming the role of pasante in Villa Pagador can bring status or shame to the couple sponsoring the fiesta, depending on how they are perceived by the people of the community.

Certain prerequisites can help ensure that the fiesta is successful and that the pasante is deemed a good sponsor by his invitees. Don Fausto said that a good pasante is one who is well-known in the community and is well liked by a lot of people. Given these good relations in the barrio, he is able to inspire other people with his energy and goodwill and move them to enthusiastic participation (as in the description of the pasante Don Felipe, above). A good pasante has ideally held several other offices in the community, such as being a leader of his sector, a leader of the potable water committee, head of the athletic league, or president of the Padres de Familia in one of the local schools. Through this participation he will have become known as a responsible person and have proven himself to be community-spirited and not an egotist (*egoísta*), one who assumes leadership roles for his own self-aggrandizement. A pasante must be a popular, well-liked person in the community or else no one is going to want to follow him or to help make his fiesta a success.

And a successful fiesta is the goal of every pasante. Everyone attending (and many people observing from without) evaluates the fiesta sponsored by each pasante and compares each to those of other pasantes of that year's fiesta, or to parties of the same fraternity in years past. Do the pasantes care for their dancers, providing them with drinks while they're dancing and good food when they're finished? Is there plenty of beer and chicha at the party? Is the band top-notch? The goal, said Don

Fausto, is to make each year's fiesta slightly better than the year before, a task that obviously becomes more difficult with the passage of time. The other goal is to win the official competition (the demostración), to be judged as having had the best dance troupe of the year.

The fiesta is thus characterized more by competition than by collaboration among dance groups, and people often express ferocious loyalty to their own group or virulent animosity against others. Prizes are given out to the best dancers and the best bands, based on their performance in Friday's entrada and Sunday's demostración; in 1996, several large, gold-plated trophies were donated by the municipal government, and a panel of judges composed of local leaders and outside dignitaries sat on a dais overlooking the football field to determine the winners of the competition. (To his lasting disappointment, Don Fausto came away empty-handed.) In addition to these formal prizes, informal judging goes on constantly during the fiesta, and the post mortem that follows the fiesta week can last for years. After the 1996 fiesta, for example, there was much gossip and criticism of the pasantes of one fraternity, who apparently hosted a very weak fiesta. The dancers in this fraternity are mostly youths and children, and the pasantes were criticized for not serving them refreshments while they danced, for providing bad food, and for generally attending inadequately to the needs of the dancers. The fact that the pasantes of this fraternity were the daughter and son-in-law of a wealthy land speculator in the community, who was presumed to be the real behind-the-scenes pasante of the event, may also have served to fuel this criticism. As a man who was ill-regarded in the barrio to begin with, an "opportunist" (oportunista) who had profited unfairly through illegal land sales, he had little credibility for sincerity and public-mindedness in the community, and people were disinclined to be sympathetic toward evidence of tight-fistedness in his fiesta.

Although the sponsorship of a fraternity in the fiesta de San Miguel is in some senses comparable to the holding of a fiesta-cargo position in a rural community, one cannot profitably understand the barrio fiesta in terms of the rural fiesta-cargo systems described in the literature (see Celestino and Meyers 1981; Doughty 1968; Fuenzalida 1976; H. Martínez 1959; Stein 1961). The San Miguel fiesta does not form part of an integrated fiesta-cargo system, in which people assume the obligations of fiesta sponsorship as part of a nested sequence of offices in the community designed to draw individuals into leadership roles (Mangin 1954) or to level wealth among individuals in the community (Wolf 1955). There is no civil-religious hierarchy in Villa Pagador as there is in the countryside, through which men pass in a cycle that lasts a lifetime, holding various offices and responsibilities in the community (Coyle 2001; Isbell 1985). Some claim that the San Miguel fiesta was initially founded in the barrio out of a desire to create cargo positions or offices that men could hold, to reproduce in the urban barrio a kind of fiesta-cargo system like that of the countryside. One friend (a student of sociology at the local university) insists that the founders of the barrio had the custom (*costumbre*) of holding offices, a holdover from life in the countryside, and that the fiesta was necessary to provide a means of achieving status in the community. This may have been the case in the early days of the barrio, when the local leaders imagined themselves to be something like *jila-qatas,* the traditional leaders of Andean peasant communities whose job it was to bridge the spiritual and secular worlds, assuming fiesta cargos as an inseparable component of their political leadership (Rasnake 1989; Ströebele-Gregor 1996). Fiesta sponsorship may have served to legitimize the authority of these early leaders of the barrio, for these men gained additional status and attached an aura of tradition to their leadership by assuming the responsibilities of pasantes.

Today, however, the sponsorship of a fiesta in Villa Pagador does not constitute the same kind of obligation that it once did in the countryside. Rather, it is an opportunity that some men seek out to position themselves as leaders of the community and to demonstrate their sense of civic responsibility. In Villa Pagador, holding the office of fiesta sponsor is a means of validating status already achieved, and not in itself a means for acquiring it. To a certain degree, the desire for prestige is a motivating factor for becoming a pasante in Villa Pagador, to the extent that a man who serves as pasante of a fiesta can claim to have established himself as an important figure in barrio life. Men of means are sometimes asked by fraternities to serve as sponsors, and this is taken as an indication of a man's status in the community. Indeed, most of the pasantes of the 1996 fiesta lived within a few blocks of each other in Primer Grupo, the oldest, wealthiest, and most established sector of the barrio. Also, as stated above, successful pasantes are men who have held other positions of responsibility in the community and so are already regarded as men of status, the fiesta serving as an additional distinction in their local career. But people scoff at the pasante who is clearly spending more than he can afford in an effort to gain prestige, and (as in the

17. Fiesta sponsors dance in the demostración, while local dignitaries and invited guests look on. Photo by the author

case of the land speculator sponsoring the fiesta in his daughter's name) fiesta sponsorship cannot compensate for other abuses or shortcomings of the individual holding the office. A pasante is just as likely to earn criticism as status for sponsoring the fiesta. Don Fausto, as noted earlier, was accused of paying for the fiesta with bribes taken through his job as a policeman, a criticism that somewhat muted his prestige. Similarly, the pasantes of the Tinku fraternity in 1995 were a couple who had been living in Argentina, but their return to the barrio to sponsor the fiesta was regarded with skepticism by some who viewed their return as a distasteful demonstration of their newly acquired wealth.

People in Villa Pagador are very sensitive to the ambitions of those known to be egoístas or *prepotentes* (domineering, overbearing people, convinced of their own superiority), individuals out for their own gain at the expense of the community, and are loath to bestow prestige on someone who is perceived to be assuming an office out of self-interest.

Thus, the effort to build a local reputation must be balanced carefully with the need to be perceived as acting out of public goodwill. In such a context, the insistence on faith in the saint as a pasante's primary motivation is critical: only by being perceived as acting out of purely selfless motives can a pasante hope to be regarded as a good or successful pasante, and so achieve a measure of prestige through his sponsorship. This is further problematized, though, by the high level of competitiveness among fraternities. A pasante must walk a fine line between serving the interests of his fraternity, by trying to win the competition and put on a fiesta better than the other fraternities in the barrio, and serving the interests of the community, which are more generalized and harder to define yet require a public demonstration of personal disinterestedness (see Albó and Preiswerk 1986).

The pasante is evaluated primarily through his efforts to build community in Villa Pagador. Although the organization and practice of the barrio fiesta does not greatly resemble that of the rural fiestas of people's places of origin, pagadoreños recognize—in something like a functionalist ethno-ethnology—that a fiesta serves to build community, in the sense of forging unity among a group of people sharing common goals and concerns. They look to the fiestas of the countryside with the hope of reproducing something like them in the barrio, with the idea of creating the same kind of community that they remember or idealize about the countryside. Many fiesta participants are young people who grew up in the barrio and have no real memory of life in the countryside, yet they nevertheless turn to the fiesta as a way to create a sense of community and cultural identity for themselves in the city. Some describe Villa Pagador as one big *ayllu*, referring to the rural Andean system of social organization whose definition, though complex, is usually glossed as "community" (Albó et al. 1990; Archondo 1991; Choque and Mamani 2001; Platt 1982a, 1982b). The fiesta is regarded as a way of communicating this sense of collective identity among people who have migrated to a new locality, whose leaders hope to build a community out of a group of displaced people. This was an important role that the barrio's founders envisioned for the fiesta, which they saw as an instrument in their project of creating not just a barrio but a unified and coherent community on the margins of Cochabamba.

A man who works honestly to create a wonderful fiesta brings prestige to the barrio as a whole, particularly if he works to publicize the fiesta outside of the barrio itself, and so can share in the prestige that his work and investment have generated. Such a man is thereafter addressed by others as "Sr. Ex-pasante," a term of great respect. But a man who is seen as putting on the fiesta for his own self-aggrandizement is regarded with contempt, for he is seen as violating a community ethos that the fiesta is supposed to help build. A pasante, then, is honored for his contribution to the *community* of Villa Pagador, and successful fiesta sponsorship is understood as a contribution to these efforts to forge unity and a sense of cultural identity in the barrio. This overarching and explicitly political dimension of the fiesta derives further significance from its connection to national-level understandings of folklore and the role of fiesta performance in the construction of a local folkloric identity.

THE FIESTA FROM WITHOUT:
THE CARNAVAL CONNECTION

Unlike rural fiestas, the fiesta de San Miguel in Villa Pagador does not constitute part of a larger annual fiesta cycle, governed by the Catholic ritual calendar, but stands alone as the singular barrio fiesta of the year. Nor can the fiesta de San Miguel be understood as a simple, linear urbanization of a rural tradition brought by migrants to the city and reproduced in the new urban environment. Rather, as the history of San Miguel indicates, the fiesta was a local event colonized by the arriving migrants and transformed according to a model that they superimposed over the existing fiesta. Though it includes features borrowed from the rural fiesta context, the larger model of the fiesta as a whole derives from Carnaval, the national folkloric festival held in the city of Oruro, capital of the department of Oruro, from which many of Pagador's residents hail.

Carnaval de Oruro serves as a frame according to which the fiesta de San Miguel has been organized since it became part of life in Villa Pagador. Of course, the experience of the fiesta varies for each participant, as do the reasons for participating. Some people dance out of devotion to the saint, some for fun, some to build community in the barrio; some people see the fiesta as a chance to party, others as an expression of their cultural traditions, others as a way of raising Villa Pagador's national profile. But whatever their differences, when asked to interpret the fiesta to an outsider people invariably invoke symbolic meanings constituted at the national level, adopting the terminology of folklore to describe their local event. For many pagadoreños, San Miguel is a *fiesta folklórica*, a festival that they perceive as a performance of *their* folklore (*nuestro folclór*), the folklore of Oruro, which in turn has become the folklore of the Bolivian nation. Especially for barrio leaders in Villa Pagador, including the people quoted below, interpreting San Miguel involves a struggle to apply folkloric meaning to their own fiesta practice in an effort to advance the political and economic interests of the local community. At the same time, barrio leaders and residents alike call on the fundamentally Oruro associations of Carnaval to lend themselves and their barrio an extraregional identification, one that sets them apart from their Cochabamba neighbors. As discussed earlier, the strength of this identification derives from the relative positions of Cochabamba and altiplano departments like Oruro in the national imaginary, in which the former is characterized as fundamentally hybridized, the latter as deeply and authentically Andean.

The prestige associated with being the self-appointed bearers of national folklore is an important instrument in battling racism and discrimination at the regional level. As migrants and orureños living in Cochabamba, the people of Villa Pagador have had to contend with prejudice and discrimination, with the insults and abuse of the native cochabambinos who characterize their migrant neighbors as inferior Indians (*indios*), "bumpkins" (*laris*), or "llama herders" (*llameros*) from the altiplano. By appealing to national identity, people circumvent the insulting regionalisms to which they are subjected. For example, the hostility against those of altiplano origin by the people of neighboring Valle Hermoso was particularly strong in the early years of barrio life. Arturo Ayma recalled that pagadoreños were not allowed to cross Valle Hermoso to reach the road beyond and risked physical assault if they tried to walk through the neighboring barrio. Elena de Ramirez told of an encounter she had with two women as they were all riding the bus into town. The bus from Pagador to the city passes through Valle Hermoso and that day was crowded with pagadoreños heading to work in the Cancha. One of these Valle Hermoso women commented to the other that these "llamas" were taking up all the seats on the bus. Doña Elena angrily informed them that migrants were not, in fact, llamas; but even if they were, she said, the llama, a prototypical emblem of the altiplano, is a prominent feature of the national seal (*escudo nacional*) of

Bolivia. Reminding people of the folkloric importance of Oruro in the national imagination similarly takes them to task for their poor treatment of altiplano natives.

To some fiesta participants, asserting the authenticity and importance of Oruro—and, by extension, themselves—is a critical goal of San Miguel. As one early pasante of the fiesta attested, "All orureños, when we travel to Oruro, to Carnaval, we bring something back, so that here in Cochabamba too, we can show what our folklore in Oruro is like. What Oruro really is like, as folklore capital." Others described the takeover of the local saint's fiesta by the migrant settlers of Villa Pagador as a necessary function of their superiority over cochabambinos in matters of folklore. Regarding the fiesta de San Miguel, for example, Don Fausto asserted that because of their altiplano origins pagadoreños knew how a fiesta should be organized; this special knowledge was responsible for the success of the fiesta, measured by its spectacular growth and orderliness: "And in this way we organized ourselves, and we made a beautiful fiesta, because at that time, here in Cochabamba, there was nothing like that. They contracted with a few small bands of eight, twelve members, no? I don't know exactly how many. And they didn't sound good, no? But we know, we understand how it is done on the altiplano, and at that time we brought a group of twenty-five musicians, well organized, that sounded good, we dressed them alike. And in that way began the fiesta, which now is big, no? Really big."

Especially when it comes to dancing, many pagadoreños believe, the orureño embodies the folkloric, possessing an almost instinctive ability in this regard:

POLICARPIO: I'm not a devotee of any saint, but I like to dance. We people from Oruro, we take pride in Carnaval. . . .
DANIEL: Yes.
POLICARPIO: Not because of any devotion to the Virgin of the Mineshaft [to whom Oruro's Carnaval is dedicated]. No. It's because I like to dance.
NESTOR: To party, no?
POLICARPIO: For the orureño, what's more, he doesn't even have to practice. He just knows how to dance.
NESTOR: That's right.
DANIEL: In his blood?
NESTOR: Exactly.

For Eleuterio Mayta, dancing ability is what distinguishes orureños from cochabambinos like those of Valle Hermoso:

DON ELEUTERIO: They don't know the steps! In Oruro, for example, the Diablada is beautiful.

DANIEL: The Diablada is a dance from . . .

DON ELEUTERIO: Oruro. Completely.

DANIEL: Oruro. But they danced it here in Valle Hermoso.

DON ELEUTERIO: Yeah, they danced it because someone, also an orureño, taught them.

DANIEL: But not very well?

DON ELEUTERIO: Not very well. No, even in Quillacollo, the Diablada is not like it is in Oruro.[16] I danced in Oruro for nine years in the Diablada. In Carnaval, it's beautiful. The dance steps as well. It's much more attractive there, the Diablada.

The power of the local discourse of folklore comes from the steady indexing of official state discourses on national culture, which have defined Oruro as a special place in the life of Bolivia (see Nash 1979). Pagadoreños reiterated their connection to Oruro in public and private speech; references to Oruro as the Folklore Capital of Bolivia punctuated everyday conversation. When asked to tell me about Oruro, for example, people would invariably speak of its wonderful traditions, a faraway look in their eyes, and then stop to remind me that Oruro is nationally recognized as Bolivia's folklore capital. I encountered this theme frequently in official barrio discourse, not only on fiesta occasions but during public civic festivities as well. For example, the cover of the program produced for the barrio's anniversary celebration in 1995 bore the phrase "Oruro . . . Capital del Folklore de Bolivia," below which appeared the official emblem of the department of Oruro, and below that the announcement of the nineteenth anniversary of Villa Sebastián Pagador. This metonymic juxtaposing of Villa Pagador with Oruro and its associated national image serves to transfer some of this prestige from Oruro to the barrio: the community of transplanted orureños stands as Oruro in miniature, just as they would have San Miguel stand as a miniature Carnaval. And publicizing this connection is regarded as critical to the life of the community; in the words of my friend Don Policarpio, "All the steps, everything, everything [in San Miguel] is like an exact copy of the original, the authentic. So each group, in this place [Villa Pagador], has to try to push itself one step further, to know how to get noticed."

Knowing How to Get Noticed:
Publicity and Festive Political Economy

Although people in the barrio have strong emotional ties to their places of origin in Oruro and to the expressive cultural traditions of the countryside, the remaking of San Miguel as a folkloric Carnaval celebration was done with explicitly political intentions. In the early days the fiesta served a unifying function within the barrio itself, as people employed fiesta practice and participation as a way to perform publicly the cultural basis of their purportedly homogeneous social identity. Later, the fiesta continued to serve as a measure of the barrio's success in establishing a new community of orureños in the city of Cochabamba, a visible public demonstration of the barrio's size, cultural affiliations, and collective solidarity. Folklore was described as a force that unified people in the barrio; it also served to attract visitors from the countryside, who came to dance in the fiesta and to marvel at the accomplishments of their countrymen who had migrated to the city. The fiesta became an instrument for broadcasting the reputation of Villa Pagador to people in various parts of Bolivia, wherever barrio residents might have kin or compadres still living in the countryside. Significantly, for Anacleto Quispe, the fiesta stands as a marker of Villa Pagador's urban identity, and it is this urbanness that gives the barrio its status in the eyes of their country cousins.

> DANIEL: And what do the people of the countryside think, when they come for the fiesta, what do they think of . . .
> DON ANACLETO: No, it's . . .
> DANIEL: . . . the city, let's say?
> DON ANACLETO: . . . enormous. It's enormous. They see us, and they admire us. They say that before, Villa Pagador was nothing. Because some of them are coming back after eight years, nine years, maybe ten years away. And back then Villa Pagador was nothing. So, back then it was full of undergrowth. No? And now, when they come after eight or nine years, it is a little city, now with a big fiesta, just like, right down to the bands that come, see. And these bands are of similar size [to Oruro bands], so they admire us, and they say, "Look, this population has progressed so much."

Many in the barrio recognized the potential significance of the fiesta to Villa Pagador's economic life, hoping that tourism could bring resources into the community, much as it has bolstered the faltering economy of Oruro. People frequently (and rather hopefully) compared San Miguel to the fiesta de Urkupiña, held in the nearby provincial town of Quillacollo. In recent years, the fiesta de Urkupiña has evolved from a small, regional fiesta celebrating the appearance of the Virgin to a peasant, into a folkloric festival of national proportions, attracting thousands of pilgrims every year and injecting millions of pesos into the local economy (Albro 1998). Visits from national-level dignitaries to observe the events are not uncommon, with the president of the Republic himself typically putting in an appearance to consecrate the festival as a nationally significant event (Lagos 1993). Looking down the road to Quillacollo, as well as to Oruro's Carnaval, pagadoreños saw the potential economic gains for their community if San Miguel could become a national tourist attraction. Though recognizing that it might be something of a pipe dream, local would-be promoters and entrepreneurs referred to the San Miguel fiesta as a "second Urkupiña," imagining the kinds of hotels they would build to attract and house the tourists who would come to watch the fiesta. In addition to tourists, such a fiesta would attract the attention of national and municipal authorities as well:

DANIEL: Is it important to maintain one's customs?

DON ELEUTERIO: It's important to maintain one's customs. And this will attract progress to the Villa, to the area.

DANIEL: How so?

DON ELEUTERIO: For one thing, in the fiesta, one sees many things. And the authorities see it growing, no? Therefore, some street needs to be improved: like that. And when tourism can come to the barrio, tourists from other countries, let's say, then there will be a need for lodgings, a hotel, all that, and one of these days for sure, someone is going to build a hotel, a [multistory] building, and the tourists will stay there. So, economically, there will be money that will stay in the Villa.

The collective self-representation of Villa Pagador as a community of oru!eños has relevance in terms of both national and regional politics. As an "island of Oruro," pagadoreños express the belief that they are performing a service to the nation, maintaining national cultural traditions though they have been uprooted from their places of origin. Because of this service, they believe they deserve not only recognition from the state as the bearers of national folklore; as in Don Eleuterio's words, they also want improved infrastructure and city services for their barrio,

18. Following several days and nights of dancing, friends drink chicha at a pasante's party. Photo by the author

better schools for their children, and an expanded voice in city-level politics. For another local leader, Demetrio Canqui, it is not merely enough for Villa Pagador to maintain folklore in Cochabamba; it is the obligation of Villa Pagador's leaders to make that fact known to municipal and national authorities.[17] The fiesta itself is a form of publicity, but Don Demetrio insists that barrio leaders also must work to publicize the fiesta, for only through active publicity can the barrio challenge its marginality and gain the recognition that it deserves:

DON DEMETRIO: What is missing here would be . . . communication. I believe that the leaders [of the barrio] are a little closed, they are not making [the barrio] known to the city of Cochabamba, not simply to the city of Cochabamba, but at the national level. We believe that, from 1981 to '96, there is so much growth [in the fiesta], nearly fourteen or fifteen fraternities. So I think it's necessary to gain recognition, at the national level, through the written and oral press. That is what is missing, the sense of communication.

DANIEL: But why? Why is it necessary that they know, or are aware of the barrio at the national level?

DON DEMETRIO: Because it is necessary to show that here too we exist, an island of Oruro. It's necessary. It's necessary.

In many ways, the initial impulse to community formation that the fiesta served still endures. Some see in the fiesta a means to forge a sense of unity and solidarity, of community, out of a group of people that is steadily getting larger and more fractious. Don Anacleto saw in the fiesta hope for building a spirit of community in the barrio and for organizing to promote other, more development-oriented projects:

DON ANACLETO: So, I believe that it has been excellent. How it has forged ahead, let's say. In every respect it seems that Villa Pagador is forging ahead, raising itself up. What I say is that, that hopefully the people understand the importance, for all of us to be unified, let's say. You have seen this fiesta, right?

DANIEL: Yes, yes.

DON ANACLETO: It was extremely unified, there were no fights, there were no insults, nothing, right?

DANIEL: It was beautiful.

DON ANACLETO: It was beautiful. And really, look, if we work like that for a, for folklore, we can also do that for a project, for the beautification of the population, we would all have to work like that, right? A small amount of resources, applying our effort, our desire, all our will. And in that way, we could have development, enormously, in our barrio, in a big way.

Like many other barrio spokespeople, Eleuterio Mayta invoked the folkloric significance of Oruro in his descriptions of San Miguel, but in his commentary below he emphasized the qualities of orderliness and organization particular to pagadoreños, using this to criticize the residents of neighboring Valle Hermoso for their ignorance in matters of folklore. Their ineptitude is evidenced in Don Eleuterio's commentary by reference to the incident in which the Diablada troupe from Valle Hermoso crashed through the lines of the Morenada Central (see introduction):

DANIEL: Others have told me that at first there were some conflicts between, prejudices by the valley people against the migrants that came here.

DON ELEUTERIO: Yes. That exists in the entrada. Yes, they wanted to enter first, because they didn't want to come after us. No, that exists. They don't enter in an orderly manner, like we do. We enter in an orderly manner, we show respect. In the demostración as well, they interrupt us. . . . They don't have order. Nor do they dance like we dance. There is a lot of difference in that.

Don Anacleto also referred to the orderliness of the fiesta, pointing to its high level of organization as a marker of its urban sophistication:

DANIEL: In the pueblos, do they know of the fiesta in Villa Pagador?
DON ANACLETO: Oh, of course, many know, the fiesta is huge. And it is getting bigger every year, a bit more, no? This year [1995] was a little bigger than the year before, next year maybe a little better, too, a little more organized, you know, in its organization. The field was totally, it was cordoned off, nobody entered, see. And for the spectators it was excellent to see us. So I think that through our organization I think that we are looking good.

For Don Anacleto, the fiesta was a full expression of modernity, its size, orderly arrangement, and urbanness impressive to his rustic rural kin. Don Anacleto's pride in the organization of the fiesta and the orderliness of the performers and spectators illustrates a more general pride in the distinctiveness of Pagador as a community that has built itself up from nothing and now hosts a fiesta that is as organized as any Carnaval could hope to be. The order of the fiesta is a reflection of the order of the city, in contrast to the image of the marginal barrio as a chaotic place, antagonistic to urban order. As a counterpoint to this orderliness, in 1996 people observing the demostración entered the field where the performance was taking place, disrupting the dancers and kicking up blinding dust storms. This collapse in organization was a source of great embarrassment for fiesta organizers and pasantes, and much criticism after the event was directed at those who spoiled the orderly spectacle.

Don Demetrio also criticized cochabambinos, whose cultural practices he saw as more "closed," less inclusive than the national culture of oruceños. Again, the fiesta is described as an instrument by which the barrio can gain publicity, broadcasting its themes of authenticity, unity, and national significance to an outside audience: "I don't want to offend the cochabambinos. You know? But those from here in the valley are somewhat closed. They want to maintain their culture, exclusively for themselves. But we have our culture as well, in spite of everything else we are from the folklore capital of Bolivia. We wanted to show what people from there are all about. With these intentions the first dances were created here, the dance fraternities of Villa Sebastián Pagador. Not to say that we have so much power, but simply because of the devotion we have in Oruro, because we have our super Carnivals. So we wanted also to say that in Oruro, this culture is practiced."

The significance that barrio leaders and fiesta sponsors place on size, orderliness, and organization in the fiesta derives from the central role that San Miguel plays in publicizing Villa Pagador to outside audiences. The fiesta stands in metonymic relationship to the barrio as a whole, its coherence, size, and precision supposedly corresponding to these same qualities in the larger life of the barrio itself. As barrio leaders frequently asserted, only a community that is itself highly organized and capable of mobilization could possibly coordinate a highly organized fiesta of such enormity and complexity. As discussed in the previous chapter, Villa Pagador was created and has grown up not just as a barrio but as a self-conscious community, one whose leaders and residents publicly represent themselves as organized and unified in pursuit of collective goals. Even as this collective solidarity has become increasingly fragmented in recent years, barrio leaders and promoters have continued to articulate a community identity and to disseminate it to outsiders in an effort to further the gains in infrastructure and political representation that they have made over the years. The fiesta is a critical device in this ongoing project of community representation, for it publicizes not only the barrio's connections to Oruro and the Bolivian nation, but also its organization and capacity for coordinated action in the arena of municipal politics. If it is true, as the architect María Hernandez claimed, that the municipal authorities view Villa Pagador as a coherent entity capable of political mobilization and potentially violent uprising, then San Miguel may be read as a kind of dress rehearsal for more violent political protest, a spectacular demonstration of local potentiality and power dressed in folkloric costume.

CONCLUSION: FESTIVITY AND THE POLITICS OF INCLUSION

The strategy adopted by barrio leaders and folklore experts to construct their community as an "island of Oruro" was based on that department's (and that city's) national identity as the Folklore Capital of Bolivia. In a context of globalization, this identity is becoming increasingly prominent. When UNESCO announced that the Oruro Carnaval had been named to the World Heritage List in 2001, it cited traits familiar to the people of Villa Pagador: "The carnival reinforces the cultural identity of the community," UNESCO observed, "and attracts more than 400,000 people." When I visited Villa Pagador shortly thereafter, different people called my attention to the fact that Oruro had received this international recognition, though most seemed to think that Oruro itself, as the Folklore Capital of Bolivia, had been named a treasure of all humanity. The point people emphasized was that this recognition by the United Nations had given international legitimacy to their claim to be masters of folklore and hence guardians not just of the Bolivian nation but of one of the "masterpieces" of human achievement.

Folklore, as it is conceived in nationalist ideology, is supposed to be a product of the essentially rural peasant community. How is it possible, then, for a barrio of urban migrants to present themselves effectively as the authentic bearers of Bolivian folklore? In making the claim to be the true custodians of what is essentially Bolivian, pagadoreños in fact tap into one of the fundamental contradictions engendered by folklorization: in becoming folklore, supposedly rural cultural practices are urbanized, while continuing to stand for the countryside that is said to have produced them. In Oruro's Carnaval, for example, an entirely urban event with many upper-class, white performers, representations of rural indigenousness provide the core of its performative content. With that in mind, urban migrants are well-positioned to make a claim for national representativeness, as, like folklore, they too can claim to be urbanized without having lost what is essentially rural in their nature. This rural/urban confusion is evident even in the UNESCO (2001) proclamation naming Carnaval a masterpiece of human heritage, which lists "urbanization" among the "threats" that Carnaval is currently facing. Though the Oruro Carnaval (at least the one that "attracts more than 400,000 people") has for ages been an urban festival, it cannot shake its rural associations—something that might be said for the migrant performers of Carnaval dances in Villa Pagador.[18]

Some writers (e.g., García Canclini 1993) have argued that the transformation of the rural fiesta into the urban folklore "show" represents the death of something fundamental and authentic in Latin American popular culture. This may be so if the only performers in these urban shows are the national elites, as many of Oruro's Carnaval dancers tend to be. As I suggested, however, the folklore performed in these same shows provides a resource to urbanized groups struggling to transform their situations, permitting efforts at political expression and identity formation that otherwise would be beyond their reach. In Villa Pagador, urban folkloric performance enables local people to negotiate new understandings of community in a diasporic context, providing them with a means to communicate the needs and demands of that community to the municipal and national authorities. The "show" in Villa Pagador is not a corrupted version of a once-authentic rural event; it is a large-scale spectacle of national belonging, a sign of hope for an expanding local economy, a demonstration of urban residence and citizenship, and itself an expression of authenticity that challenges the injustice of the municipal and state politics of exclusion.

Just what have been the results for pagadoreños of this massive cultural effort to produce local identity and publicize it to outside audiences? That is not easy to assess. The annual performance of the fiesta continues to be a significant event in the barrio routine, providing a performative context within which local collective identity can be constituted and expressed. This has become increasingly critical in recent years, as the barrio has grown and its social and political cohesiveness has fragmented, though fragmentation continues despite the ongoing performance of San Miguel. Contrary to the expectations of functionalist ethnology, the fiesta de San Miguel is not an effective instrument for plastering these cracks in collective solidarity. However, the fiesta continues to be an important venue for barrio performers to enact and publicly display the *idea* of community to outsiders, that is, to perform unity among what is increasingly a disunified group. It is unclear to what extent this process has had the desired effect of influencing outside perceptions of Villa Pagador. In many ways, it has fallen on deaf ears: the number of outside observers coming to visit the barrio and watch the fiesta has not increased substantially over the years, and the fiesta is as far from becoming a "second Urkupiña" today as it ever was. But in other ways the barrio's self-performance has produced improvements in local conditions, as municipal authorities respond to the demands of an apparently organized and unified community.

At the same time, however, constructing public identity through performative culture has necessarily been exclusive, barring significant sectors of the local population from meaningful participation. Evangelical Christians, for example, who make up a sizable portion of the barrio population, are precluded from drinking, dancing, or worshiping what they call "false idols" (such as San Miguel) by the strictures of their faith. For these people, the fiesta time is a period for prayer, reflection, and,

19. Boys in costume. Photo by the author

sometimes, cheerful spectatorship, though not for active participation in the central organizing event of the community (see Goldstein 2003a). Similarly, the poorer residents of the barrio lack the funds to participate even as dancers in the fiesta and so can only watch from the sidelines. As the barrio continues to grow and diversify, the fiesta may be becoming more an artifact of the original barrio, an event that belongs only to those residing in the oldest sectors of Villa Pagador; rather than strengthening ties of community, the fiesta may be deepening the divisions that exist between those who can afford to participate and those who can only observe. Women, though active participants in the fiesta as cooks, organizers, dancers, and clean-up crews, are not the principal actors in the public life of the fiesta. Though they may function officially as pasantes of the dance troupes, women do not gain prestige from such participation, nor do they become eligible for other kinds of political office holding. Men plan the fiesta, men lead the fiesta, and in public representations (including many of my own interviews) men interpret what the fiesta means. Ultimately, the critical publicity that the fiesta affords the barrio is under the control of the predominantly male barrio leadership. The fiesta, intended to challenge the unjust exclusion of the marginal barrio from membership in the city and the nation, has itself developed its own forms of belonging and exclusion.

Thus, despite its importance in building and disseminating ideas about community in Villa Pagador, the fiesta de San Miguel is not an all-inclusive spectacle, but a selective one whose meanings have to be negotiated in the face of what is actually a highly differentiated local group. And those excluded from participation in the spectacle of the fiesta may be seeking other, more violent avenues for expressing their dissatisfaction, their anger, and their desire for substantive inclusion in the life of the city and the nation. It is to this other kind of spectacular performance that I turn in the next chapter.

5

Spectacular Violence
and Citizen Security

When they begin to find a voice, people who see themselves as disadvantaged often do so either by speaking back in the language of the law or by disrupting its means and ends. The crucial challenge we face . . . is to establish when and why some seek legal remedies for their sense of dispossession and disempowerment; when and why others resort to illegalities, to techniques of silent subversion or to carnivals of violence.—John L. Comaroff, from the Foreword to *Contested States: Law, Hegemony, Resistance,* edited by M. Lazarus-Black and S. F. Hirsch

Hatred and truculence: it was as though the labourers had at last realised that they were not Englishmen with rights, but slaves; that their demand for the modest and subaltern life in a stable hierarchical but not in principle *unjust* society had been a mistake, because the rest of society did not accept that there was justice and that they had rights.—Eric Hobsbawm and George Rudé, *Captain Swing: A Social History of the Great English Agricultural Uprising of 1830*

Lynchings—*linchamientos* or *ajusticiamientos,* the murder or attempted murder of suspected thieves by an angry mob—have occurred with increasing frequency in the marginal barrios surrounding Cochabamba city. During the first few years of the new millennium, groups of enraged barrio residents carried out hundreds of these lynchings, typically citing police corruption and lack of access to formal institutions of justice administration as the primary factors motivating their violence. In 1995, during my fieldwork in Cochabamba, one of the earliest in this spate of lynchings occurred in Villa Sebastián Pagador (Goldstein 2003b). As recounted in the police report of the incident, this event involved not only the attempted execution of three accused thieves, but also a violent assault by the crowd on police officers who responded to the incident. In attempting to account for this violence after the fact, barrio leaders and residents explained that if they were to have any hope of seeing justice done, they had no choice but to take the law into their own hands. This chapter explores the significance of this claim: what it says about the relationship between state law and local people's ideas about justice, rights, and citizenship, and the ways people in Villa Pagador have used spectacular displays of violence to contest their marginalization within Bolivian sociopolitical space.

In Bolivia, the absence of what is generally referred to as "citizen security" (*seguridad ciudadana*) is an important component of the "crisis" facing Bolivian society today. As the Bolivian state has wholeheartedly pursued a neoliberal democratic model emphasizing free market reforms, privatization or "capitalization" of state-owned industries, and the withdrawal of the state from social service provision, escalating levels of crime and violence, particularly in the marginal zones of the nation's cities, have produced heightened fear, anxiety, and social tension among the populace. The Bolivian national police force is widely viewed as corrupt, and the judicial system, never a model of efficiency, is almost entirely unavailable to the many people in need of its services. Globalization of the U.S.-sponsored "War on Drugs" has placed additional burdens on an already beleaguered Bolivian justice system. The costs of prosecuting the war (particularly the enforcement of the draconian Law 1008, aimed at curbing the production of coca and the trafficking of its cocaine derivative) have been astronomical, filling the nation's prisons with petty drug offenders and creating an enormous case backlog in the court system (Laserna 1995).[1] Prosecuting the War on Drugs has also led to worsening police corruption, as the heavy sentences associated with conviction under Law 1008 intensify the levels of bribery and extortion to which the accused are willing to submit in order to secure their liberty (Andean Information Network [AIN] 1993). Violations of human rights by state authorities and violent clashes between police and coca producers have also intensified in recent years (Farthing 1997). Protesting their inadequate salaries and benefits under the austerity of the neoliberal regime, in February 2003 police themselves took to the streets in a massive protest that lasted several days and led to armed conflict between police officers, their supporters, and the Bolivian military (Ledebur 2003).

In Cochabamba city, levels of violent crime, police corruption, and the exasperation of people confronting these conditions have likewise mounted. The promises of political candidates to enhance citizen security ("Our government will give security to the people," boasts Ronald MacLean of the Acción Democrática Nacionalista (ADN) party, "and will make the delinquents nervous, very nervous"; quoted in Marinkovic Uzqueda 2002) are regarded with scorn in the marginal barrios of Cochabamba, whose residents are quite familiar with the daily consequences of the neoliberal model. In Villa Pagador, for example, a total of three police officers are stationed full time in the barrio, and rather than patrolling the streets they stay close to their station house on the corner by the school, responding laconically to complaints brought to them by residents. Meanwhile, gangs of youths roam the unlit barrio streets, making travel after dark hazardous for the average resident. Murders, rapes, and other violent crimes are common in the barrio, as are alcoholism, domestic abuse, and abandonment. Because most people work in the city center they must leave their homes unattended during the day, and so are vulnerable to the predations of thieves, who often steal the most basic of household items: clothing, food stores, canisters of cooking gas. For people who can count themselves among the poorest in a country ranked among the poorest in the Western hemisphere, such losses are devastating. It is perhaps not surprising, then, that people in these communities are increasingly looking for alternatives to the state's own system of law enforcement: "When the institutions of order fail to provide proper arbitration of conflict, legitimate forms of revenge, and security, private citizens are likely to act on their own" (Caldeira 2000: 209). In neoliberal Bolivia, where the ethic of privatization has been elevated to something akin to a national religion, taking the law into one's own hands—the "privatization of justice" (Caldeira 1996)—is an ironic response to the lack of official state law enforcement.

But of course, the privatization of justice administration is not a playful intercession by citizens into the domain of the state, like the folkloric manipulations of national identity described in chapter 4. In the case of vigilante lynchings, the appropriation of the state's authority to punish criminals has deadly consequences, and whereas lynchings may assuage some of the anger people feel over the conditions in which they live, they ultimately serve to perpetuate the cycle of vengeful violence in which they are ensnared (Caldeira 2000; Girard 1977; Guerrero 2001; Huggins 1991). But vigilante lynchings in Cochabamba are more than just attempts at vengeance, efforts to satisfy individual or collective psychological cravings for reprisal.[2] They also must be seen as expressive moments in the lives of people historically silenced, denied avenues to communicate their demands or to lament their conditions to an audience that might be able to offer them official redress. Lynchings in this context are not merely parallel justice systems intended to substitute for the inadequate enforcement of state law; nor can they be seen simply as "mob violence," the spasmodic reflex of enraged sociopaths bent on retribution (see Thompson 1971). Lynchings are also spectacles, intended to catch the eye of an inattentive state and to perform for it visually and unmistakably the consequences of its own inaction. Violent spectacles are intended to call attention to the predicament of insecurity in which the actors currently find themselves, as well as to criticize the failures of the democratic state and its claim to a rule of law (Caldeira and Holston 1999; Pinheiro 1999). Through such violent practices, the politically marginalized find an avenue for the expression of grievances against the inadequacies of the state's official legal order, while at the same time deploying the rhetoric of justice and law to police their communities against crime. As with the nineteenth-century English peasants described by Hobsbawm and Rudé (1968), violence emerges as the socially subordinate and politically and economically powerless attempt to communicate—to themselves as well as to those powerholders whom they regard as having failed them—their grievances, their anger, and their political potential.[3]

This chapter explores the idea that lynching in Bolivia can be profitably understood as a form of public spectacle, focusing on one particular "carnival of violence," an attempted lynching of suspected thieves that took place in Villa Pagador on 10 March 1995. I examine the panoply of competing interpretations offered by observers of and participants in this violent event, situating that conversation within broader discourses of law and order extant in Cochabamba. I analyze the prevailing discourses about lynchings that abound in Bolivian media and official legal circles, as well as those that are deployed by the vigilante actors and community residents themselves, examining the ways these discourses intersect, overlap, and blend to produce compelling narratives about justice, power, and law in a context of urban migration and marginality (see Nagel 1999; Orlove 1994; Poole 1994). Throughout, I examine questions of motivation and the hoped-for outcomes held by the different parties to the event, particularly the gendered dimensions of participation in and interpretation of the attempted lynching in Villa Pagador. In the final section of the chapter, I describe the consequences of the lynching phenomenon in Cochabamba, which has exploded after the turn of the millennium and which in large measure was anticipated by the attempted lynching in Villa Pagador in 1995. Though in many ways a spontaneous, uncoordinated event, the Pagador lynching helped to establish a model for subsequent spectacles of violence in Cochabamba by demonstrating that such actions could attract the public eye to a community whose needs had long been neglected, its cries for assistance ignored.

DANGER AND DISORDER IN COCHABAMBA

The attempted lynching that took place in Villa Pagador on 10 March 1995 was not an isolated incident.[4] Rather, it was one of the first instances of what has since become an everyday practice of vigilantism by the residents of poor barrios in response to rising crime levels in the southern zone of Cochabamba and the apparent inability or unwillingness of the state to police their communities effectively. According to official reports (e.g., "Bolivia ocupa el segundo lugar en el mundo en casos de linchamientos" 2003), sixty-seven lynchings or attempted lynchings took place between January 2002 and June 2003 in Bolivia, though given the faulty reporting requirements of the Bolivian national police and people's reluctance to provide information to investigators in such cases (see below), these numbers likely underrepresent the actual frequency of such events during this period.[5] Many of these attempted lynchings took place in the marginal communities of Cochabamba's southern sector; according to my own inquiries, eight attempted lynchings took place in Villa Pagador in the month of January 2002 alone. In the southeastern zone of the city, as a *Los Tiempos* article reported, Villa Pagador is considered to be one of the two "most dangerous zones and where the most delinquents have been detained" ("Vecinos carbonizan el 'taxi del delito'" 2001). What is unclear from this statement is whether Villa Pagador is to be considered dangerous because of the many "delinquents" to be found there, or because of the violent nature of the pagadoreños themselves, who are prone to lynch thieves without submitting to formal legal dictates.

This conception of Villa Pagador and the zona sur as places of danger, disorder, and violence is widespread in public discourse throughout Cochabamba, and lynchings are taken as an indicator of the inherent viciousness of the people who live there. The conception of the marginal barrio as a dangerous place was presented to me on several occasions during my fieldwork in Cochabamba. Friends in the city center would often caution me against working in Villa Pagador and were aghast at the thought that I lived there with my wife and infant son. "They'll set you on fire!" I was warned, with only a hint of irony implied in the suggestion. Others more intimately involved in the criminal justice system shared this perception. The district attorney in charge of prosecuting the attempted lynching in Villa Pagador was extremely cooperative in my attempts to learn more about the case, sharing with me the official police records cited in this chapter; she also shared with me her personal opinion that the root of the problem was that "these people" ("esa gente") have no respect for justice, by which she meant the police and the judiciary. A secretary in the DA's office told me that she saw Villa Pagador mentioned on the nightly news and would be too terrified to go there herself. It would appear that even in the halls of justice itself, people harbor fears of the lawlessness of the margins (see Rotker 2002).

Though the violence in Cochabamba's southern zone is real, perceptions of the marginal barrio as a dangerous place must be understood as historically constituted; such perceptions color and condition the ways vigilante violence, subsequently dehistoricized, is perceived by people in the government, the media, and the better parts of the city. As explored in chapter 2, these perceptions emerged over the course of the past thirty or forty years as the barrios of the zona sur began to experience exponential growth on the margins of Cochabamba city. Villa Pagador and other barrios of the zona sur are widely regarded in the better parts of Cochabamba as dangerous, the source of this danger being both the people of the barrios (themselves criminalized in public discourse) and those who commit crimes of person and property against them. This is evident in newspaper interpretations of vigilantism in the barrios of the zona sur, much of which employs language familiar from the ways migrant settlers were characterized in an earlier period of the city's history. Those people once accused of bringing chaos and disorder to Cochabamba in their violation of the norms of urbanization, threatening the very life of the city with their reckless settlement patterns, unsanitary homes and bodies, and violations of the edicts contained in the city's regulatory plan, now are accused of disordering the justice system, whose fabric of laws and regulations is seen as binding together the human community. Attempted lynchings are described by commentators as "a form of chaos and loss of control over citizen security" by state authorities; they threaten to make Cochabamba "a city where the people are on the side of barbarism" ("A barbarie ante el delito" 2002). To allow these unauthorized forms of justice administration to continue would be "to accept the social chaos or anarchy in which the enraged masses have carte blanche to commit crimes" ("Linchamientos e impunidad" 2002). "Apparently," remarks an editorial writer for *Los Tiempos*, "Bolivian sociology has a new object of study: the lynching. It reveals the level of social degradation to which Bolivian society is descending" (Tórres 2001).

Described as an "attack on social institutions" ("Linchamiento: Atacan a instituciones sociales" 2001), the violence of lynching seems to threaten to undermine social order entirely, and so is perceived as an assault on the democratic nation. For example, sociologist and editorial writer Yuri Tórres (2001) observes that the phenomenon of the lynching "is an example of democratic retrocession," which "should serve as a red light causing us to stop and reflect on this problem, unless we want to end up with a society devoid of any juridical regulation." Justice and law are the province of the state, according to this discourse, not of a mob. "We cannot punish crimes with crimes," remarks one Bolivian newspaper commentator: "Society cannot sanction acts which by their commission violate what is called in law Due Process because constitutionally speaking, only the jurisdictional body can and should try someone accused of committing a crime and determine a discontinuance (by declaring his innocence) or else his eventual condemnation" (Gutiérrez Sánz 2001). "Nobody can take justice into their own hands," chief of police Col. Hernán Miranda more prosaically reminds us. "We have judges and prosecutors for that" ("Ojo con los linchamientos dice PTJ" 2001).

Criminal behavior, including lynchings, is portrayed as moving Cochabamba even further from what it formerly was, a peaceful city with a quiet, harmonious public face, the Garden City of Bolivia: "The tranquil and secure city, chosen by so many as a place to relax, which Cochabamba once was, seems to be a thing of the past owing to the amount of delinquency and the macabre crimes that have occurred in the last few months, which not only trouble the population but provoke a reaction, in various cases leading to justice by one's own hands" ("Cochabamba ya no es una ciudad tranquila" 2001). The romanticizing of the city's past, it must be remembered, recalls an era prior to the migration boom of the past several decades, before the arrival of rural migrants who expanded and diversified the city. Now vigilantism is described as a reflection of these people's disrespect for the laws and institutions of civilized society, a "sign of barbarism," according to one observer, a practice "typical of the intolerant mentality of the Middle Ages" ("Linchar: Señal de barbarie" 2001). To many media analysts, lynchings in the marginal barrios are expressions of the inherent savagery and primitive mentality of the actors themselves, the indigenous and illegally settled migrants who lack an appropriate knowledge of and respect for "civilization." Another commentator remarks: "In the movies of the Savage American West the sheriff appears, just in time, and gun in hand confronts the mob that wanted to hang the presumed *bandido*. 'We'll hang him after a trial'—he warns them. . . . Here [in Bolivia] things are more savage, and the police arrive late" (Peña Cazas 2001). Indeed, some commentators view the lynchings as a stigma on the entire Bolivian nation. Calling lynchings "primitive and cruel," an editorial writer states, "The lynchings make Bolivia one of the most backward countries on earth. . . . The image of Bolivia, of all of us, should not be marked by the primitive conduct of certain groups of people" ("Los linchamientos se repiten porque las autoridades no hacen nada para evitarlos" 2002). Imagining a conversation with his "fat aunt," a lady who "divides her time between the club, the beauty parlor, and her commentaries on virtually everything and nothing at all," another media analyst gives us some insight into how these images of primitive savagery find their way into the discourse of upper-class cochabambinos. Reflecting on one particular event in the recent spate of lynchings, the writer envisions this fine lady telling him, "The incident seems to me atrocious, an embarrassment, *hijo*, something out of a truly underdeveloped country, full of savages, what would the Chileans say, ¡ay hijo!" (Gonzáles Quintanilla 2001).

For residents of Villa Pagador and other barrios of the zona sur, such accusations are infuriating. "For the rich, for those who live well, it is easy to say: 'How can you lynch someone, you are savages,'" remarks Doña Justina, a barrio resident. "But they don't know how we suffer, how we kill ourselves working and still we can't afford to go to the doctor when we're sick, and on top of that the thieves come and take from us all that we have" (Achá 2003: 56). It is because of their poverty and suffering, barrio residents (and barrio women in particular) assert, that they live in constant fear of the thieves who prey on them; states pagadoreña Doña Elisa: "We live with fear. . . . There are many problems with fights and robberies around here but we have to endure it because no authority ever comes and says: We are going to solve this problem in this way. We can't live in peace because of the anxiety . . . because they rob us . . . we are afraid to leave our children alone in the house . . . because the thieves take anything they can get" (27). As Doña Elisa's statement suggests, from what might be called a barrio perspective it is not only the predations of thieves but the inaction of the police and other authorities to resolve these issues that are at the root of the problems of insecurity in Villa Pagador (see "Valle Hermoso cansado de delincuencia" 1999; "Supuesto ladrón de ganado se salva por un pelo de ser linchado: En la comunidad de Calli Pampa" 2002). Barrio residents hate and fear the police, whom they generally suspect of corruption and collaboration with the thieves themselves. Mistrust of the judicial system is widespread; Don Cirilo, an older resident of Villa Pagador, remarks, "I don't know whose fault it is, the police or the judges, but the thieves are never punished, we know that they always return to rob us again" (Achá 2003: 27).[6]

The police themselves generally concur with the assessment that the authorities are incapable of controlling crime or adequately policing the barrios. Underpaid, underequipped, and undertrained (issues over which they went on strike in February 2003), the police have little motivation or ability to vigorously pursue criminal investigations. One officer, for example, admits, "We don't have the resources to protect everyone, even here [in police headquarters], we don't have typewriters or cars or anything to investigate with when there are complaints. What can we do? Sometimes the people want us to do everything and that we can't do" (Achá 2003: 56). Privately, individual police officers confess a certain sympathy for the lynchings, which commonly occur in barrios where they themselves reside. Police officers often find themselves of two minds in confronting the lynchings, condemning them as violations of the law while at the same time appreciating their logic and the factors that motivate their violence.

In response to this generalized insecurity and suspicion (what I characterized in an earlier chapter as desconfianza) and a complete lack of trust in the police or judicial system to protect them, their families, and their property from crime, many barrio residents are turning to their own local mechanisms for policing their community. In Villa Pagador, barrio residents have organized their own local patrols, and many families have whistles with which they can sound the alarm in the event of a robbery or other crime discovered in their neighborhood. Lynching is another response to this insecurity, something that people do not openly admit to participating in, but an action whose logic they can fully comprehend and explain. At its most fundamental basis, pagadoreños say, lynching stems from a lack of confidence in attaining justice in any other way: "It is well known," says Don Mario, a leader of the zone known as Alto Pagador, in which the 1995 lynching occurred, "that for poor people there is never justice. Therefore, we have to protect ourselves, by ourselves" (Achá 2003: 28).

Danger, disorder, an embarrassment to a nation aspiring to modernity and civility: these themes reverberate through media interpretations of vigilante violence from 1995 to the present. Lacking in what the Spanish called policía (roughly, "civilization"), lynch mob participants are portrayed as representing a fundamental challenge to a democratic Bolivian society based on a rule of law and respect for the institutions of justice. From the perspective of barrio residents themselves, however, lynching is the inevitable result of state neglect and a legitimate response to the violence and fear that color their daily lives. It was in this context that an attempted lynching took place in Villa Pagador on 10 March 1995, and against such critical discourses as those described above that barrio leaders and residents subsequently found themselves struggling, as they tried to control the way their community would be viewed in the public eye.

10 MARCH 1995

On Friday, 10 March of this year, at approximately 10:30 A.M., the señora Sonia D., 48 years old, with her two children Sandro, 18 years old, and Mónica, 17 years of age, left their home in Cruce Taquiña and traveled to Villa Sebastián Pagador, so that the daughter Mónica could collect money from her former live-in lover Nelsón H., arriving at the location at 11:00 in the morning, they went up to Nelsón's house, and were told that he was not in, so they opted to wait and moved one block away from the house, during which time the señora Sonia D., with her son Sandro, went into a thicket of bushes to attend to their biological necessities, leaving Mónica alone, and she, taking advantage of the solitude of the place and seeing a house completely unprotected, opted to enter the dwelling of señor José C., breaking the glass in the window, and succeeded in entering, removing a radio-tape recorder, a gas tank, a small stove, blankets and clothing, then her mother and brother returned from the bathroom and were surprised to find Mónica with these bundles, in that interim a resident of the place, Ana de V., realized that a robbery was taking place, and gave shouts of alarm and in an instant almost immediately the residents of the place gathered, armed with shovels, wires and stones, trapping the thieves and beating them with the aforementioned objects, with fists and kicks, after which they tied them to a high-tension tower, where they cut off their hair, blindfolded them, insulted them with coarse words, attacking them they tried to get them to confess to other robberies that had been committed in the area, after which they doused them with gasoline, first they set fire to Sandro who screamed in pain, this happened at 1:00 P.M., at which time police officers arrived and disrupted the lynching of the three, rescuing them from the mob of enraged people, who then threw stones at the police breaking the windshields and glass of the vehicles of Radio Patrol "110" and destroying the cars' metal plating, after which the rescued people were taken to Hospital Viedma, Emergency Section, where they were given a meticulous examination, two of them remained in the hospital, Sonia with injuries, lesions and severe burns and Sandro with injuries, lesions and severe burns, the latter remains hospitalized, in the men's surgical ward.

In addition . . . in the place where the incident occurred nobody wants to furnish any information about the events, to the contrary threats have been received to the effect that if any authority were to go to the area he would receive the same punishment as the thieves. (Report of the investigating officer, Policía Técnica Judicial, Case no. 2700451, Cochabamba, Bolivia, 5 April 1995)

Most residents of Villa Pagador accept the sequence of events as described in the police report of the attempted lynching on 10 March 1995. Three individuals were apprehended in broad daylight, stolen goods in hand, on a street in one of the poorest sectors of Villa Pagador. An alert neighbor, noticing something strange going on in the house next door, began shouting the alarm. Others, hearing her cries, began to blow whistles and in seconds a crowd gathered, seizing the astonished thieves and tying their hands behind their backs with plastic strips. (One of the thieves later recounted in her statement to the police that she had been captured by a "mob" of people, appearing out of nowhere, "like ants.") The prisoners were marched up a hill to a high-tension electrical tower, where they were tied up, insulted, beaten and stoned, their hair cut off, and finally doused in gasoline. One of them was set on fire by the angry crowd, his skin falling from him, in the words of one woman, "like a potato peel." He reported to the police that had his plastic bindings not melted in the fire, allowing him to roll on the ground and extinguish the flames, he surely would have been incinerated.[7] Though some present attempted to exhort the crowd not to go through with the lynching (one man, Bible in hand, even lectured the assembled on the proscription against murder in the Ten Commandments; Achá 2003), the vast majority of those present were angry and derisive, intent on exacting punishment.

After several hours, the police arrived to disrupt the lynching. First on the scene were the three local police officers, who ran the length of the barrio from their station near the plaza, only to be showered with stones and abuse by the barrio residents. These officers called in reinforcements, who later arrived in patrol cars, dressed in full riot gear. These policemen, too, were attacked with stones thrown by people in the crowd, which shattered the windows of three of the police cars parked at the bottom of the hill where the lynching was taking place.[8] At some point a van from a local TV news station arrived, and according to one report, this vehicle also was stoned by the crowd ("Una madre y tres de sus hijos casi linchados en V. Pagador" 1995[9]). The police responded more forcefully following this attack, and dispersed the crowd with tear gas and police dogs. From start to finish, the entire event lasted more than seven hours.

Though presented in official police language, the breathless style of the investigating officer's report captures the texture of the event: the outrage of the barrio residents, the terror of the victims, the bewilderment of the police. The protagonists of this particular, official narrative are the police officers, who arrive on the scene in the nick of time and rescue the victims from the people's rage. Though the three thieves are the official suspects named in the police report, the real criminals would seem to be the people of Villa Pagador, inflamed with passion and bent on revenge, who take the law into their own hands and interfere with the authorities' attempts to restore order. The barrio residents' disrespect for the law and the people who enforce it would appear to be demonstrated in the last paragraph of the report, which describes the lack of cooperation by barrio residents in investigating the case and the threats received by the police warning them to stay out of Villa Pagador. These themes were picked up by the news media, which characterized the lynching as an act of savagery, committed by people with no decency or respect for the laws of civilized society.

Press coverage of the attempted lynching in Villa Pagador provoked strong reactions among the barrio populace. People in Pagador expressed outrage at the journalists' reports and news commentaries that described the barrio residents as "savages," denouncing those who were using the episode to destroy the barrio's good name. Criticism of the press coverage of the lynching was extended in people's conversation to a more general critique of the media as an institution and of its failure to speak on behalf of the poor people of the marginal barrios. The leaders of the barrio were particularly vocal in their denunciations. Don Lucho, head of the parents' group at one of the local schools, complained to me of "the yellow press," which reports on the marginal barrios when something bad happens—a murder, a robbery, or some violent event—but otherwise only reports on issues of concern to the *q'aras* (Quechua: whites; rich people). At a leaders' meeting called to discuss the event and its consequences, my compadre Nestor, his normally placid demeanor evaporating, bitterly recounted a report on the national radio network Metro-Policial, which had characterized the barrio residents as crazed savages, completely out of control, and Villa Pagador as a dangerous place where no sane person should visit. This report also made the criminals out to be victims, he said, painting the barrio residents as the real criminals. Another television news report featured a call-in program, which residents of Cochabamba (those with both TVs and telephones, which most barrio residents then lacked) had phoned to denounce the residents of Pagador as heinous savages.

In the days following the attempted lynching, Villa Pagador was abuzz with discussion and analysis of the event, in particular the effect that the incident would have on the barrio's reputation in greater Cochabamba. Barrio leaders in particular were concerned that Pagador's good reputation for community organization and collaboration was threatened by this media criticism. As discussed in previous chapters, though widely viewed in the city as a marginal barrio, illegally settled by thieves of public space, Villa Pagador also has a reputation in Cochabamba as a highly organized and progressive community, politically active in making demands of the local authorities and in trying to bring needed services and development initiatives into the community. To this end, individual barrio leaders rely on the public perception of Villa Pagador as a community of good citizens and willing collaborators, people who are capable of participating in self-help development schemes. For example, the efforts to bring water service to the barrio (see chapter 3) were successful because of the World Bank's perception that the community was organized and willing to work in collaboration with external agencies to create change in their neighborhood. The effort to bring a school to the barrio succeeded for the same reasons. Barrio leaders were thus fearful that the negative reputation Villa Pagador seemed to have acquired after the attempted lynching might imperil these other efforts, as NGOs and government officials would begin to regard the community as violent and retrograde, a danger to order and reason, rather than as a worthy and progressive collaborator in development enterprises.

Ultimately, much of the outrage over press characterizations of Villa Pagador stemmed from people's general discomfort with having outsiders control how the barrio was being represented, and the potential consequences of those representations for barrio residents. Thus began a local effort to counter images of the barrio being produced and disseminated through channels outside of local control. Barrio leaders and residents offered their own narratives and interpretations of what took place during the attempted lynching and what its larger political significance was, whenever possible seeking avenues to present this interpretation to a wider audience. Mostly, these efforts targeted the media, but in my role as ethnographer and author I, too, was offered "insiders'" interpretations of events.[10] In people's attempts to explain the deeper meaning of the attempted lynching, the political significance of spectacular violence begins to emerge.

BARRIO PERSPECTIVES ON EXTRALEGAL VIOLENCE

If you as the authority do not make justice, then we are going to make it with our hands.—Celestino Loayza

Though admitting that he did not witness the lynching firsthand, Don Celestino Loayza, a local leader and resident of Villa Pagador, related the event in the following manner, offering an account that differs in many respects from the one contained in the official police report cited above:

> These little thieves have always tried to harm humble people, no? Because they have no feelings. And besides, this is their work. They never want to work, to make sacrifices. So, they look for the easiest thing to do. . . . But also the people, all the residents of Villa Pagador, how many times have we caught [thieves], and delivered them to the police, to the National Police, no? To the National Guard. But this National Guard doesn't respond like it should. They hold him in prison, the thief, then, he pays a few pesos. . . . So from that perspective they [the police] are also participants in the crime. And that's why Villa Sebastián Pagador reacted. . . . And the police, truly, instead of defending the pueblo they go and defend the wrongdoers, against the pueblo, no? And suspecting that the police were opposed to the pueblo, the pueblo reacted.
>
> Then, the police called in reinforcements from the central station, so that they'd have more officers there, no? And they called them in from the central station, and there came a large number of soldiers, and they released tear gas, and after that those rockets that they have, and they released those. And seeing these abuses, the pueblo rose up, see? Then they rose up. And they reacted with the only weapon that they had to use, in their hands: the stone. So the police began first, releasing tear gas, and after that the people began to react. And they rose up, with stones. Then, after that, they brought in police dogs to pacify all those people. But the pueblo joined together tremendously then, and there was a confrontation between the groups. Even the dogs, even the dogs were stoned. But in that way they decided, when they [the police] went to defend the wrongdoers, then they [the pueblo] decided to set fire to that wrongdoer. In that way, they came to be burned. . . . Because the people themselves said . . . "Where is the justice? What justice are you going to make?" Then, "If you as the authority do not make justice, then we are going to make it with our hands." Now, "If you want to take us in, fine, take all the people." That was the key.
>
> So that was the reaction of the people. We defended the pueblo itself.

This narrative presents a number of themes that later became prominent elements in the wider public discourse about lynchings in Cochabamba. A rhetorical element deployed in this account is the trope of community, glossed here by the narrator's frequent use of the term "pueblo." Though generically translatable in locational terms, meaning simply "town" or "village," pueblo also refers to people, the inhabitants of the space so identified, as well as to the community that joins individuals to each other and to the place inhabited by them (Nugent 1993: 34). The term also has a much broader range of meaning, in other contexts being used to refer to larger sociopolitical collectivities, including the city (the pueblo of Cochabamba) or the nation (the *pueblo boliviano,* or Bolivian people), though in these cases, too, borrowing the sense of unified community implied in reference to smaller groups (Anderson 1983). Even more poignantly, the term pueblo resonates with a collectivist ideology long-standing in Bolivian politics, in which *el pueblo* is consonant with "the people," the bedrock of the national social formation. By invoking this term, Don Celestino suggests that it is the people themselves who are the ultimate arbiters of justice, unified and mobilized against the injustices they confront at the hands of both thieves and police. This gives the people of the barrio the moral high ground, for it is as "the people" that they are justified in taking matters into their own hands. At the same time, use of the term pueblo enables the narrator to be deliberately vague, making reference to the people in a general collective sense without having to identify which specific people he is actually talking about (and thus guarding their identity against retribution). In describing the violence as a community action, the narrator shifts voices to speak authoritatively from the position of the community as a whole: the pueblo, a single entity with a single, unitary voice. In juxtaposition stand the thieves, described as "wrongdoers" (*malhechores*) or "antisocial elements" (*antisociales*), people without commitment to the pueblo and so indefensible and deserving of any punishment the community sees fit to give them.[11] So, too, are the police deserving of just retribution, for their failure to protect the pueblo is a failure in both the local and national senses of this term: the police, as an arm of the state, are charged with defending the people, from whom they ultimately derive their legitimacy. The pueblo speaks to the police, chastising them for their failure to meet their responsibilities to the community and warning them of the potential consequences: "If you as the authority do not make justice, then we are going to make it with our hands."

In addition to exacting justice on the bodies of suspected criminals, the residents of Villa Pagador also launched a violent assault against the police who came to disrupt the lynching. As stated above, mistrust of the police and suspicions about their allegiances are endemic in the marginal barrios of Cochabamba, and people in Villa Pagador share this mistrust.[12] In Villa Pagador it is widely accepted that the police are in league with the criminals, taking money to look the other way in the event of a crime. Many people told me that the crowd was certain that, once back at the station, the thieves would have bribed the police into freeing them, allowing them to prey once again on the residents of Pagador: "They are accomplices of the delinquents," said a lynching participant, "the police are accomplices." In Villa Pagador, some people asserted that the burning never would have taken place had the police not shown up and attempted to defend and rescue the criminals. People thus regard the police as another threat to their security: though officially an arm of the law, the police themselves are seen as lawbreakers, incapable of providing justice because they, too, are unjust.

Accusations of corruption are made against perceived violations of social norms and appropriate standards of conduct; corruption is not inherent in an action itself, but depends on the social position and group identification of the person making the accusation (Herzfeld 1992: 77). Designations of corruption also may be applied to behaviors that appear to violate local standards of accountability, when public officials are viewed as working against the interests of the people they are supposed to serve: "Expectations of 'right' behavior, standards of accountability, and norms of conduct for state officials, in other words, come from social groups as well as 'the state.' Sometimes these standards and norms converge; more often, they do not. Thus, there are always divergent and conflicting assessments of whether a particular course of action is 'corrupt'" (Gupta 1995: 388). From the perspective of state law, a police officer intervening to stop an illegal lynching is acting in accordance with his assigned duties, but for a barrio resident this same action is perceived as a violation of the moral precepts of the community, a defense of the thieves against the people, and thus is a corrupt action. It also is informed by the bribe taking generally imputed to corrupt individual officers. This set of perspectives creates an impossible situation for the police, who disrupt the lynching in the name of law and order, but in doing so appear to the people in the crowd to be rescuing their accomplices, the thieves whom the crowd is attempting to punish (see Brass 1997). In trying to impose the state's law (including right to a trial, or due process, instead of summary judgment) by rescuing the thieves, the police's actions put them in opposition to the pueblo. From a police perspective, the subsequent attack demonstrates the lawlessness of the crowd; seen differently, police corruption has delegitimized the law as a means of securing justice, requiring the crowd to pursue it through other means (see Pinheiro 1999; Sarat 2001a; Sarat and Kearns 1996; Sunstein 1996).

This idea is expressed in Don Celestino's narrative, in which the sequence of events is critical to accomplishing one of the narrator's rhetorical objectives: establishing responsibility. In contradiction to the official narrative contained in the police report, in Don Celestino's account the burning did not occur until after the police came to defend the wrongdoers, thus transferring responsibility for the event to the police authorities. Such a rhetorical move is important as a way of protecting individuals and the community itself from possible retribution, both from "delinquents" returning to seek revenge on the people of the barrio and by the police seeking to do the same. Indeed, Don Celestino's narrative closes with a defiant remark by the pueblo to the police, reminding the authorities of their inability to prosecute the community for the attack, and of the "safety in numbers" that the group action provides ("Now, 'If you want to take us in, fine, take all the people.' That was the key."). This is complemented by the refusal on the part of those involved to identify individual perpetrators: the lament that one hears in the final lines of the official police report ("in the place where the incident occurred nobody wants to furnish any information about the events") attests to the effectiveness of this tactic of unanimity. Transferring responsibility for the lynching from the people of the community to the police is intended to stave off the possibly violent retribution by the state against the people who challenged its authority. It asserts that only after the police had demonstrated their complicity with the thieves, thereby opposing themselves to the interests of justice, did the people respond by assaulting the police.

Despite their patent illegality, lynchings remain impervious to the Bolivian legal system in its efforts to prosecute via formal legal channels both the people doing the lynching (*los linchadores*) and those whom they lynch, the suspected criminals (*los linchados*). This is due to features of the law itself. According to the New Penal Procedural Code of the Bolivian state, intended to limit arbitrariness in police procedures, for a crime to be investigated by the police there needs to be both proof that a crime has been committed and someone to make a formal accusation ("Linchadores y linchados quedan en la impunidad" 2001). This requirement means that the linchadores are rarely if ever arrested, as the police are unable to establish proof of the culpability of any single individual. Similarly, because they lack faith in the honesty of the police and the efficacy of the justice system, the linchadores rarely make formal denunciations of suspected thieves to the authorities, preferring to send a warning to thieves by means of the lynching, hoping to recover the items that were stolen from them thereafter. Also, were an individual to step forward to make a formal denunciation, he or she would in effect surrender the cloak of anonymity given by membership in the crowd and thereby risk prosecution as a linchador. Thus, despite the obvious violence and other illegalities that have occurred, in the absence of a perpetrator and an accusation the police and the DA find themselves unable to gather sufficient evidence to establish the existence of any crime at all. This situation is especially galling to the legal authorities, as it essentially confirms the critique of the justice system as ineffective and inadequate. The police are forced to concur with the vigilantes' own reading of their behavior, that is, that no crime has been committed, because the formal requirements of the system prevent an investigation, thus compelling the police to participate publicly in their own discrediting.[13] The failure to prosecute or punish vigilantes has itself been interpreted as an indictment of the police and the formal justice system; as one federal prosecutor puts it, "If the State were more efficient in the investigation of these acts, it would jail all those who instigate and carry them out, but since the legal entities charged by law with guaranteeing personal security have failed to do so, they lack the moral authority to try the lynch mob, and so these cases fizzle out and are forgotten" ("Los linchamientos no son actos salidos de la cultura ni tradición" 2001).

"So that was the reaction of the people," Don Celestino confirms. "We defended the pueblo itself." Throughout his testimony, Don Celestino narratively constructs a coherent, unified community that is both actor and object in the lynching/self-defense action of 10 March. I have suggested that this is in part a strategy to protect individuals from retribution through the posture of unanimity. But equally important is the effort to represent the community to outside audiences as unified and indivisible, capable of securing its own defense in much the same way as it once secured its own water supply. Don Celestino's narrative may be read as an effort to put forth an interpretation of the attempted lynching that counters the prevailing discourses about violence and savagery circulating in media and other public interpretations of the meaning of the incident, by representing the attempted lynching as a community effort to secure justice in the face of another kind of violence coming from the representatives of the state and the law (see Greenhouse 1992; Weisberg 1992; Wolff 1971). The attempted lynching, from this perspective, was not just a simple, reflexive act of resistance to the authority of the state. Rather, the event is better understood as a spectacular demonstration in the context of ongoing efforts by barrio leaders like Don Celestino to foster inclusion within the city and the nation, part of a larger effort to bring the rights of citizenship to the people of Villa Pagador.

CITIZENSHIP AND VIOLENCE IN VILLA PAGADOR

> The residents of Villa "Sebastián Pagador" meeting in grand Extraordinary Assembly and confronting the events that occurred on Friday March 10 of this year in which unfortunately . . . enraged residents, the great majority of them women . . . decided to take justice into their own hands . . . Resolve: Not to permit the repetition of other similar acts [of thievery], as the population of this barrio is in a constant state of emergency and therefore we cannot be responsible for the measures taken by the residents against the delinquents. . . . We want the people of Cochabamba to know, that the residents of "Sebastián Pagador" are peaceful people, of limited economic resources, in a place where robberies of our homes frequently occur and the authorities named by Law haven't been able to stop these abuses that have caused us so much sorrow and therefore we are organized and ready to act in case of a repetition of similar acts. . . . Should the residents of "Sebastián Pagador" again suffer the aggressions of antisocial elements, we will rise up as one man and punish this act, knowing as we do that the security forces lack the personnel and the means necessary to do it. ("Voto resolutivo" ["Resolution"], published in *Los Tiempos* 22 March 1995)

In addition to many personal accounts like Don Celestino's, the lynching met with several "official" barrio responses (i.e., statements issued by barrio leaders in the name of the community as a whole). The incident occurred on a Friday, and Saturday was market day, so the barrio was absolutely still, as most residents went into town to sell or to buy; but by Sunday the leaders had begun to coordinate a response. By that time, much of the negative publicity had come out in the press, and people realized that much potential damage to the barrio's reputation could result. In a meeting of the barrio leaders on Sunday afternoon, it was decided that a rally should be called for the following day and that the commandant of the Cochabamba section of the National Police be invited to the barrio to hear the demands of the residents for improved police protection in the zone.

On Monday morning it was raining, and the unpaved streets of the barrio had turned to mud. The commandant had been scheduled to arrive at 8:00 A.M., but when he hadn't shown up by 10:00 a delegation was organized to go downtown to the prefectura, seat of departmental government in Cochabamba, to demand an explanation. The timing of this visit of the delegation to the prefectura was provident, for it happened to be covered by both the radio and the print news media. An article in *Los Tiempos* reported that the residents of Villa Pagador wanted to replace the corrupt National Police; it quoted one barrio resident as saying, "We want our own police force for our pueblo" ("Villa S. Pagador quiere organizar su propia policía" 1995). Meanwhile, in the barrio, the leaders' group organized an effort to catalogue everything that had been stolen from people's homes in the barrio during the preceeding few months. A partial list was compiled for presentation to the police.[14]

The news coverage that the barrio residents received on their visit to the prefectura was remarkable in that it was the first positive coverage they had gotten from the media, stressing the ineffectiveness of the police in meeting the needs of barrio residents. The article also picked up on one of the key themes that the leaders were attempting to put forth to the authorities: the barrio's potential for self-reliance and collective action. Viewed positively, this image connects with the barrio's reputation for collaboration and self-help; viewed negatively, it suggests the barrio's threatening disrespect for the authorities and the law. These themes were reiterated during the visit of the commandant later that same day. A colonel of the National Police, the commandant spoke to a group of several hundred barrio residents gathered on the football field, promising to augment police protection in the barrio and to provide a patrol car to the area one night a week. Following his address, Don Juan Mamani, a leader speaking on behalf of the community, offered this response, attributing the violence of the lynching to the inadequacy of police protection in the barrio:

Sr. Colonel, on a previous occasion there occurred something similar to what is happening to us now. At that time you promised to grant us the personnel necessary for the tranquility of the barrio. Again we were promised twenty-four-hour protection, and shortly thereafter it was forgotten. And these are the consequences, when we can't count on the support of the authorities. We understand, Colonel, that there are very few police personnel. But also it is necessary that you give them to the areas where their protection is most required for the well-being of the citizenry itself. The promise that you just made, we would like to ask you very respectfully that you fulfill it, and that here, we don't want to go to extremes, Colonel! . . . We are beseeching you that you grant us this security. And if there is not going to be the security that we are asking you for, Colonel, I think that this place that now welcomes you will have to take matters in a direct form. And we don't want to do that. We are very respectful of the authorities. We are citizens that, we are battling here in order to be able to live. But also we need the cooperation of you all. That is what I ask for, as a citizen, and as a resident of Sebastián Pagador.

This speech reflects the dual themes that appear throughout local discourse on the lynching: a desire for protection under the law (including incorporation within the official justice system of the state) against a willingness to take the enforcement of justice under local authority when the legal apparatus of the state is unwilling or unable to provide it. Don Juan, as a spokesman for the community, invokes the inclusive discourse of citizenship to call for improved police protection for the barrio. This is again followed by the threat to take matters into their own hands, directly referencing the violence of the lynching as a warning to the state to meet the needs of its citizenry ("We don't want to go to extremes, Colonel!"). The residents of the barrio are presented as loyal subjects of the state ("We are very respectful of the authorities"), an amusing irony given the steady criticism of the police and suspicion of their legitimacy by barrio residents, but a statement that reiterates the positive side of the barrio's reputation as worthy and cooperative collaborators. Rather than blaming police corruption, as people frequently do in their private conversations, in his public speech Don Juan emphasizes the structural predicament created by a state that lacks the resources to provide adequate police personnel to the zone. Nonetheless, the violence of 10 March is invoked as the predictable and coordinated re-

20. Pagadoreños meet to denounce media characterizations of barrio "savagery" following the attempted lynching in Villa Pagador, 13 March 1995.
Photo by the author

sponse of an organized community demonstrating its dissatisfaction with the current authorities for neglecting the needs of their citizens.

After the colonel's departure, an impromptu gathering was called on the football field. Several leaders addressed the crowd, among them Don Lucho of the parents' group from the local school. He denounced the negative characterization of barrio residents by the news media, calling on the pueblo to take charge of its own reputation. A hat was passed around, and the crowd responded enthusiastically with a flood of coins. The money was publicly counted and displayed, its intended purpose being to pay for publication of a statement by "the pueblo itself" in defense of its actions during the attempted lynching. The leaders adjourned to Doña Lidia's pharmacy, where a small core of the local leadership gathered to draft the statement that would be sent to the newspaper. A number of people sat on the floor, wrestling with the language to find just the right words to express their intent. The result was the statement of "Resolution" ("Voto Resolutivo"), dated 13 March 1995 and published in *Los Tiempos* on 22 March of that year. This resolution, like Don Juan's speech to the commandant, places the blame for the lynching on the "the authorities named by Law," whose failure to provide citizen security is identified as the root cause of the "sorrow" that barrio residents experience.

Local Contradictions: Gender and the Attempted Lynching
Curiously, the published resolution points out that the great majority of the participants in the attempted lynching were women. Despite this recognition of women's active role, however, in the resolution the pueblo itself is conceptualized in the masculine: in defense of itself, the pueblo "will rise up as one man" to punish those who prey on the community. As the leaders sat around in the pharmacy, composing the text that would later be published as the resolution, the gendering of the pueblo became a point of some contention. Don Lucho, an agronomist and college graduate, had taken charge of the writing, and it was he who coined the phrase "as one man" ("como un solo hombre"). Seated nearby on the floor of the pharmacy, Doña Felipa, head of the local women's organization (*club de madres*) and one of only two women in attendance (Doña Lidia was the other), suddenly piped up: "As one *woman* [Como una sola *mujer*]!" All eyes fastened upon her. Well, she said, not backing down under the steady gaze of the men, everyone knows that the women in this community participated more actively in the lynching than the men. This point was acknowledged by the men, who nodded their heads in agreement, though the text of the resolution retained its masculine emphasis.

Women did indeed participate actively in the attempted lynching of 10 March, though their interpretations of the event after the fact differed in some important ways from those of their male counterparts. Much has been written about Andean women and the political sphere (e.g., Babb 1989; Paulson and Calla 2000; Rivera Cusicanqui 1996), but here I want to refer to women's involvement in the attempted lynching in Villa Pagador as a way of pointing to the diversity—in this case, gender diversity—that existed in interpreting the violence in that one locality, and to indicate the ways different people in the barrio justified their participation in it. This consideration is interesting for another reason as well: according to scholars of vigilantism, women are not supposed to be participants in such events. In his synthetic, cross-cultural survey of vigilantism around the world, Abrahams (1998: 137) comments, "I am confident that the large majority of those who are currently and historically identifiable as vigilantes are and have been men, and few women have apparently been keen to stake their claim to an active share in the proceedings." The strong involvement of women in the lynching in Villa Pagador clearly contradicts this historical generalization.

It was widely acknowledged in the barrio that in the events of 10 March women did the greater part of the violence against the thieves, and that it was women who threw the gasoline and then the match that set the young man on fire. Women openly expressed their approval of the violence, saying that the thieves deserved the punishment they got and worse. Far from showing remorse about the burning, many women in Villa Pagador endorsed it, fearing only that the thieves might return to take their revenge on the community. Doña María Chamani, a widow and mother of three grown children and a respected vendor of soft drinks in the local market, put it this way, in a conversation about the attempted lynching:

DOÑA MARÍA: They shouldn't have burned him. Because he suffered!
DANIEL: This . . .
DOÑA MARÍA: The young man. They should have killed him.
DANIEL: Killed him? That would have been better?
DOÑA MARÍA: Yes. Better. That way he wouldn't suffer. Now some say that he's died, some say that he's still alive. If he lives, he will return.
DANIEL: He will come back?
DOÑA MARÍA: Yes.
DANIEL: I don't believe it!
DOÑA MARÍA: He will. Because there was a lot of, "I'm going to get revenge."
DANIEL: Yeah?
DOÑA MARÍA: Mmm hmm.
DANIEL: But, no, how's he going to do it?
DOÑA MARÍA: Just by getting himself healthy.
DANIEL: The people are afraid, that he will get revenge?
DOÑA MARÍA: Mmm hmm.
DANIEL: But, they should have done something, no?
DOÑA MARÍA: They should have killed him.

Women explained their participation in the violence in terms of their roles as women and mothers, sacrificing to provide for their children and defending their homes and property with their lives. This they saw as an obvious and essential aspect of women's lives, and the attempted lynching was described as an extension of this role. Not only were women in attendance in greater numbers than men at the lynch-

21. Residents of Villa Pagador. Photo by the author

ing, but women asserted that they were also angrier than the men and committed the actual violence against the thieves. My comadre Doña Juana described it this way: "They are the suffering ones, the women. More do they sacrifice themselves [than men], more do they work, sometimes they arrive home at night from selling in the market, they arrive home and wash the clothes, the next day again, making food for their children, going back out to sell. They sacrifice, the women. They defend fiercely, fiercely." Another local woman, Doña Julia, observed, "We here are poor and with much sacrifice we are able to care for our children, but the worst thing for us is that these damned thieves come and rob from us" (Achá 2003: 27).

A woman in Villa Pagador, as in poor households elsewhere, works constantly, both in the home and outside of it. This work, the difficulty of women's lives, and the near impossibility of making real improvements in their standard of living is characterized as suffering and sacrifice, qualities of their lives that women in the barrio see themselves as sharing. The discourse of suffering and sacrifice serves as a device used by women to interpret the lynching, as in the following excerpt from Doña Juana's narrative of the event. Speaking in a voice even softer than her usual tones, Doña Juana, like Don Celestino above, invokes the voice of the pueblo; here, however, it is a voice that speaks in a distinctly female register, as a woman and a mother. Here the pueblo speaks directly to one of the thieves, herself a woman and a mother:

> Many, many have had their houses robbed, poor people they are, so, because they sacrifice so much to have things in their houses, they said, "I, we were working for our children, for their daily bread, of that sacrifice you are robbing us." They [the thieves] had gold rings, gold teeth. "You, well dressed with our sacrifice, and we, not one nice skirt do we have, so that our children can have something to eat, so that we can have in our houses a good plate of food—this we wanted with our sacrifice, but you have robbed us of this." They cursed her like this, terribly, terribly they scolded her. "Now, now it is your turn to suffer, now you are going to die," [the pueblo] says, "in the fire," it says. They [the thieves] cried, "I will never do it again!" "You have already done harm to the people. So many people you have made cry. It is your fault that we hit our children, that we have made them suffer. Leaving our children, we have gone out to sell, we have sacrificed, and that you have taken advantage of, that you have exploited. Now for you it is too late. Now you are going to die. In fire," they said. They wanted to burn the three of them, the police defended them.

The voice of the pueblo is harsh, unforgiving. It gains force in its critique of the thief by addressing her as a mother herself, caught robbing from other mothers in the company of her two children. "How could she do such a thing?" women asked each other, incredulous that a woman could be so despicable as to teach her children to prey on other women and their families. Everything that is difficult about their lives—their lack of personal items like nice clothing, the stress and abuse in the household, the daily struggle just to feed their families—the women see condensed into the person of the thief, who is first chastised, then beaten, and then forced to watch as her own son is burned. The voice of the pueblo as a woman is also the voice of justice, as it utters the death sentence over the captured thieves: "Now you are going to die. In fire."

Women, like men, see the police as being in league with the thieves, so when the police intervene to stop the lynching the people turn their rage on them. Doña Juana concluded her narrative with this comment on the police, here speaking in the voice of the police: "And the police said to the pueblo, 'We are the ones who defend. You should have burned them before we arrived. And now you can't,' they told them. The police told them. 'Order is made by us, with us. And now we are here, now you can't do anything.'" The voice of the police, like that of the pueblo, is a single, unitary voice; but whereas the pueblo speaks with the conviction of righteous rage, the voice of the police mocks and threatens, cognizant of the arbitrariness of its own authority ("You should have burned them before we arrived. And now you can't"). It denies the women their power, depriving them of their right to defend their homes and families ("We are the ones who defend," say the police). It is the (corrupt) police who deal in order, and their arrival marks the end of the women's power to create justice. It is this power the women attempt to regain in their attack on the police, asserting their own ability to defend their homes even in the face of an abusive authority.

Women's participation in the attempted lynching would thus seem to be associated with their roles as mothers and homemakers, one of whose duties is the defense of the home against threats from outside. Women's political participation in Latin American social movements has often been theorized in this manner, with women's involvement in demonstrations and political movements seen as emerging from their role as organizer of the family's social reproduction (Bennett 1992; A. Scott 1994), or being constructed on the power inherent in their social identity as mothers (Navarro 1989). Because of the constraints placed on them by their domestic and economic responsibilities, women in Villa Pagador tend to participate less in formal, institutionalized organizations than in protest movements that emerge in moments of crisis, requiring less of a commitment of time and energy and encountering less opposition from men who object to women being involved in political activity (Díaz Barriga 1998; Radcliffe and Westwood 1993). Women in Villa Pagador rarely hold office or attend meetings and participate only intermittently in formal political functions of barrio leadership. Those women who do participate more frequently are either widows (and so are said to lack a man who controls them and keeps them home) or else are full masters of masculinist forms of discourse; Doña Lidia, for instance, spent her career as a pharmacist and physician in the Bolivian military and so was well-equipped to take on the presidency of the local leaders' group.

Yet women's participation in the attempted lynching should not be downplayed as merely spontaneous and uncoordinated, as though it lacked any political content. Indeed, women had distinct political goals in their participation in and subsequent interpretations of the lynching, which differed markedly from those of the male leaders. Men, concerned with the political ramifications of the act and its effect on local reputation, sought to moderate the negative impact by suggesting that the violence, committed by women, was a justified act of self-defense. In their public speech, men emphasized the collective nature of the violence as an expression of community solidarity, while reiterating the barrio's continued loyalty to and acknowledgment of state authority, in order to leave open possible avenues for receiving support for future projects in the barrio. Women, on the other hand, are not involved in ongoing, formal political activities, and so are less concerned with the "good" reputation of the barrio. Still enraged and living in fear of retaliation, women preferred to maintain the image of the barrio as hostile to all outsiders. Whereas for many male leaders the characterization of the people of Pagador as savages was a cause for grave concern (with some even suggesting a march on the prefectura just to protest this representation of the community in the media), women were not nearly so adamant. Many women, in fact, confessed to me that they were not at all unhappy with being characterized as savages, or the barrio as a dangerous place. Such an image, they felt, could only serve to frighten off future delinquents and criminals, who might recognize the barrio's reputation and so choose to commit their crimes somewhere else. This advantage of a negative image was also recognized by some men, though they sought to moderate it with public statements insisting on the nature of the population as "peaceful people" as opposed to savages.

Finally, it is interesting to note that this gendered difference in interpretive aims is paralleled by socioeconomic divisions within the community. The interpretive goals of women in the barrio were also shared by many in the poorer sections of Villa Pagador (including Alto Pagador, the sector of the barrio in which the lynching actually occurred), those who are most vulnerable to crime and who participated most actively in the attempted lynching. For these people, too, political office is less attainable than it is for those men living in the older, more established sections of the community, and their recent arrival in the city means they are less likely to have ongoing relationships with politicians and bureaucrats in the city center. For these poorest people, then, as for women of all social classes in the barrio, the negative side of the barrio's reputation for savagery and danger is more efficacious as a tool in warding off delinquents than is the positive side, the collaborative nature of the barrio emphasized by the male leaders. The "official" response of barrio leaders to the attempted lynching was in one sense an attempt to put a positive spin on an action undertaken by a sector of the barrio population that did not share their political objectives. With their institutional authority and greater access to external media, barrio leaders were able to articulate a specific, situated response to the attempted lynching in Villa Pagador, and to have that response accepted as the voice of the community on the subject.

Given this diversity of goals and interpretive perspectives among the participants in and observers of the attempted lynching in Villa Pagador, the event itself can be understood as having multiple levels of significance in the life of the community and its residents. On the one hand, and perhaps most obviously, the lynching was an expression of rage and dissatisfaction with the loss of property, the wasted sacrifice that such loss represents, and the fear and anxiety that come with living in an environment in which such loss is a daily affair. As a corollary to that, the lynching was also a warning to thieves, a deliberate reaffirmation of the image of Villa Pagador and other marginal barrios as dangerous places on the urban periphery. In similar fashion, the lynching was also a statement to the police and the political authorities whom they represent, a warning to them as well to live up to their obligations and provide real security to the barrio. In each of these expressions, the lynching served as a highly visible and dramatic vehicle of communication—a fact that barrio residents themselves clearly understood. In the words of Doña Nelly, a vendor in the barrio market, commenting on the efficacy of violent protest in Villa Pagador: "All of us have to participate if we want the authorities to listen to our problems. So we follow our leaders, because we are the forgotten ones to the authorities, no authority is interested in solving our problems, even though they are very serious problems. They only listen to us when we mobilize ourselves, when we apply pressure" (Achá 2003: 27).

NEW FORMS OF VIOLENCE AND PERFORMANCE

In Villa Pagador, the publication of the resolution turned out to be the final word in the lynching episode of 1995. The sensation in the news media died out, the authorities made promises of a very limited extent that were not kept, and the anger of the barrio residents moderated with time and a return to the exhausting routine of daily life. But the representations of the barrio and its residents produced by the news media endured, impacting the ideas that urban cochabambinos continued to hold of the people inhabiting the city's margins. These representations returned to the fore in early 2001, as Cochabamba once again attempted to grapple with the issues raised by vigilante violence in the city's zona sur. As before, this new round of lynchings seemed to confirm the fears of native urban cochabambinos that their city was once again under siege by altiplano migrants, who were bringing disorder and lawlessness to the city.[15]

In 2001, though, a new kind of interpretive frame began to find its way into media analyses of lynchings, resonating in surprising ways with the discourses of vigilantes themselves. In contrast to media interpretations that place the blame for lynching squarely on the shoulders of the lynch mob, this new strain of commentary points to the inadequacies of the Bolivian judicial system as being at least partially to blame for the upsurge in violence in Cochabamba. For example, an article in *Los Tiempos* suggests that "mass hysteria" is the cause of the lynchings, resulting from living conditions that create "grave psychosocial stress, both acute and chronic" ("Lincharían por histeria y estrés" 2001). In the article, Daniel Moreno, a Bolivian sociologist, observes that the sources of chronic stress for poor barrio residents include the absence of effective policing and the failure of state institutions such as the justice system to control and punish criminals. People don't respect the law, Moreno comments, nor do they feel like citizens or have an attachment to state institutions: "That's why these people take justice into their own hands." Some articles cite legal authorities, themselves critical of the failures of the state justice system. One of these commentators, described as an ex-judge, observes that poverty, compounded by anxiety in the face of mounting crime, is the real cause of the lynchings: "The problem is that in this country justice does not exist, and the Police have abandoned citizen security" ("Linchamiento: Más de 100 sospechosos en lista" 2001). Others take a broader view, attributing the failures of the police to that institution's "reduced budget, small number of officers, and insufficient technical and logistical provisioning. Owing to these factors, the institution of order can't be present everywhere in the city," a fact that the "antisociales" exploit to their own advantage ("Una práctica condenable" 2002). For their part, the police blame the prosecutors for inadequately enforcing the law once accused criminals have been apprehended, and they blame the new criminal procedural code, which requires them to attain proof of a suspect's culpability in order to detain

him. Col. Hugo Velasco, director of the Policía Técnica Judicial, attributes the rising crime rates everywhere in Bolivia to the economy in
general (*la cuestion económica*), which is driving the poor to steal from
the poor in an effort to feed their families (" 'Los ladrones están matando para evitar que los linchen.' Habla el director de la Policía Técnica
Judicial" 2002). Teresa Rivero, president of Cochabamba's Judiciary
Council, speaks in the voice of an aggrieved barrio resident as she describes the need for spectacular display by those who take the law into
their own hands: "We are left unprotected . . . by the authorities," she
says. "We feel like we shout and nobody hears us" ("Explican la causa de
los 'linchamientos' " 2002).

The willingness of observers to look beyond the supposed savagery of
the actors to more structural explanations of vigilantism is, I would
argue, a measure of the success of the lynch mobs in communicating
their messages to outsiders. Many of the themes expressed in the barrio
residents' discourse about the lynching—critiques of police corruption
and inadequacy, of the state's failure to enforce the law and protect its
citizens, statements of the rights of citizens to defend themselves in the
absence of an overarching authority—now appear regularly in mainstream media commentary. Official media and government spokespeople now articulate what amounts to an exculpation of barrio lynch
mobs, placing the blame instead on those national social institutions
that have failed to live up to their public mandates. Increasingly, media
commentators express a sympathy with the victims of crime and a willingness to view the lynching problem from the perspectives of the
linchadores: "The disgust of people who suffer from robberies is under-
standable," remarks an editorial writer for *Los Tiempos*: "But here the
responsibility for citizen security and vigilance is that of the Police,
therefore we must point out that it's not the thief who occasions this
violence, rather the primary responsibility lies with the Institution of
Order that does not fulfill its job of providing citizen security" (Quiroga
Oblitas 2002).

Discursive intersections between this media commentary and the
rhetoric of vigilantism suggest that as "la Crisis" continues to worsen in
Bolivia, accompanied by mounting violence and decreasing confidence
in the ability of the state to control crime and provide security, the
Bolivian middle class is increasingly coming to sympathize with the
aims of the lynch mobs patrolling the barrios of the urban periphery.
Indeed, while the poor and marginalized are "privatizing justice" by

taking the law into their own hands, the Bolivian middle class is turning to private security firms to patrol their neighborhoods and enforce order. Dressed in paramilitary garb and armed with truncheons and mirrored sunglasses, the young men in the employ of these firms (companies with English-language names like Men in Black and Bolivian Pest Control) are largely unregulated by any state authority and frequently commit their own acts of violence against criminal suspects (e.g., "Vecinos entregan vivos a ladrones pero dicen que será la última vez" 2002). Indeed, the cycle of violence is escalating nationwide: Ronald MacLean, running as the ADN party's presidential candidate in 2002, advocated introducing the death penalty into Bolivian national law, a proposal endorsed by some 80 percent of the population, according to a television news poll. Observes one Bolivian supporter of the death penalty, in words that might also have been used to justify vigilantism in the barrios: "Those responsible for citizen security have to search out whatever mechanisms are necessary to defend the population" (García Prada 2002).

The actions of the vigilantes in Cochabamba have begun to produce a response from the federal government as well, which is co-opting the language and the practice of vigilantism in an attempt to curb unregulated violence in the barrios. In 2002, the Bolivian government announced the creation of the Program of Participatory Vigilance (Programa de Vigilancia Participativa, or PROVIPA), part of the state's broader Plan for Citizen Security. Funded by the national government to the tune of US$10 million, the program calls for the creation of Neighborhood Security Brigades (Brigadas Vecinales de Seguridad) in different barrios in the cities of Cochabamba, La Paz, and Santa Cruz ("El plan de serenazgo vecinal empieza con fallas de coordinación" 2002). The largest investment in the program is being made in Cochabamba, which has exhibited the highest levels of vigilante activity in the country. Some two thousand barrio residents are being employed as neighborhood watchdogs. These "neighborhood vigilantes" (as they are called in the lingo of the program) will be trained by officers of the national police force, uniformed in distinctive ponchos, and supplied with whistles to alert barrio residents of trouble in their neighborhood. These vigilantes will be paid a salary of Bs120 (US$17) per week for their services. Governmental authorities in charge of the program state that vigilantes will be chosen "from among the best barrio residents" and promise to turn delinquents whom they apprehend over to the police for prosecution ("El gobierno ensaya carísimo e incierto plan de vigilancia" 2002). Villa Pagador has been chosen as one of the first sites in which a Neighborhood Security Brigade will be created, and residents of the barrio, according to news reports, "consider the program beneficial not only for its economic aspects but also for the security advantages it offers them. They hope that this will lead to increased attention from the Police and a reduction in attempted lynchings" ("Arranca la formación de 2.000 vigilantes zonales" 2002).

The spectacle, it would appear, has gained an audience. Vigilantism, which began as an attempt to violently appropriate state authority, is now itself being appropriated by the state in an effort to incorporate and hence control vigilante activity. This, it will be recalled, is precisely the goal articulated by the people of Villa Pagador: sociopolitical inclusion, recognition as citizens, and the bestowal of the full rights of citizenship (including honest police protection) by the state authorities. Whether these increased measures of control will have the desired effects of reducing crime and curbing extralegal violence in the barrios remains to be seen.

Despite the increased attention from the state judicial authorities, however, incidents of lynchings and attempted lynchings have not diminished in the barrios and surrounding towns of Cochabamba city. To the contrary, they have continued apace: June 2002, for example, saw another eighteen such incidents, even as the efforts to institute PROVIPA proceeded. What is becoming apparent is that the vigilantes themselves have gained a more explicit recognition of the power of the spectacular lynching to create social change. Increasingly, people in the barrios are using the press coverage that the lynchings have gained them to communicate their dissatisfaction with the state to a wider audience, which they are finding is increasingly receptive to their message. At the same time, the practice of lynching has experienced some alterations. Consider three examples:

− Following an incident in a barrio on Cochabamba's south side, where a young man was caught in the act of burglarizing a home and verbally abused by angry barrio residents, an unidentified individual was quoted in the paper in defense of his community: "The residents here behaved with restraint, we didn't try to lynch him, we called the Police and the press" ("¿Paranoia? Casi linchan a dos inocentes" 2001).

- In barrio El Paso, part of neighboring Quillacollo, a mob of residents apprehended three thieves in the act of robbing a home; but rather than lynch them, the residents made the young men run in circles around the barrio plaza while bombarding them with verbal insults and a few swats with a eucalyptus branch. Following this "moral punishment" (*castigo moral*), the residents turned the accused thieves over to the police, announcing that they had decided to "pardon" them for their crimes, warning that they would not be so lenient in the future ("El Paso 'perdona' la vida de tres presuntos antisociales" 2002).
- In a barrio in the city of El Alto, outside Bolivia's capital, La Paz, a group of residents burnt in effigy figures representing "antisociales," demanding greater police attention and a reduction in levels of delinquency in their neighborhood. According to participants, the burning was intended to serve as a warning to delinquents that if they are caught committing crimes in the barrio, they would suffer the same fate as the dummies. "In light of the disinterest shown by the police authorities with respect to our request to augment the number of police officers in the zone to counter delinquency, we decided to make our protest public," commented the president of the local neighborhood organization ("Amenazan con tomar la justicia en sus manos: Vecinos impondrán castigos a los delincuentes" 2002).

Threats and warnings, couched in the language of the law, together with symbolic forms of punishment are increasingly emerging as spectacular counterparts to the violence of lynching. In reviewing the reports of lynchings from barrios throughout Cochabamba between 2000 and 2002, one is indeed struck by the large number of "attempted" lynchings (i.e., lynchings in which no one was actually killed) that took place, far outnumbering the lynchings that resulted in the death of the victims. Even more surprising is the fact that in almost every one of these cases of attempted lynching, the police arrived "in the nick of time" to rescue the victims from the rage of the mob. In a city where police attention is recognized by all sides to be woefully inadequate, the police seem to have a remarkable track record in disrupting lynchings. This perhaps makes sense if one considers the attempted lynching as a spectacular performance, one that cannot take place without an audience. For example, in the Villa Pagador lynching in 1995, the vigilantes waited around for almost seven hours for the police to arrive, their victims tied to electrical poles, before setting one individual on fire. It is likely that in many cases of attempted lynching, the "attempt" is to gain the attention of the authorities through the threat of violence more than it is the actual commission of the violent act itself. Consider another example, reported in the daily *Opinión* on 18 June 2002: "On Monday morning, four persons were almost lynched by infuriated residents of Cerro San Miguel. . . . The residents threatened to kill the detainees, to burn them and hang them, but instead they doused them in cold water, cut off their hair and hit them . . . until finally police officials were able to convince them to turn over the suspects" ("Se salvaron de ser linchados" 2002). In another case from Cochabamba's south side, a group of barrio residents apprehended three thieves whom (in the linchadores' own words) they "symbolically lynched," tying them to a tree and chastising them while they waited for the police to arrive ("No lo lincharon, pero ¡como! lo golpearon" 2001). The strategy of attracting publicity through spectacular lynching is abetted by the fact that the police are usually accompanied by a journalist, a print or television reporter who had been working the police beat down at the local station house and visited the scene of the lynching with the responding officers, thus providing publicity for the lynch mob. Though these journalists insist that they are appalled by the events they witness (Achá 2003), they are not averse to increasing newspaper sales or television ratings through sensationalizing such events.

What this suggests is that barrio residents throughout Cochabamba are discovering what the people of Villa Pagador figured out earlier: the attempted lynching is a spectacular vehicle for the communication of demands and an instrument to attract the attention of an audience that has otherwise ignored them. As the lynching performance has been repeated over and over again—in the barrios of Cochabamba, in the surrounding towns and hamlets, and in other cities elsewhere in Bolivia— it has become routinized, and this predictability allows residents to creatively manipulate its performance and outcomes, even developing "symbolic" alternatives to violent punishment. As the economic crisis in Bolivia shows no signs of abating, the future dimensions of the lynching or attempted lynching are difficult to anticipate. What is clear, however, is that as this crisis continues to impact people at all levels of Bolivian society, spectacular forms of protest will continue to be deployed, reaching an ever more sympathetic audience.

Conclusion: Theaters of Memory
and the Violence of Citizenship

Torture forms part of a ritual. It is an element in the liturgy of punishment and meets two demands. It must mark the victim: it is intended, either by the scar it leaves on the body, or by the spectacle that accompanies it, to brand the victim with infamy. . . . In any case, men will remember public exhibition, the pillory, torture and pain duly observed. And, from the point of view of the law that imposes it, public torture and execution must be spectacular, it must be seen by all almost as its triumph. The very excess of the violence employed is one of the elements of its glory: the fact that the guilty man should moan and cry out under the blows is not a shameful side-effect, it is the very ceremonial of justice being expressed in all its force. . . . Justice pursues the body beyond all possible pain.—Michel Foucault, *Discipline and Punish: The Birth of the Prison*

In his writing on seventeenth- and eighteenth-century European techniques for the punishment of criminals and the prosecution of justice, Foucault (1977) identified the public execution as a form of political ritual, an instrument intended not only to punish the wrongdoer but to express and reinforce the sovereign's power to govern. For Foucault, all crime is ultimately an attack not just on crime's victims but on the state whose law the criminal violates, and hence an attack on the prince himself; by violating the law, the criminal flaunts the authority of the prince to make the law and rule the land. Thus, the public execution was designed to be a highly visible demonstration of the prince's might and capacity for vengeance, a spectacular, ritualized restoration of the prince's authority, for which the criminal had shown such utter contempt. "The public execution did not re-establish justice," Foucault asserts, "it reactivated power" (49). In this ceremonial display, the force of the law was demonstrated with bloody and awesome ferocity, inscribing the power of the sovereign on the body of the condemned. Not only for the benefit of the condemned: key to the entire spectacle was the presence of the audience, the crowd of spectators drawn to watch this public display and to witness the demonstration of the supremacy of the sovereign and his law. The engaged participation of these observers ("the people," for Foucault) was critical to the effective performance of the sovereign's "theater of terror": "The ceremony of the public torture and execution displayed for all to see the power relation that gave his force to the law" (50). The performance engraved upon the observer's memory a vivid image of the sovereign's might.[1]

But Foucault did not envision that "the people" might take upon themselves the power of the executioner. Foucault commented on the potential rebelliousness of the spectators at a public execution, their sometimes realized ability to disrupt an execution that they deemed unjust, thereby embarrassing the authorities attempting to carry it out and subverting the effort to reactivate the sovereign's power. But the administration of justice ultimately remained in the sovereign's hands, and in Foucault's historical vision the bloody spectacle of the public execution became diffusely incorporated into milder, less spectacular means of producing docile bodies through the carceral continuum.

Meanwhile, in Bolivia, "the people" have indeed come to discover that the public execution remains a productive political ritual, not only for punishing criminals but for challenging the legitimacy of the powers that be. In much the same way as it provided the sovereign with an instrument for the public display of his power, lynching in Cochabamba today is an instrument that marginalized groups can employ to demonstrate, in a sense, their powerlessness: their vulnerability to crime and their frustration with and lack of recourse to an official justice system that honestly serves their interests. At the same time, lynching is also a demonstration of power: by taking the law into their own hands, people in Villa Pagador and elsewhere in Cochabamba express their dissatisfaction with a state that seems to be in league with the very criminals it is supposed to combat, and by punishing (or threatening to punish) criminals under their own authority, they push the state toward reform.

Lynching in Cochabamba fulfills by inversion the criteria described by Foucault: it marks the body of the (presumed) criminal with the anger and vengeance of the executioners, while displaying the potential power of the people (el pueblo, recalling Villa Pagador's Don Celestino) to the legally constituted authorities who may be watching. The inscription that the public lynching leaves on the body of the condemned in Villa Pagador is a warning to the state to live up to its self-proclaimed obligations to its citizens. The delay in executing the suspects that invariably seems to accompany the lynching ritual (resulting, frequently, in its becoming an attempted lynching) allows the authorities and the press—the audience—time to arrive and witness the proceedings.

Lynchings in Cochabamba, of course, are not without precedent in the annals of violent political protest. Executions, whether unofficial or legally sanctioned, have a long history as spectacular forms of communication, protest, and entertainment. The spectacular history of public execution includes the beheadings of the "enemies of the people" in the French Revolution, in which the removal of a "traitor's" head constituted an expression of the sovereignty of the people and (following the institution of the guillotine as an instrument of execution by the revolutionary regime) a means of restoring order and returning control of capital punishment to the authorities (Janes 1993). The so-called spectacle lynchings in the southern United States that followed the Civil War and continued into the twentieth century were also highly visible methods of prosecuting racist "justice" in an effort to render humble and mute a subjugated black population, while at the same time expressing the rage of a white population that longed for a restoration of the antebellum slaveholding social order (J. Allen et al. 2000; Dray 2002; Tolnay and Beck 1995).[2] And the death penalty in the United States has been described as a spectacular form of punishment and communication, a means of "sending a message" to potential criminals and a ritual for restoring order in the cosmos (see the essays in Sarat 2001b). In all of these forms of spectacular punishment it is the practice of violence, the public administration of violent death or its implied threat, that expresses the power of the executioners and inscribes that power on the bodies of the victims (Scarry 1985).

Conceptualizing the attempted lynching as a spectacle has allowed me to link it to other forms of public display intended to produce similar effects. In chapter 4, I described Villa Pagador's folkloric fiesta de San Miguel as another kind of spectacle, not characterized by violence though very much concerned with the construction and performance of community and collective identity and with effecting change in the sociopolitical order. Like the attempted lynching, the fiesta de San Miguel contains what I described in the introduction as a pedagogical dimension: it is intended not only to critique, but to educate its audience as to the unfairness of the current social order, motivating observers to accept the need for and to work toward social reform. For many participants in and observers of the fiesta in Villa Pagador, San Miguel represents a performance of the centrality of this marginal barrio to the cultural life of the nation, and hence a statement about the illegitimate exclusion of the barrio from membership in both the city of Cochabamba and the larger national formation of which it is part. Communication of this idea is facilitated by the spectacular performance of the fiesta itself. Like the lynching, the fiesta is big, loud, and visually arresting. The vividness of folkloric dancing captures the eye and resonates with the national imagination; it stays in the memories of the observers, and it draws participants and spectators back year after year. This visual and auditory intensity is also what makes the fiesta a productive stage for the performance of identity and community, as it provides the participants with a venue for communicating their messages of collective solidarity and national belonging to a diverse set of observers. Like the lynching, the fiesta is a theater of memory within which pagadoreños display their critique of what they perceive to be their unjust exclusion from the benefits of citizenship, and impress this idea into the consciousness of all those who witness it.

But to analyze the communicative and pedagogical capacity of spectacular performance is not to presume unanimity of goals or intentions among the actors. Critical to this analysis has been the exploration of the actually existing diversity within a single locality, what is usually glossed as "the local community" in anthropological writing. As I have observed, the local community in Villa Pagador is itself a highly charged and politicized construct, one that conceals a great deal of conflict and dissensus beneath a public veneer of unity and homogeneity. Ethnographic analysis of both fiesta and lynching in Villa Pagador reveals the deep interpretive discord that exists in this one locality, as different groups within and without the barrio struggle to understand and explain, both to themselves and to concerned observers, the meanings and goals of the spectacular events in which they or their neighbors engage. Often, this interpretive struggle is between barrio residents and other,

22. Villa Pagador, with downtown Cochabamba in the distance. Photo by the author

external forces—the media, municipal authorities, or visiting anthropologists—who would otherwise control the public interpretations or representations of local practices. At other times, the interpretive conflict is joined by various groups within the locality itself, as people of different genders, sectors, socioeconomic status, religions, or places of origin debate the meanings emergent from both violent and festive practices. The interpretive process, therefore, is not merely secondary to the performance itself, but is fundamental to its basic definition and efficacy as a form of communication and pedagogy. Spectacular performance on its own is not enough to get one's message across; controlling spectacle's subsequent interpretation and evaluation by the audience is critical to enabling one's view of events to compete for recognition in public discourse.

What is perhaps most interesting about these internal conflicts in Villa Pagador is that their end product, from the time of the barrio's founding to the present day, has been a consistently coherent ideal of community elaborated on the public stage. Even in moments of profound crisis, such as that which followed the attempted lynching in 1995, barrio leaders have been able to mediate the competing interpretations of local practices and to elaborate a unified public identity for the barrio, one that masks the internal divisions and maintains the barrio's reputation for solidarity and collective action. My historical and ethnographic discussion of the neighborhood known as Villa Sebastián Pagador reveals the hard physical and ideological labor that individuals and groups invest in the construction of locality itself, particularly in a diasporic context like contemporary urbanizing Bolivia. Defined as "a structure of feeling, a property of social life, and an ideology of situated community" (Appadurai 1996: 189), locality becomes both the site of political organizing and the subject in whose name such organizing is undertaken. Community in this process reveals itself to be not the authentic and spontaneous nature of a given locality, but the carefully constructed public face of that locality, produced both for local consumption and for extralocal audiences with the power to affect life in the barrio. Community does not spring fully formed from a homogeneous and unified population, but is a political tool by which a diverse and conflicted group of people can come together and mobilize in pursuit of specific goals.

EXCLUSION AND THE RIGHTS OF CITIZENS

As this book has explored, the exclusion of large segments of the urban and indigenous populations in Latin America has long been conceptualized in terms of marginality, a geospatial distancing from the urban center that physically reflects the political, racial, and ideological distance of the groups so marginalized from the center of national identity and socioeconomic life. From the perspective of the marginalized themselves, the illegal settlers and poor urbanites of contemporary Latin American society, urban marginality is today being conceptualized as a denial of citizenship, the exclusion of poor urban residents (particularly urban migrants) from full membership in the nation, and a denial of the political, economic, and social rights that such membership entails.

Though citizenship has been a powerful component of political discourse in Latin America since the beginnings of the Republican period (e.g., Chambers 1999), with the emergence of democratic forms of political governance in recent years the idea of citizenship has taken on renewed power as a source of political identification and challenge. Citizenship is an inherently inclusive concept, defining the membership of the national polity and the rights and duties that such membership confers. But formal inclusion in the nation is insufficient to the needs of many contemporary urban people who may officially be citizens (i.e., they hold an identity card issued by the state and, if the polls in their neighborhood are open, are allowed to vote in local and national elections) but who do not enjoy the legal or social rights of citizens to live free of fear, want, and violence (Holston and Appadurai 1999: 4). For even as democratic rhetoric and nominally democratic political forms begin to take hold throughout Latin America, offering promises of inclusion and citizenship for all beneath the nation-state's supposedly egalitarian umbrella, neoliberal economic plans and the externally imposed constraints of structural adjustment are producing states incapable of providing full rights of citizenship to all of their subjects. The failure of newly democratic regimes to live up to their own rhetoric of providing inclusive citizenship to all members of the national polity is provoking angry reactions in marginalized urban populations across the region. In response to the gulf between expectations and promises of inclusion and the lived reality of an ongoing exclusion from the benefits of membership in the national polity, the residents of the marginal zones of many Latin American cities are employing the language of citizenship and rights to characterize their experience of poverty, violence, and crime and to coordinate their political protest.

In Bolivia, the insistence on full political and social inclusion articulated by some marginalized urbanites increasingly is encountering a receptive audience in the shifting terrain of national politics, where since 1993 the national state has itself been attempting to reimagine Bolivian nationhood. In chapter 2 I described the Law of Popular Participation as an effort by the Bolivian government to decentralize the state, extending nominal decision-making power and rights of financial allocation to "base communities" and indigenous groups. At the same time, the old class-based model of nationhood in place since the 1952 revolution (one that purported to hold all members of the polity equal regardless of origin or economic status) has been supplanted by an ideology (encoded in an amended national Constitution) emphasizing the "multiethnic and pluricultural" composition of the Bolivian nation. This attempt to construct a more inclusive national identity, one that specifically recognizes "indigenous people" as members of and contributors to the Bolivian national fabric (Van Cott 2000: 176), is encoded in other reforms introduced by the first Sanchez de Lozada regime in the mid-1990s (including the educational reform law, which brought the instruction of indigenous languages into the schools). These reforms have not produced substantial changes in the distribution of power or wealth across the Bolivian ethnic landscape, but they have created a rhetorical space within which claims to indigenousness resonate more potently than ever before. Once antithetical to the very idea of the modern nation, indigenousness now holds a more central position in Bolivian national politics and identity. For the people of Villa Pagador, this means that their claims to mastery of national folklore, at once fully urban and modern, yet possessed of a rustic, indigenous authenticity, are doubly powerful as assertions of belonging to the Bolivian nation. As the "new" Bolivia expands its definition of who and what constitutes the nation, new opportunities are created for pagadoreños to push for greater substantive inclusion as national citizens (see Lagos 1997).

Meanwhile, in spite of these rhetorical efforts, the failures of and fissures within the Bolivian state have led to a further diminution of social stability and citizen's rights, as they have under so many other states in Latin America now restructured according to the neoliberal model. This is particularly evident in the domain of citizen security. As Caldeira and Holston (1999) have observed, urban collective violence throughout Latin America in recent years is an indicator of democratic "disjuncture," a rupture between the democratic rhetoric of neoliberal states that promise inclusion, security, and prosperity to all their citizens, and the realities of life for many in these democracies, who experience poverty, violence, and abandonment by a state that fails to live up to its promises. Though formally democratic in the political sphere (especially in contrast to the authoritarian regimes of the recent past), when considered in terms of the basic rights of citizens to justice, security, and freedom to live without fear of violence, these societies come up far short of the democratic ideal. This overall failure of "civil citizenship" has many consequences for weak democratic states and the vulnerable urban populations they purport to serve; these consequences include "the delegitimation of many institutions of law and justice, an escalation of both violent crime and police abuse, the criminalization of the poor, a significant increase in support for illegal measures of control, the pervasive obstruction of the principle of legality, and an unequal and uneven distribution of citizen rights" (692).

The dislocation and migration of rural populations to Cochabamba created a massive population on the urban periphery deprived of access to economic opportunity and state services, including law enforcement and justice administration. For these migrants, the disjuncture between a democratic politics and the lived reality of fear, violence, and insecurity is all too real. Excluded from membership in the city and the nation by a range of legal impositions and cultural beliefs that have defined them as marginal, these migrants have come to understand their vulnerability to crime in much the same way as they view their lack of paved roads or public illumination: as a denial of the rights of citizens by an inattentive state. The response of many people to this failure of civil citizenship has been violence, a way to express their dissatisfaction and to reverse the exclusion they have experienced. In Cochabamba city, as the neoliberal state has retreated further and further from its self-proclaimed obligations to its citizens, marginalized groups increasingly have turned to "self-help" justice administration in the form of attempted lynchings to police their communities against crime, explaining them as the last resort of people desperate for self-defense.[3] Though interpreted by some observers as another expression of indigenous migrants' lack of policía, a civilized urban disposition, such violence is clearly more than a pathology produced by urban social relations, and the city is more than a spatial metaphor of those relations. Rather, collective violence of the kind described here is an effort by marginalized groups to insist on their rights of belonging in the city itself: "The point is that people use violence to make claims on the city and use the city to make violent claims. They appropriate a space to which they then declare they belong; they violate a space that others claim. Such acts generate a city-specific violence of citizenship" (Holston and Appadurai 1999: 15–16).

But violence does not characterize all attempts to make claims on the city and on citizenship, as the preceding chapters have explored. Claims to social inclusion lie at the heart of both violent and nonviolent spectacles in Villa Pagador, as well as other, more quotidian events and forms of political expression in the barrio's history. These include the efforts to create a school, found a bus line, and attract World Bank funding for a water system in the barrio, all described in chapter 3, all intended to establish the legitimate urban presence of Villa Pagador and its residents within Cochabamba's cityscape. Individually, barrio residents have undergone the rigors of the land legalization process (chapter 2), complying with the arduous bureaucratic requirements of the municipality, all to establish themselves as legitimate landowners in the eyes of the state and hence as legitimate claimants of the rights of citizens of the nation. In important ways for barrio residents, staking a claim to the city itself is a critical step in the effort to establish oneself as a citizen: the Spanish word for citizen, *ciudadano* (meaning both national citizen and denizen of the city, an urban person), neatly captures the multiple levels at which this concept is operative.

What links all the different political struggles and assertions of citizenship issued by barrio residents is the quest for publicity that each deploys, often in spectacular fashion, to overcome the invisibility and silence that the processes of marginalization and social exclusion have imposed. The ability to attract an audience of potentially influential observers—including municipal authorities, development groups, and even anthropologists like myself (chapter 1)—is key to this endeavor. The effort to achieve publicity also attempts to put forth a particular vision of what the marginal barrio in fact is, what its collective identity— or what I have preferred to call its public reputation, a term that better emphasizes its politicized and constructed nature—should be in the public eye. In spectacular public demonstrations and events, local reputation is formed around the idea of community, a unified, socially coherent group of people, ready to act in response to perceived abuse or neglect by the state, the municipality, or so-called antisocial elements that seek to take advantage of local vulnerabilities. This reputation is not contradicted by the deep rifts in local collective solidarity that my discussion of barrio history reveals, nor by the ethnographic descriptions of the fiesta and the lynching, each of which is characterized more by interpretive conflict and competition than by consensus among barrio actors and spokespersons. Rather, what such analysis reveals is the tremendous energy and political will that go into the fashioning and dissemination of collective representations and the difficulties that must be overcome for marginalized people to attain the kind of publicity they seek for themselves and their community.

Notes

INTRODUCTION

1   All translations from the Spanish are my own. Except for recognized public figures (e.g., the mayor of Cochabamba), the names of individuals appearing in newspaper articles, interview transcripts, and ethnographic descriptions have been disguised or replaced by pseudonyms to protect individual identities. I have retained the actual names of places (including Villa Sebastián Pagador) throughout.

2   The violence I'm describing as centered on issues of law and law enforcement is paralleled in other Latin American countries by recent violence in response to economic uncertainty, which has led to food riots, looting, and other forms of protest in Argentina, Brazil, and Peru; for other parallels, see Orlove (1997); Serulnikov (1994).

3   Not all cities in colonial Spanish America fit this description, as Hardoy (1975: 30) points out. Port cities, for example, typically served as docking areas for loading and unloading ships before they became cities, and their expansion followed the pragmatic and apparently chaotic pattern laid down during this earlier phase of their development. Mining centers also tended to be built on irregular topography, which made an orderly grid pattern difficult to implement. On urban public space in Latin America, see Low (1996, 2000).

4   One of the few aspects of Inca society to elicit admiration from the Spanish was the highly ordered and organized physical design of their cities (Kagan 2000).

5   A circular or ring design was an alternative to the checkerboard pattern found in Renaissance Europe. Even more than the grid, the circular design expressed

the hierarchical nature of society, with governmental authority at the center and the residential areas associated with different social strata radiating out from the central hub (Rama 1996: 5).

6   The adjective *civilizado* (civilized), which shares many of the same connotations as *policía*, did not appear in Spanish until the early eighteenth century (Lechner 1981: 397).

7   The picota was a monument erected by the Spanish colonizers at the time of a new city's founding to symbolize justice and guarantee its provision within the colonial city. Typically located on the city's central square, the picota often stood alongside the town pillory, where the public administration of justice was invoked.

8   According to Kagan (2000: 209), the earliest use of the term policía to mean something like the contemporary English word "police" can be found in a 1737 Spanish dictionary, which defined policía as "la buena orden que se observa y guarda en las Ciudades y Repúblicas, cumpliendo las leyes u ordenanzas, establecidas para su mejor gobierno."

9   Hygiene (or what Rotenberg [1993] calls "salubrity") in this context extends beyond mere attributions of physical cleanliness to issues of moral purity as well, which in the Andes correlates with race. Cleanliness, which may be indexed by the absence of dirt under one's fingernails or stains on one's apron but which goes well beyond such material signs, is a quality reserved for the white upper class: "It also requires sexual restraint and morally upright behavior, which are qualities that, according to whites, the poor, by definition, do not possess" (Gill 1994: 116). Securing the health of the city's elites (and, by extension, of the city itself) requires the sanitizing of its landscape and the careful management of interactions between upper and lower classes, whites and Indians; this in turn requires the maintenance of order, civility, and things properly in their places—that is, of policía.

10   Although my emphasis here is on the visual components of spectacular performance, aural display also may have a role in urban identity formation (e.g., R. Allen and Wilcken 2001).

11   The fashioning and performance of personal identity can in this sense be a kind of spectacle, putting oneself on display before the public. In contemporary urban settings, membership in the fashionable classes may be performed through conspicuous consumption and display, consumerism being a prerequisite to being "seen" in the modern city (García Canclini 2001; S. Hall 1996; Hebdige 1979). This is the "theatrical quality" of the modernist city (as Guano [2002: 190] notes for Buenos Aires), the city as stage on which spectacles of identity, both personal and collective, are performed (Wilson 1991).

12   In their ideal form, particularly during the phases of redress and reintegration, social dramas were intended to permit the continued existence of society, either through continuity or schism, creating new social wholes from a

previously integrated totality (V. Turner 1957). However, Turner (1986: 35) also recognized that where consensus over core social values was completely lost, redress might be impossible, leading to crisis or full-scale social revolution.

13   In Bolivia, neoliberalism has been elevated to something like an official state ideology, and the state's Nueva Política Económica has been accompanied by a political restructuring that combines a rhetoric of democratization and human rights with a set of policies for expanding citizen participation in governmental affairs and economic development decision making (e.g., the Law of Popular Participation, or Participación Popular, discussed in chapter 2).

14   In its rejection of the state, vigilantism of the sort I describe here has certain commonalties with what Merry (1993: 47) has called "anarchic popular justice" and Cain (1985) "wildcat popular justice." Foucault (1980: 30) defines popular justice as an attack by the masses on an enemy in reaction to a specific event or injury.

1 URBAN LIFE

1   This is particularly so in regard to policing. Following the lynching in March 1995, police scrutiny of Villa Pagador momentarily increased, but was short-lived. The contradictions inherent in the desire for more surveillance by police, who are regarded locally as corrupt and abusive, are explored in chapter 5.

2   The term "informant" has some negative connotations in anthropology, suggesting something more akin to a stool pigeon than a research collaborator. However, other terms that have emerged to substitute for informant in the anthropological lexicon (e.g., collaborator) have similarly negative implications in other cultural contexts. I have therefore chosen to stick with the familiar "informant" in this chapter.

3   If ethnographic writing is to serve to advance the collective political goals of ethnographic subjects, then the anthropologist must struggle with knowledge that may contradict those goals. This problem arises for me in my portrayals of community organization and the extent to which it is appropriate for me to discuss internal conflicts of the barrio. This raises the question of the possibility of anthropological advocacy and whether the goals of knowledge creation and political allegiance may or may not be in opposition; see Hastrup and Elsass (1990); Scheper-Hughes (1992).

4   The problem of collusion in a context of political conflict and division can make any kind of simple advocacy impossible. As Terence Turner (1992: 7) observes in regard to visual-image production: "An outsider attempting to facilitate the use of video by a community, either for political or research purposes, by donating a camera or arranging access to editing facilities, quickly

finds that she or he does not escape the invidious implications and responsibilities of 'intervention' simply through handing over the camera to 'them.' Precisely *whom* she/he hands it to can become a very touchy question, and may involve consequences for which the researcher bears inescapable responsibility."

5 While not wishing to sound overly instrumental in my approach to fieldwork, it should not be surprising that an ethnographer would try to put these very confounding tensions to work in the service of the ethnographic enterprise. As García (2000: 97) points out, "Just as local informants develop tactics to negotiate with ethnographers, so do anthropologists negotiate and manipulate their positions within local networks in order to gain access to informants and to ethnographic information."

6 The department of Cochabamba, in its tropical lowland zone, is a major coca-producing region of Bolivia, and as such is a target of operations for the U.S. Drug Enforcement Agency (DEA).

7 Another reason for people to mistake an academic anthropologist for a development practitioner is that the academic/applied distinction does not exist in such cut-and-dried terms in places outside of the United States. CERES, for example, though an academic research institute, has done development-oriented work in barrios of Cochabamba (e.g., CERES/FORHUM 1993); its director, with a social science PhD, has been a candidate for mayor of Cochabamba. CEDIB (Centro de Documentación e Información Bolivia), a research center and newspaper archive, also runs development projects in Villa Pagador.

8 The Bolivian state relies on a remarkably draconian technique for gathering census data. On the day of the national census all Bolivians are subject to virtual house arrest, being required to remain in their home so that the census takers may come by and count them. Consumption of alcoholic beverages is forbidden on census day, though one wonders how closely this particular requirement is followed (see Schultz 2001).

2 URBANISM, MODERNITY, AND MIGRATION

1 Hardoy (1975: 32) describes life in Spanish America during these centuries as basically "monotonous," as the routine operations of the Spanish empire established a strong continuity over the years.

2 What is today known as "the Cancha" is the product of a late nineteenth-century movement to consolidate around Plaza San Antonio a number of different markets that had previously been located along the Avenida Aroma and neighboring streets on the city's (then) southernmost fringe.

3 In Cochabamba today, the Cancha is regarded as the city's most distinctive

feature as well as its only internationally recognized tourist attraction (according to one popular tourist guide; see Swaney and Strauss 1992). The Cancha thus is important not only for the economic function it serves but for its role as icon of urban Cochabamba society.

4 Cholas have typically been characterized in the anthropological literature as serving this function of economic intermediary, articulating "peasant" and "capitalist" (Seligmann 1989) or "formal" and "informal" economies (Babb 1989; see also Paulson 1996; Rivera Cusicanqui 1996). Albro (2000b) has described the role of the cholita as a kind of symbolic intermediary in Bolivian electoral politics.

5 This migration of ex-combatants to Cochabamba was accompanied by the arrival of a small but significant number of European Jews fleeing the Nazi expansions of the 1930s (Solares Serrano 1990: 309). A number of ex-Nazis also migrated to Cochabamba before and after World War II (see Spitzer 1998).

6 In many ways, this attempt at urban planning was a pioneering effort in Bolivia. As Solares Serrano (1990: 350) observes, Bolivia was one of the last countries in the Americas to address in any public way the planning and management of its cities. Prior to the national revolution of 1952, the issues of urban growth and development were barely addressed, and the country didn't even have a Ministry of Urbanism in the prerevolutionary period.

7 This was not Cochabamba's first Plano Regulador: an earlier plan created in 1910 had by this time become completely obsolete. The Plano Regulador drafted by Urquidi and his team was accompanied by a Plan Regional that sought to coordinate urban, suburban, and rural development within the Cochabamba valley, and a plan for the urban development of the old city center (Anteproyecto de Urbanización).

8 In Cochabamba today, these three rings correspond to Avenida Ramón Rivera, bordering the Rio Rocha to the north; Avenida América, north of the river; and Avenida Circunvalación, beyond that. Few in Cochabamba today are aware of this history or can recognize the imprint of the urban planners on the contemporary city.

9 This discussion presents an interesting parallel with Rotenberg's (1993) study of urban gardens in present-day Vienna, in which gardens are seen as healthy reserves against the polluting effects of urban growth. "Urban agglomeration is pestilential in character," claims Rotenberg. "Only by reserving certain enclosed protected places can the urbanite insure a salubrious precinct" (27–28).

10 One should not infer, from the brief history I am offering here, that migration into Cochabamba in the twentieth century was without any kind of historical precedent. Indeed, migration has perhaps always been a characteristic of life in the Andean vertical archipelago (Larson and Harris 1995). The nineteenth

century was a period of frequent migration into and out of the Cochabamba valley, as the mining economy of the altiplano fluctuated in its demand for valley labor. Later, Rodríguez Ostria and Solares (1990: 47) refer to "el éxodo cochabambino" of the 1870s, as artisans and peasants left Cochabamba to work in the saltpeter refineries of the Pacific coast. But the migration boom of the mid- to late twentieth century in Cochabamba, as elsewhere around Andean Latin America, exhibited a pace unlike anything previously known in the region.

11 The Census Bureau does not disaggregate the urban population of Cochabamba city from some of its adjacent provincial towns, instead providing statistics for the Cochabamba "metropolitan area" (INE 2001). Thus, the census figures for urban Cochabamba include people living in Quillacollo, Sacaba, Tiquipaya, Vinto, and Colcapirhua. This is a fair reflection of reality, as these contiguous urban centers tend to blend into one another despite their political boundaries, creating one large metropolitan area. A full 91 percent of the department's total urban population resides in this single metropole.

12 The total national population of Bolivia in 2001 was 8,280,184 people (INE 2001).

13 In addition to the warm climate's just being pleasant, the desire to live in such a place has an ecological basis as well. As Laserna (1995) points out, for poor people lacking resources for an adequate diet, survival in a warm climate requires lower caloric intake, and hence lower monetary expenditure, than it does in a cold climate.

14 The idea of open spaces as the "lungs of the city" is derived directly from Le Corbusier ([1929] 1996: 370), who wrote, "Modern toil demands quiet and fresh air, not stale air. The towns of to-day can only increase in density at the expense of the open spaces which are the lungs of a city."

15 Despite this image of "old Cochabamba" as an entirely white, elite city, indigenous people have always been a presence in Cochabamba. For example, Larson (1988: 177) points out that as early as 1802, a census indicated that about a thousand "Indians" could be found living in "poor urban barrios" in different parts of the city, working as domestic servants, artisans, or merchants. Many of these indigenous urban residents were monolingual Quechua speakers, who "clung to fragments of their own culture in the midst of urban life" (178).

16 Begun in 1991, the Talleres Zonales were in some ways an experimental precursor for the Law of Popular Participation. Some in Cochabamba today claim that the Talleres were in fact the originators of Popular Participation, that the national program instituted by Goni was deliberately modeled on the Taller Zonal project.

17 In addition, several of them were students of Humberto Solares, a prominent Cochabamba architect, historian, and urban critic, whose works include the historical study of Cochabamba (Solares Serrano 1990) cited in this chapter.

1   The trámite is an experience with which anthropologists are well familiar. Arriving in Bolivia in 1994 as a Fulbright scholar certainly expedited my passage through the rigors of the trámites involved in securing permission to live and study in the country, but the process was not without its difficulties. When we finally left Bolivia after a year and a half, by then with a baby born during the fieldwork period, the trámites involved in leaving the country were similarly arduous.

2   Though many of the people in the barrios work in the city center, they can't easily slip in a trámite on their lunch break. People working as ambulant vendors or construction workers can ill afford to take a few hours in the heart of the workday to stand in line at some bureaucratic office to process paperwork. The trámite thus requires an extra trip downtown in one's scarce free time, or else time away from paid employment.

3   The material on local history and the founding of Villa Pagador presented in this section is derived largely from oral histories collected from participants in the settlement of the community and from original documents possessed by barrio residents (including *libros de actas,* locally kept records of public events, minutes of meetings, and the like). Due to the unregulated nature of migration and settlement, no official archives or registries exist to document the history of places like Villa Pagador.

4   Van den Berg and Schiffers (1992) describe the complexity of "community" for rural Aymara people, pointing out that ideas about community come into play in various contexts, including the formation of relationships with people not in one's own local village but in the same general region (the *marka*); relationships with the dead (*comunidad con los difuntos*) and other supernatural beings; with the natural world; and with Christian saints and deities.

5   As Lloyd (1980) shows for the *pueblos jovenes* (literally, young towns, or marginal barrios) of Lima, collective action and the ability of a group to work in concert toward common goals are locally regarded as critical measures of the extent to which a locality can be called a "community." In a Brazilian context, see Shirley (1990).

6   In practical terms, the alcaldía would recognize each individual land claim as legal, and on that basis the community itself would take on the aspect of a legal settlement. Strictly speaking, however, the alcaldía's rules of legalization apply to individuals, not collectivities.

7   For example, shortly after the founding of the barrio, Domingo Mollo invited compadres of his from Oruro to migrate to Cochabamba, enticing them to leave the countryside with an offer of a parcel of land in the city.

8   The emphasis on the qualities of the land in people's recollections also connects with the project of building a local identity for the barrio based on its

ties to Oruro. Arturo Ayma said that many of Villa Pagador's native geographical qualities disposed it to this kind of project. Like Oruro, he said, Villa Pagador is "an extremely uninhabitable place. . . . It doesn't have any kind of vegetation. The wind is very characteristic [of Oruro], we have that here too."

9   That such a project was part of the original vision of the barrios' founders and early residents demonstrates a high degree of political awareness and ability to act with calculation, quite the opposite of the stereotype of the dissolute, marginalized rural migrant (Park 1928; see Gay 1994; Lloyd 1979).

10   The term "to struggle" (luchar) is widely used in Villa Pagador in reference not only to political processes like the ones I discuss, but also to describe the difficulties of daily life under conditions of poverty. The highest compliment that people pay to a good leader is to call him a luchador (a "struggler"), and residents of Villa Pagador often refer to their community as a barrio luchador.

11   Fé y Alegría (Faith and Happiness) is a system of school administration instituted in Bolivia by the Catholic Church in collaboration with a Spanish NGO. Though schools in the system are publicly owned and funded, administrative responsibilities are turned over to Fé y Alegría. The directors and administrators of the schools are generally nuns from Spain.

12   The rules about what qualifies a school as urban as described here may not reflect the realities of the process from the state's perspective, but this is how local people understood it. Accurate or not, the description reflects the different qualities attributed to "rural" and "urban" in local estimation.

13   It should be mentioned that although some land speculators were motivated entirely by greed and self-interest (especially those who left town after the illegal sales had been transacted), others in the community were less pernicious. The men who founded the barrio and served as the first leaders are loath to discuss their involvement in the land sales in Villa Pagador. They seem to feel, however, that they were providing a service to the community in their role as loteadores and that the problem of legalization was not something they had anticipated or intentionally ignored.

14   The story goes that the helicopter kicked up so much dust landing on the dirt football field that barrio residents who had come to greet the representative had to flee for their lives, nearly consumed by the giant dust storm. The World Bank representative had to retreat, and returned the following day in a car.

15   This is particularly true in relation to water. For example, a recent study undertaken by CESU (Centro de Estudios Superiores de la Universidad Mayor de San Simón) found that whereas residents of the wealthier northern zone of the city consume 165 liters of water per day per person, in the poor southeastern zone of the city (where Villa Pagador is located) consumption of water measures 125 liters per day per family. This discrepancy correlates with markedly higher rates of infant mortality in the southeastern zone ("Entre zonas sud y norte hay grandes diferencias en el consumo de agua" 1994).

1 Indeed, UNESCO is aware of this contradiction, as Nas (2002: 142) points out.

2 In a presidential decree of 1970, the Bolivian state declared the city of Oruro to be the "Folklore Capital of Bolivia" (Guerra Gutierrez 1990), part of the state's larger effort to categorize and enumerate all aspects of "its" national folk culture.

3 This is a strategy that benefits from the Bolivian nation-state's own self-reimagining and embrace of its multicultural composition, part of the effort to reimagine Bolivia as a "pluricultural" and "multiethnic" nation (Bigenho 2002).

4 Regionalism in a context of urban migration is addressed by the contributors to Altamirano and Hirabayashi (1997).

5 Historicizing cultural performance and festivity is key to breaking down the sense of it as a timeless device in maintaining a stable community, as Guss (2000: 8) points out.

6 The Diablada is also from the altiplano, but for Don Fausto the Morenada is a more significant representative of that region's folklore, perhaps because of the visual distinctiveness and sonorous beat of the music associated with the dance. Others would surely disagree.

7 The population of evangelical Christians in the barrio is large, though people dispute the actual figure. In general, evangelicals in Villa Pagador have an ambivalent relationship with the fiesta de San Miguel; see Goldstein (2003a).

8 The division of the fiesta into dancers and spectators is a feature that distinguishes the rural fiesta from the urban "show" (García Canclini 1993). In the traditional rural fiesta, participation is more generalized throughout the community. In the urban fiesta, by contrast, the community is more segregated as performers/audience. This is particularly evident in the entrada and demostración.

9 In San Miguel, the manner in which the ch'alla blessing is performed varies according to the province of origin of the individual pasante. In other contexts, see Albro (2001); G. Martínez (1987); Rocha (1990).

10 This style of hat indicates the altiplano (Aymara) origin of the woman wearing it.

11 Compared to the sometimes elaborate matrakas used by Carnaval dancers, these were very simple and unadorned, indicating the financial limitations of the pasante and his dancers.

12 The term *misa* is sometimes used to describe the entire ritual here termed the q'owa.

13 In most Catholic churches the saint would be represented by a mannequin or sculpted figure, but in Valle Hermoso's chapel he is depicted in an oil painting.

14 Typically, the first thing that outsiders assume about fiesta sponsorship in

Villa Pagador is that it was paid for with coca money. For reasons discussed in chapter 1, the place of coca in the barrio economy is a closely guarded secret, and not one that I will explore here. The topics of coca and cocaine production, consumption, and distribution have received their share of scholarly attention in the Andes (see C. Allen 1988; Gill 1987; Healy 1988; Henkel 1988; Léons and Sanabria 1997; Sanabria 1993).

15 This claim—that a religious wedding in the Catholic Church obliges one to host an elaborate party afterward—is vigorously denied by the Church itself. The local priest in Villa Pagador also insisted to me that the Catholic Church does not encourage drinking, but views drunkenness as a grave social ill that it is committed to combating. Nevertheless, the priest did acknowledge that "Andean custom" requires the routine consumption of alcohol in ritual functions like the Saint's Day celebration, and that this is part of the "social dimension" of Latin American Catholicism.

16 The mention of Quillacollo is a reference to the fiesta of Urkupiña, the largest folkloric celebration in the Cochabamba valley, held in the nearby provincial town of Quillacollo.

17 Local applications of the energy generated by the fiesta are in some ways more practical and important than is the hope that the fiesta could help the barrio to achieve national recognition. It is not at all certain that the national government would even be pleased to find a community of orureños engaged in folklore-based self-representation on the margins of Cochabamba.

18 Both Salomon (1981) and Mendoza (2000) have remarked on the problematic aspect of festive performance in a context neither fully rural nor fully urban.

5 SPECTACULAR VIOLENCE

1 Although Law 1008 created a parallel policing and court system intended to investigate and process the surplus of cases generated by the drug war, these have spilled over into the ordinary judicial and penal systems, swamping the entire system with caseloads.

2 It is important to underline here the cultural and historical specificity of the phenomenon I describe. Despite the familiar resonance of the word, lynchings in Bolivia are fundamentally different from those in the southern United States during the nineteenth and early twentieth centuries, and the analysis of the Cochabamba lynchings offered here is for the most part not applicable to the U.S. context. It bears repeating that my analysis should not be read as an expression of sympathy for racist lynch mobs, or for violence of any kind. Rather, it is an attempt to understand one particular set of circumstances within the specific context in which it has unfolded.

3 The comparison with the agricultural uprising of 1830 described by Hobsbawm and Rudé (1968) raises the question of typology. I find it exceedingly

difficult and, for my purposes, fruitless to attempt to classify lynchings like the one described in this chapter as one type of public manifestation or another, a problem of "framing" collective action (Tarrow 1994). Are they "uprisings," to use the terminology of Hobsbawm and Rudé (for Latin America, see Chasteen 1993)? Following Brass (1997), we might call lynchings "riotous behavior" or (if we focus on the second part of the incident described here) "police-people confrontations." More broadly, by looking at the political significance of these events, they might be better characterized as components of a social movement, of the sort described by the contributors to Escobar and Alvarez (1992) or Alvarez, Dagnino, and Escobar (1998). But such efforts to typologize obscure more than they clarify. What is more relevant here is an understanding of the violence of the lynching, looking to what Coronil and Skurski (1991: 289) call its "specific manifestations, to the way its effects are inseparably related to the means through which it is exerted, and to the meanings that inform its deployment and interpretation."

4   Violence of the kind described in this chapter is widely referred to as "lynching" (*linchamiento* in Spanish) or "attempted lynching" (*casi-linchamiento*), the latter being distinguished from the former by the fact that no one was actually killed in the event. A lynching need not involve hanging to merit the appellation; lynchings in the U.S. South often involved other means of dispensing with victims, including burning, as in the case described here (see J. Allen et al. 2000; Dray 2002; Tolnay and Beck 1995; White [1929] 2002). Other work on lynchings or other forms of collective or "popular" violence in Latin America and elsewhere includes Benevides and Fisher Ferreira (1991); Burrell (2002); Colloredo-Mansfeld (2002); Fleisher (2000); Fuentes Díaz and Binford (2001); Godoy (2002); Guerrero (2001); Quinones (2001); Souza Martins (1991); and Vilas (2001a, 2001b).

5   For example, based on my own survey of newspaper accounts, between January and July 2002 alone, sixty-eight incidents of lynching or attempted lynching took place in Cochabamba's southern zone. The newspapers I surveyed, and which I have cited in this chapter, range across the political spectrum in their orientation and generally have specific party affiliations. *Los Tiempos*, for example, has historically supported the ruling MNR Party, and *Opinión* has more recently been affiliated with Manfred Reyes Villa and the Nueva Fuerza Republicana (NFR).

6   Rose Marie Achá (2003) of Acción Andina has written a fascinating life history of one of the victims of the attempted lynching in Villa Pagador.

7   A prominent theme in the interpretation of lynchings in the U.S. South has been to view them as a form of ritualized human sacrifice; see Patterson (1998), following ideas put forth by Douglas (1966) and Hubert and Mauss (1964). Though I don't take this approach here, there are some compelling parallels that warrant comparative analysis (e.g., Castillo Claudett 2000: 222).

The ritual/symbolic aspects of lynching that find expression in other forms of political protest in Cochabamba include the burning of a figure in effigy at political rallies, another way that immolation serves as a form of symbolic communication, there again conceptualized in terms of a debate over citizenship/noncitizenship or the unfair denial of rights to the poor and disenfranchised in national politics.

8 Stoning has a long history as a form of collective punishment in rural Andean society. Community members accused of violations of local norms could be banished from the village after being stoned by angry neighbors. The ritualized performance of the *t'inku* also may be accompanied by stoning of one's opponents (see Platt 1987). In urban Cochabamba, hurled stones were the most common weapons deployed by rioting crowds in that city's Water War of 2000. All of these examples suggest a broader field of practice within which the actions of the lynching can be understood.

9 Newspaper accounts of this incident varied in the accuracy of their reporting. The story cited here, for example, from the newspaper *Opinión*, misstated the number of victims.

10 Fortunately, I was spared the kind of soul-searching that Starn (1999) experienced following his witnessing of a lynch mob in Peru. Though I have obtained data about the events described in this chapter from a variety of sources (including a videotape of the attempted lynching shot by the TV crew that was on the scene), I was not physically present at the time of the event.

11 Most accounts of lynchings that I have read describe the accused as outsiders to the local community. In those few cases where the accused criminal is in fact a resident of the barrio in which the crime took place, he seems to have been treated in the same way as would an outsider.

12 For example, Asteria Chamani, director of the Small Merchants Federation, complains, "Not only do the police protect the delinquents, but they set them free and attack us with tear gas" ("Comerciantes se cansaron de promesas, exigen hechos" 2001). Recent exposés of massive police corruption in the Bolivian national police force (including the Blas Valencia scandal; see, e.g., "'Banda de Blas' se infiltró entre militantes de ADN" 2002) seem to confirm these suspicions.

13 Indeed, the police are actively antagonistic to the New Penal Code, as it limits their ability to use force indiscriminately by imposing legal restrictions on their investigative and coercive capacity. The police may in fact discourage complainants from lodging formal denunciations, blaming the law itself for their failure to prosecute.

14 I helped to compile this list, using a manual typewriter to record the testimony of losses by robbery victims. The quotidian nature of the items stolen—propane gas tanks, items of clothing, packages of food—attests to the direct impact of these thefts on people's attempts to preserve basic domestic econ-

omy. The absence of any luxury items on the list (apart from an occasional boombox) is also telling.

15 The extent to which community self-policing and punishment in the urban barrio are direct extensions of rural "traditions" is another topic of debate by Bolivian intellectuals and the media (e.g., "Los linchamientos no son actos salidos de la cultura ni tradición" 2001; Santivañez Soria 2002).

CONCLUSION

1 For a more general consideration of the role of spectacle in modern life, see Debord (1995).

2 Tolnay and Beck (1995: 90) remark on the "expressive potential" of the lynch mob for reinforcing racial hierarchy and social norms.

3 This interpretation of the lynching phenomenon in urban Latin America is much more compelling, to my mind, than the assumption that urban lynching today somehow represents a wholesale importation of "traditional" forms of justice administration from the countryside (e.g., Santivañez Soria 2002). It may in fact be the case that lynching practitioners invoke the language of communalism and "custom" to justify their actions as legitimate defense of the community (in a manner similar to what Mayer [1991] has suggested); but to then view these practices as though they were unmediated expressions of a timeless indigenous legal vision is to overlook hundreds of years (particularly the past thirty years) of dislocation and disarticulation of these purportedly timeless and isolated rural villages. On forms of justice administration in rural Bolivia, see Ministerio de Justicia y Derechos Humanos (1997).

References

"A barbarie ante el delito." 2002, 22 March. *Opinión* (Cochabamba).

Abercrombie, Thomas A. 1991. "To be Indian, to be Bolivian: 'Ethnic' and 'national' discourses of identity." In *Nation-states and Indians in Latin America*. G. Urban and J. Sherzer, eds., 95–130. Austin: University of Texas Press.

———. 1992. "La fiesta del Carnaval postcolonial en Oruro: Clase, etnicidad y nacionalismo en la danza folklórica." *Revista Andina* 10(2): 279–325.

———. 1998. *Pathways of memory and power: Ethnography and history among an Andean people*. Madison: University of Wisconsin Press.

Abrahams, Ray. 1998. *Vigilant citizens: Vigilantism and the state*. Cambridge, England: Polity.

Abrams, Philip. [1977] 1988. "Notes on the difficulty of studying the state." *Journal of Historical Sociology* 1(1): 58–89.

Achá, Gloria. 2003. *Huellas de fuego: Crónica de un linchamiento*. Cochabamba: Acción Andina.

Adams, Abigail E. 1998. "Gringas, ghouls and Guatemala: 1994 attacks on North American women accused of body organ trafficking." *Journal of Latin American Anthropology* 4(1): 112–133.

Adams, Laura L. 1999. "The mascot researcher: Identity, power, and knowledge in fieldwork." *Journal of Contemporary Ethnography* 28(4): 331–363.

Adams, Richard N. 1959. *A community in the Andes: Problems and progress in Muquiyauyo*. Seattle: University of Washington Press.

———. 1962. "The community in Latin America: A changing myth." *Centennial Review* 6(3): 409–434.

Águilo, Federico. 1985. *La inmigración extra-departamental en la ciudad de Cochabamba*. Cochabamba: Editorial Universitaria.

Albó, Xavier. 1985. *Desafíos de la solidaridad Aymara*. La Paz: CIPCA.

——. 1987a. "From MNRistas to kataristas to Katari." In *Resistance, rebellion, and consciousness in the Andean peasant world, 18th to 20th centuries*. S. J. Stern, ed., 379–419. Madison: University of Wisconsin Press.

——. 1987b. "Por qué el campesino qochalo es diferente?" *Cuarto intermedio* 2: 43–59.

——. 1994. "And from kataristas to MNRistas? The surprising and bold alliance between Aymaras and neoliberals in Bolivia." In *Indigenous peoples and democracy in Latin America*. D. Van Cott, ed., 55–82. New York: St. Martin's.

Albó, Xavier, Thomas Greaves, and Godofredo Sandoval. 1981. *Chukiyawu: La cara Aymara de La Paz*. Vol. 1 (Cuadernos de investigación, tomo 20). La Paz: CIPCA.

Albó, Xavier, Kitula Libermann, Armando Godínez, and Francisco Pifarré. 1990. *Para comprender las culturas rurales en Bolivia*. La Paz: MEC-CIPCA-UNICEF.

Albó, Xavier, and Matias Preiswerk. 1986. *Los señores del Gran Poder*. La Paz: Centro de Teología Popular.

Albro, Robert. 1997. "Virtual patriliny: Image mutability and populist politics in Quillacollo, Bolivia." *Political and Legal Anthropology Review* 20(1): 73–92.

——. 1998. "Neoliberal ritualists of Urkupiña: Bedeviling patrimonial identity in a Bolivian patronal fiesta." *Ethnology* 37(2): 133–164.

——. 2000a. "The humble origins of popular publics in Quillacollo, Bolivia." Paper presented at the annual meeting of the American Anthropological Association, San Francisco, November 17.

——. 2000b. "The populist chola: Cultural mediation and the political imagination in Quillacollo, Bolivia." *Journal of Latin American Anthropology* 5(2): 30–88.

——. 2001. "Reciprocity and realpolitik: Image, career, and factional genealogies in provincial Bolivia." *American Ethnologist* 28(1): 56–93.

——. 2002. "A spectacular genealogy for Bolivia's new popular political subject." Paper presented at the annual meeting of the New England Council of Latin American Studies, Worcester, Mass., October 19.

Albro, Robert, and Jeffrey Himpele, eds. N.d. "New public appearances of the popular in Latin America: Regional variations from north and south." Unpublished manuscript. Forthcoming.

Allen, Catherine J. 1988. *The hold life has: Coca and cultural identity in an Andean community*. Washington, DC: Smithsonian Institution Press.

Allen, James, et al. 2000. *Without sanctuary: Lynching photography in America*. Santa Fe: Twin Palms.

Allen, Ray, and Lois Wilcken, eds. 2001. *Island sounds in the global city: Caribbean popular music and identity in New York*. Urbana: University of Illinois Press.

Alonso, Ana María. 1988. "The effects of truth: Re-presentations of the past and the imagining of community." *Journal of Historical Sociology* 1(1): 33–57.

Altamirano, Teófilo. 1985. *Migrantes campesinos en la ciudad: Aproximaciones teóricas para el estudio*. Lima: Pontificia Universidad Católica del Perú.

Altamirano, Teófilo, and Lane Ryo Hirabayashi, eds. 1997. *Migrants, regional identities and Latin American cities.* Washington, DC: American Anthropological Association.

Alvarez, Sonia E., Evelina Dagnino, and Arturo Escobar, eds. 1998. *Cultures of politics, politics of cultures: Re-visioning Latin American social movements.* Boulder, Colo.: Westview.

"Amenazan con tomar la justicia en sus manos: Vecinos impondrán castigos a los delincuentes." 2002, 21 April. *El Diario* (La Paz).

Anaya, Franklin. 1947. "Informe sobre las labores de la Dirección de Obras Publicas Municipales durante el año 1946." 10 January. *El Pais* (Cochabamba).

Andean Information Network (AIN). 1993. *Human rights violations stemming from the "War on Drugs" in Bolivia.* Cochabamba: Andean Information Network.

Anderson, Benedict. 1983. *Imagined communities: Reflections on the origin and spread of nationalism.* London: Verso.

Appadurai, Arjun. 1996. *Modernity at large: Cultural dimensions of globalization.* Minneapolis: University of Minnesota Press.

Archondo, Rafael. 1991. *Compadres al micrófono: La resurrección metropolitana del ayllu.* La Paz: Hisbol.

"Arranca la formación de 2.000 vigilantes zonales." 2002, 30 April. *Los Tiempos* (Cochabamba).

Arze Aguirre, René Danilo. 1987. *Guerra y conflictos sociales: El caso rural boliviano durante la campaña del Chaco.* La Paz: CERES.

Auyero, Javier. 1999. "The hypershantytown: Ethnographic portraits of neo-liberal violence(s)." *Ethnography* 1(1): 93–116.

———. 2000. *Poor people's politics: Peronist survival networks and the legacy of Evita.* Durham, N.C.: Duke University Press.

Babb, Florence. 1989. *Between field and cooking pot: The political economy of market-women in Peru.* Austin: University of Texas Press.

Babcock, Barbara. 1978. *The reversible world: Symbolic inversion in art and society.* Ithaca: Cornell University Press.

Bakewell, Liza. 1998. "Image acts." *American Anthropologist* 100(1): 22–32.

Bakhtin, Mikhail. 1981. *The dialogic imagination.* Austin: University of Texas Press.

———. 1984. *Rabelais and his world.* H. Iswolsky, trans. Bloomington: Indiana University Press.

" 'Banda de Blas' se infiltró entre militantes de ADN." 2002, 10 January. *La Prensa* (La Paz).

Barragán, Rossana. 1992. "Las ciudades, lo urbano, y lo rural: Descuentros y convergencias." *Allpanchis* 28(27): 11–60.

Bateson, Gregory. 1958. *Naven.* Stanford: Stanford University Press.

Battaglia, Debbora. 1995. "On practical nostalgia: Self-prospecting among urban Trobrianders." In *Rhetorics of self-making.* D. Battaglia, ed., 77–96. Berkeley: University of California Press.

Bauman, Richard. 1986. "Performance and honor in 13th-century Iceland." *Journal of American Folklore* 99: 131–150.

Bauman, Richard, and Charles L. Briggs. 1990. "Poetics and performance as critical perspectives on language and social life." *Annual Review of Anthropology* 19: 59–88.

Beeman, William O. 1993. "The anthropology of theater and spectacle." *Annual Review of Anthropology* 22: 369–393.

Behar, Ruth. 1995. "Rage and redemption: Reading the life story of a Mexican marketing woman." In *The dialogic emergence of culture.* D. Tedlock and B. Mannheim, eds., 148–178. Urbana: University of Illinois Press.

Bendix, Regina. 1997. *In search of authenticity: The formation of folklore studies.* Madison: University of Wisconsin Press.

Benevides, Maria-Victoria, and Rosa Maria Fisher Ferreira. 1991. "Popular responses and urban violence: Lynching in Brazil." In *Vigilantism and the state in modern Latin America: Essays on extralegal violence.* M. K. Huggins, ed., 33–46. New York: Praeger.

Bennett, Vivienne. 1992. "The evolution of urban popular movements in Mexico between 1968 and 1988." In *The making of social movements in Latin America: Identity, strategy, and democracy.* A. Escobar and S. E. Alvarez, eds., 240–259. Boulder, Colo.: Westview.

Beyer, Glenn H., ed. 1967. *The urban explosion in Latin America: A continent in process of modernization.* Ithaca: Cornell University Press.

Bigenho, Michelle. 1999. "Sensing locality in Yura: Rituals of carnival and of the Bolivian state." *American Ethnologist* 26(4): 957–980.

——. 2002. *Sounding indigenous: Authenticity in Bolivian music performance.* New York: Palgrave.

Boero Rojo, Hugo. 1991. *Fiesta boliviana.* La Paz: Editorial "Los Amigos del Libro."

"Bolivia ocupa el segundo lugar en el mundo en casos de linchamientos." 2003, 14 July. *Opinión* (Cochabamba), 4A.

Bouysee-Cassagne, Thérèse, et al. 1987. *Tres reflexiones sobre el pensamiento andino.* La Paz: Hisbol.

Bowie, Katherine A. 1997. *Rituals of national loyalty.* New York: Columbia University Press.

Brass, Paul R. 1997. *Theft of an idol: Text and context in the representation of collective violence.* Princeton: Princeton University Press.

Brow, James. 1990. "Notes on community, hegemony, and the uses of the past." *Anthropological Quarterly* 63(1): 1–16.

Brown, Michael F. 1996. "On resisting resistance." *American Anthropologist* 98(4): 729–749.

Brown, Richard Maxwell. 1975. *The strain of violence.* New York: Oxford University Press.

Brusco, Elizabeth E. 1995. *The reformation of machismo: Evangelical conversion and gender in Colombia.* Austin: University of Texas Press.

Brush, Stephen. 1977. *Mountain, field, and family: The economy and human ecology of an Andean valley.* Philadelphia: University of Pennsylvania Press.

Buechler, Hans. 1970. "The ritual dimension of rural-urban networks: The fiesta system in the northern highlands of Bolivia." In *Peasants in cities.* W. Mangin, ed., 36–51. Boston: Houghton Mifflin.

——. 1980. *The masked media: Aymara fiestas and social interaction in the Bolivian highlands.* The Hague: Mouton.

Bullrich, Francisco, ed. 1969. *New directions in Latin American architecture.* New York: George Braziller.

Burchell, Graham. 1996. "Liberal government and the techniques of the self." In *Foucault and political reason: Liberalism, neo-liberalism and rationalities of government.* A. Barry, T. Osborne, and N. Rose, eds., 19–36. Chicago: University of Chicago Press.

Burdick, John. 1992. "Rethinking the study of social movements: The case of Christian base communities in urban Brazil." In *The making of social movements in Latin America: Identity, strategy, and democracy.* A. Escobar and S. E. Alvarez, eds., 171–184. Boulder, Colo.: Westview.

Burke, Kenneth. 1966. *Language as symbolic action: Essays on life, literature, and method.* Berkeley: University of California Press.

Burns, Allan F. 1995. "Video production as dialogue: The story of Lynch Hammock." In *The dialogic emergence of culture.* D. Tedlock and B. Mannheim, eds. Urbana: University of Illinois Press.

Burrell, Jennifer. 2002. "Intimate violence: After lynching in Todos Santos Cuchumatán." Paper presented at the 101st annual meeting of the American Anthropological Association, New Orleans, November 21.

Butler, Judith. 1990. *Gender trouble: Feminism and the subversion of identity.* New York: Routledge.

Cain, Maureen. 1985. "Beyond informal justice." *Contemporary Crises* 9: 303–328.

Caldeira, Teresa P. R. 1996. "Fortified enclaves: The new urban segregation." *Public Culture* 8: 303–328.

——. 2000. *City of walls: Crime, segregation, and citizenship in São Paulo.* Berkeley: University of California Press.

Caldeira, Teresa P. R., and James Holston. 1999. "Democracy and violence in Brazil." *Comparative Studies in Society and History* 41(4): 691–729.

Calderón G., Fernando. 1984. *Urbanización y etnicidad: El caso de La Paz.* Cochabamba: CERES.

Calkowski, Maria S. 1991. "A day at the Tibetan opera: Actualized performance and spectacular discourse." *American Ethnologist* 18(4): 643–657.

Cancian, Frank. 1965. *Economics and prestige in a Maya community: The religious cargo system in Zinacantan.* Stanford: Stanford University Press.

Canessa, Andrew. 2000. "Fear and loathing on the *kharisiri* trail: Alterity and identity in the Andes." *Journal of the Royal Anthropological Institute* 6(4): 705–720.

Castillo Claudett, Eduardo. 2000. "La justicia en tiempos de la ira: Linchamientos
populares urbanos en América Latina." *Ecuador Debate* 51: 207–226.

Celestino, Olinda, and Albert Meyers. 1981. *Las cofradías en el Perú: Region central.*
Frankfurt: Editionen der Iberoamericana.

Centro de Estudios de Población (CEP). 1993. "Departamento de Cochabamba:
Información sobre población y vivienda 1976–1992." In *Boletín de Población* no.
1. Cochabamba: Universidad Mayor de San Simón.

———. N.d. *La migración interna en Cochabamba.* Cochabamba: Universidad Mayor
de San Simón.

CERES/FORHUM. 1993. *La influencia de las organizaciones externas en la gestión
barrial: El caso de Villa Sebastián Pagador y Alto Cochabamba.* Cochabamba:
CERES.

Chambers, Sarah C. 1999. *From subjects to citizens: Honor, gender, and politics in
Arequipa, Peru, 1780–1854.* University Park: Pennsylvania State University Press.

Chasteen, John Charles. 1993. "Fighting words: The discourse of insurgency in
Latin American history." *Latin American Research Review* 28(3): 83–112.

Choque, María Eugenia, and Carlos Mamani. 2001. "Reconstitución del ayllu y
derechos de los pueblos indígenas: El movimiento indio en los Andes de Bolivia." *Journal of Latin American Anthropology* 6(1): 202–224.

"Cochabamba ya no es una ciudad tranquila." 2001, 16 April. *Los Tiempos* (Cochabamba).

Cohen, Abner. 1980. "Drama and politics in the development of a London carnival." *Man* 15: 65–87.

———. 1993. *Masquerade politics: Explorations in the structure of urban cultural movements.* Berkeley: University of California Press.

"El colegio de arquitectos de Cochabamba frente a las arbitrarias cesiones de
parques públicos." 1980. *Los Tiempos* (Cochabamba).

Colloredo-Mansfeld, Rudi. 1998. " 'Dirty indians,' radical *indígenas,* and the political economy of social difference in modern Ecuador." *Bulletin of Latin American
Research* 17(2): 185–205.

———. 1999. *The native leisure class: Consumption and cultural creativity in the Andes.*
Chicago: University of Chicago Press.

———. 2002. " 'Don't be lazy, don't lie, don't steal': Community justice in the neoliberal Andes." *American Ethnologist* 29(3): 637–662.

Comaroff, Jean, and John L. Comaroff. 2001. "Millennial capitalism: First thoughts
on a second coming." In *Millennial capitalism and the culture of neoliberalism.* J.
Comaroff and J. L. Comaroff, eds., 1–56. Durham, N.C.: Duke University Press.

Comaroff, John L. 1994. Foreword to *Contested states: Law, hegemony, resistance.* M.
Lazarus-Black and S. F. Hirsch, eds., ix–xiii. New York: Routledge.

"Comerciantes se cansaron de promesas, exigen hechos." 2001, 28 March. *Los Tiempos* (Cochabamba).

"Concejo creará dirección municipal para atender las zonas periurbanas." 1994, 24 January. *Opinión* (Cochabamba), 4A.

Connerton, Paul. 1989. *How societies remember.* Cambridge, England: Cambridge University Press.

Cornblit, Oscar. 1995. *Power and violence in the colonial city: Oruro from the mining renaissance to the rebellion of Tupac Amaru (1740–1782).* E. L. Glick, trans. Cambridge, England: Cambridge University Press.

Coronil, Fernando. 1997. *The magical state: Nature, money, and modernity in Venezuela.* Chicago: University of Chicago Press.

Coronil, Fernando, and Julie Skurski. 1991. "Dismembering and remembering the nation: The semantics of political violence in Venezuela." *Comparative Studies in Society and History* 33(2): 288–337.

Corrigan, Phillip, and Derek Sayer. 1985. *The great arch: English state formation as cultural revolution.* London: Basil Blackwell.

Coyle, Philip E. 2001. *Nayari history, politics, and violence: From flowers to ash.* Tucson: University of Arizona Press.

Crandon-Malamud, Libbet. 1993. "Blessings of the virgin in capitalist society: The transformation of a rural Bolivian fiesta." *American Anthropologist* 95(3): 574–596.

Crespo, Ramiro Julio. 1995. "La plaza del vicio." *Cuarto Poder* (Cochabamba), 8–9.

Cueto, Marcos. 1991. "*Indigenismo* and rural medicine in Peru: The Indian Sanitary Brigade and Manuel Nuñez Butrón." *Bulletin of the History of Medicine* 65(1): 22–41.

DaMatta, Roberto. 1991. *Carnivals, rogues, and heroes: An interpretation of the Brazilian dilemma.* Notre Dame: University of Notre Dame Press.

Dandler, Jorge. 1969. *El sindicalismo campesino en Bolivia: Los cambios estructurales en Ucureña.* Mexico City: Instituto Indigenista Interamericano.

———. 1971. "Politics of leadership, brokerage, and patronage in the campesino movement in Cochabamba, Bolivia 1935–1954." PhD diss., University of Wisconsin.

Davis, Susan G. 1986. *Parades and power: Street theatre in nineteenth century Philadelphia.* Berkeley: University of California Press.

Debord, Guy. 1995. *The society of the spectacle.* D. Nicholson-Smith, trans. New York: Zone.

de la Cadena, Marisol. 2000. *Indigenous mestizos: The politics of race and culture in Cuzco, Peru, 1919–1991.* Durham, N.C.: Duke University Press.

Desmond, Jane, ed. 1997. *Meaning in motion: New cultural studies of dance.* Durham, N.C.: Duke University Press.

Díaz-Barriga, Miguel. 1996. "*Necesidad:* Notes on the discourse of urban politics in the Ajusco foothills of Mexico City." *American Ethnologist* 23(2): 291–310.

——. 1998."Beyond the domestic and the public: *Colonas* participation in urban movements in Mexico City." In *Cultures of politics, politics of cultures: Revisioning Latin American social movements.* S. E. Alvarez, E. Dagnino, and A. Escobar, eds., 252–277. Boulder, Colo.: Westview.

Dirección Social Universitaria (DISU). 1996. *Estudio socioéconomico, Villa Sebastían Pagador.* Cochabamba: Universidad Mayor de San Simón.

Dobyns, Henry F. 1964. *The social matrix of Peruvian indigenous communities.* Ithaca: Cornell University Press.

Dominguez, Ana María. 1994. "The 'talleres zonales': An alternative strategy of people's participation." Architecture and Development, Compendium of Independent Studies by the Course Participants, 77–100. Department of Architecture and Development Studies, Lund Centre for Habitat Studies, Lund University, Lund, Sweden.

Doughty, Paul L. 1968. *Huaylas: An Andean district in search of progress.* Ithaca: Cornell University Press.

Douglas, Mary. 1966. *Purity and danger: An analysis of the concepts of pollution and taboo.* London: ARK Paperbacks.

Drake, Paul W., and Eric Hershberg. 2001. "Crises in the Andes." Social Science Research Council, unpublished manuscript.

Dray, Philip. 2002. *At the hands of persons unknown: The lynching of black America.* New York: Random House.

Dundes, Alan, and Alessandro Falassi. 1975. *La terra in piazza: An interpretation of the Palio of Siena.* Berkeley: University of California Press.

Dunkerley, James, and Rolando Morales. 1986. "The crisis in Bolivia." *New Left Review* 155: 86–104.

"80% de urbanizaciones periféricas son clandestinas, reconoce Concejo." 1993, 20 July. *Opinión* (Cochabamba).

"El Paso 'perdona' la vida de tres presuntos antisociales." 2002, 9 April. *Los Tiempos* (Cochabamba).

"Enajenación de áreas verdes en Cochabamba, 1." 1974. *Los Tiempos* (Cochabamba).

"Enajenación de áreas verdes en Cochabamba, 2." 1974. *Los Tiempos* (Cochabamba).

"Entre zonas sud y norte hay grandes diferencias en el consumo de agua." 1994, 3 March. *Opinión* (Cochabamba).

Escobar, Arturo, and Sonia E. Alvarez, eds. 1992. *The making of social movements in Latin America: Identity, strategy, and democracy.* Boulder, Colo.: Westview.

Escobar de Pabón, Silvia, and Carmen Ledo García. 1988. *Urbanización, migraciones y empleo en la ciudad de Cochabamba.* La Paz: CEDLA/CIDRE.

"Explican la causa de los 'linchamientos.'" 2002, 28 March. *Los Tiempos* (Cochabamba).

Farcau, Bruce W. 1996. *The Chaco War: Bolivia and Paraguay, 1932–1935.* Westview, Conn.: Praeger.

Farthing, Linda. 1997. "Social impacts associated with antidrug law 1008." In *Coca, cocaine, and the Bolivian reality.* M. B. Léons and H. Sanabria, eds., 253–369. Albany: State University of New York Press.

Ferrufino Llach, Clara. 1987. *Tamayo y el hombre boliviano.* La Paz: Editorial Gisbert.

Fishman, Robert. 1982. *Urban utopias in the twentieth century: Ebenezer Howard, Frank Lloyd Wright and Le Corbusier.* Cambridge, Mass.: MIT Press.

Fleisher, Michael L. 2000. *Kuria cattle raiders: Violence and vigilantism on the Tanzania/Kenya frontier.* Ann Arbor: University of Michigan Press.

Flores Galindo, Alberto. 1988. *Buscando un Inca.* Lima: Editorial Horizonte.

"El 40% de la población está asentada en barrios clandestinos." 1993, 11 April. *Presencia* (Cochabamba).

"El 40% de viviendas de la periferia se considera ilegal y 'clandestina.'" 1993, 23 March. *Opinión* (Cochabamba).

Foster, George M. 1967. *Tzintzuntzan: Mexican peasants in a changing world.* Boston: Little, Brown.

Foster, George M., and Robert V. Kemper. 1974. "Introduction: A perspective on anthropological fieldwork in cities." In *Anthropologists in cities.* G. M. Foster and R. V. Kemper, eds., 1–18. Boston: Little, Brown.

Foucault, Michel. 1977. *Discipline and punish: The birth of the prison.* New York: Vintage.

——. 1980. "On popular justice: A discussion with Maoists." In *Power/knowledge: Selected interviews and other writings 1972–1977.* C. Gordon, ed. New York: Pantheon.

——. 1991. "Governmentality." In *The Foucault effect: Studies in governmentality.* G. Burchell, C. Gordon, and P. Miller, eds., 87–104. Chicago: University of Chicago Press.

Frampton, Kenneth. 2001. *Le Corbusier.* New York: Thames and Hudson.

Francovich, Guillermo. 1956. *El pensamiento boliviano en el siglo veinte.* Mexico City: Fondo de Cultura Económica.

Fraser, Valerie. 1990. *The arquitecture of conquest: Building in the viceroyalty of Peru, 1535–1635.* Cambridge, England: Cambridge University Press.

Freitag, Sandria B. 1989. *Collective action and community: Public arenas and the emergence of communalism in North India.* Berkeley: University of California Press.

Fuentes Díaz, Antonio, and Leigh Binford. 2001. "Linchamientos en Mexico: Una respuesta a Carlos Vilas." *Bajo el Volcán* 2(3): 143–156.

Fuenzalida, Fernando. 1976. "Estructura de la comunidad indígena tradicional: Una hipótesis de trabajo." In *Hacienda, comunidad y campesinado en el Perú.* J. Matos Mar, ed., 219–263. Lima: Instituto de Estudios Peruanos.

Gamarra, Eduardo. 1994. "Market-oriented reforms and democratization in Latin America: Challenges of the 1990s." In *Latin American political economy in the age of neoliberal reform.* W. C. Smith, C. H. Acuña, and E. Gamarra, eds., 1–14. Miami: Transaction.

García, María Elena. 2000. "Ethnographic responsibility and the anthropological endeavor: Beyond identity discourse." *Anthropological Quarterly* 73(2): 89–101.

García Canclini, Nestor. 1993. *Transforming modernity: Popular culture in Mexico.* Austin: University of Texas Press.

——. 1995. *Hybrid cultures: Strategies for entering and leaving modernity.* C. L. Chiappari and S. L. Lopez, trans. Minneapolis: University of Minnesota Press.

——. 2001. *Consumers and citizens: Globablization and multicultural conflicts.* G. Yudice, trans. Minneapolis: University of Minnesota Press.

García Linera, Alvaro. 1998. *Reproletarización: Nueva clase obrera y desarrollo del capital industrial en Bolivia (1952–1998).* La Paz: Muela del Diablo Editores.

García Prada, Hernán. 2002, 17 May. "La pena de muerte." *Los Tiempos* (Cochabamba).

Gay, Robert. 1994. *Popular organization and democracy in Rio de Janeiro: A tale of two favelas.* Philadelphia: Temple University Press.

Geertz, Clifford. 1973. *The interpretation of cultures: Selected essays by Clifford Geertz.* New York: Basic.

Gill, Lesley. 1987. *Peasants, entrepreneurs, and social change: Frontier development in lowland Bolivia.* Boulder, Colo.: Westview.

——. 1994. *Precarious dependencies: Gender, class, and domestic service in Bolivia.* New York: Columbia University Press.

——. 2000. *Teetering on the rim: Global restructuring, daily life, and the armed retreat of the Bolivian state.* New York: Columbia University Press.

Ginsburg, Faye. 1995. "Production values: Indigenous media and the rhetoric of self-determination." In *Rhetorics of self-making.* D. Battaglia, ed., 121–138. Berkeley: University of California Press.

Girard, René. 1977. *Violence and the sacred.* Baltimore: Johns Hopkins University Press.

"El gobierno ensaya carísimo e incierto plan de vigilancia." 2002, 4 May. *La Prensa* (La Paz).

"Gobierno municipal declara lucha a muerte a loteadores." 1993, 25 February. *Los Tiempos* (Cochabamba).

Godoy, Angelina Snodgrass. 2002. "Lynchings and the democratization of terror in post-war Guatemala: Implications for human rights." *Human Rights Quarterly* 24: 640–661.

Goffman, Erving. 1959. *The presentation of self in everyday life.* Garden City, N.Y.: Doubleday Anchor.

Goldstein, Daniel M. 1998a. "Dancing on the margins: Transforming urban marginality through popular performance." *City and Society* 4: 201–215.

——. 1998b. "Performing national culture in a Bolivian migrant community." *Ethnology* 37(2): 117–132.

——. 2000. "Names, places, and power: The politics of identity in the Miss Oruro

Pageant, Cochabamba, Bolivia." *Political and Legal Anthropology Review* 23(1): 1–24.

——. 2003a. "The customs of the faithful: Evangelicals and the politics of Catholic fiesta in Bolivia." *Journal of Latin American Lore* 21(2): 179–200.

——. 2003b. "In our own hands: Lynching, justice, and the law in Bolivia." *American Ethnologist* 30(1): 22–43.

Gomes da Cunha, Olivia Maria. 1998. "Black movements and the politics of identity in Brazil." In *Cultures of politics, politics of cultures: Re-visioning Latin American social movements*. S. E. Alvarez, E. Dagnino, and A. Escobar, eds., 220–251. Boulder, Colo.: Westview.

Gonzales Quintanilla, Luis. 2001, 19 April. "Del linchamiento a otra clase de violencias peores." *Los Tiempos* (Cochabamba).

"Gonzalo Terceros Rojas: Cochabamba se está quedando sin pulmones para respirar." 1993, 14 September. *Opinión* (Cochabamba).

Gordillo, José M. 1987. *El proceso de extinción del yanaconaje en el valle de Cochabamba*. Cochabamba: Universidad Mayor de San Simon.

Greenhouse, Carol J. 1992. "Reading violence." In *Law's violence*. A. Sarat and T. R. Kearns, eds., 105–139. Ann Arbor: University of Michigan Press.

Gregory, Steven. 1998. *Black Corona: Race and the politics of place in an urban community*. Princeton: Princeton University Press.

Guano, Emanuela. 2002. "Spectacles of modernity: Transnational imagination and local hegemonies in neoliberal Buenos Aires." *Cultural Anthropology* 17(2): 181–209.

Guerra Gutierrez, Alberto. 1990. *Folklore boliviano*. La Paz: Los Amigos del Libro.

Guerrero, Andrés. 2001. "Los linchamientos en las comunidades indígenas: ¿La política perversa de una modernidad marginal?" *Ecuador Debate* 53: 197–226.

Gulick, J. 1973. "Urban anthropology." In *Handbook of social and cultural anthropology*. J. J. Honigmann, ed., 979–1029. Chicago: Rand McNally.

Gupta, Akhil. 1995. "Blurred boundaries: The discourse of corruption, the culture of politics, and the imagined state." *American Ethnologist* 22(2): 375–402.

Gupta, Akhil, and James Ferguson. 2002. "Spatializing states: Toward an ethnography of neoliberal governmentality." *American Ethnologist* 29(4): 981–1002.

Guss, David M. 1993. "The selling of San Juan: The performance of history in an Afro-Venezuelan community." *American Ethnologist* 20(3): 451–473.

——. 2000. *The festive state: Race, ethnicity, and nationalism as cultural performance*. Berkeley: University of California Press.

——. N.d. "The good, the bad, and the uppity: Life and struggle in the streets of La Paz." Paper presented at the 101st annual meeting of the American Anthropological Association, New Orleans.

Gutiérrez Sánz, Bernardo. 2001, 18 April. "Injusticia por mano propia." *Los Tiempos* (Cochabamba).

Gutkind, Peter C. W. 1974. *Urban anthropology: Perspectives on "Third World" urbanization and urbanism.* Assen, The Netherlands: Van Gorcum.

Gutmann, Matthew C. 2002. *The romance of democracy: Compliant defiance in contemporary Mexico.* Berkeley: University of California Press.

Guzman, Augusto. 1972. *Cochabamba.* Cochabamba: Editorial "Los Amigos del Libro."

Hall, Peter. 1990. *Cities of tomorrow: An intellectual history of urban planning and design in the twentieth century.* Cambridge, England: Basil Blackwell.

Hall, Stuart. 1996. "Introduction: Who needs 'identity'?" In *Questions of cultural identity.* S. Hall and P. du Gay, eds., 1–17. London: Sage.

Handelman, Don. 1990. *Models and mirrors: Towards an anthropology of public events.* Cambridge, England: Cambridge University Press.

——. 1997. "Rituals/spectacles." *International Social Science Journal* 153: 387–399.

Hannerz, Ulf. 1980. *Exploring the city: Inquiries toward an urban anthropology.* New York: Columbia University Press.

Hardoy, Jorge. 1972. *Las ciudades en América Latina: Seis ensayos sobre la urbanización contemporánea.* Buenos Aires: Paidós.

——. 1975. *Urbanization in Latin America: Approaches and issues.* Garden City, N.Y.: Anchor.

——. 1992. "Theory and practice of urban planning in Europe, 1850–1930: Its transfer to Latin America." In *Rethinking the Latin American city.* R. M. Morse and J. E. Hardoy, eds. Washington, D.C.: Woodrow Wilson Center Press.

Harris, Marvin. 1964. *Patterns of race in the Americas.* New York: Walker.

Harris, Olivia. 1994. "Comments to O. Starn, Rethinking the politics of anthropology, the case of the Andes." *Current Anthropology* 35(1): 27.

Harvey, David. 2001. *Spaces of capital: Towards a critical geography.* Edinburgh: University of Edinburgh Press.

Hastrup, Kirstin, and Peter Elsass. 1990. "Anthropological advocacy: A contradiction in terms?" *Current Anthropology* 31(3): 301–311.

Healy, Kevin. 1988. "Coca, the state, and the peasantry in Bolivia, 1982–1988." *Journal of Interamerican Studies and World Affairs* 30(2–3): 105–125.

Healy, Kevin, and Susan Paulson. 2000. "Introduction: Political economies of identity in Bolivia, 1952–1998." *Journal of Latin American Anthropology* 5(2): 2–29.

Hebdige, Dick. 1979. *Subculture, the meaning of style.* London: Methuen.

Henkel, Ray. 1988. "The Bolivian cocaine industry." In *Drugs in Latin America.* E. Morales, ed., 53–81. Williamsburg, Va.: Department of Anthropology, College of William and Mary.

Herzfeld, Michael. 1992. *The social production of indifference: Exploring the symbolic roots of Western bureaucracy.* Chicago: University of Chicago Press.

Hill, Jane H. 1991. "In nēca gobierno de Puebla: Mexicano penetrations of the Mexican state." *In Nation-states and Indians in Latin America.* G. Urban and J. Sherzer, eds., 72–94. Austin: University of Texas Press.

Himpele, Jeffrey. 1996. "Distributing difference: The distribution and displacement of media, spectacle, and identity in La Paz, Bolivia." PhD diss., Princeton University.

Hirst, Paul, and Grahame F. Thompson. 1996. *Globalization in question: The international economy and the possibilities of governance.* Cambridge, England: Polity.

Hobsbawn, Eric, and George Rudé. 1968. *Captain Swing: A social history of the great English agricultural uprising of 1830.* New York: Norton.

Holston, James. 1989. *The modernist city: An anthropological critique of Brasília.* Chicago: University of Chicago Press.

——. 1991a. "Autoconstruction in working-class Brazil." *Cultural Anthropology* 6(4): 446–463.

——. 1991b. "The misrule of law: Land and usurpation in Brazil." *Comparative Studies in Society and History* 33(4): 695–725.

——. 1999. "Spaces of insurgent citizenship." In *Cities and citizenship.* J. Holston, ed., 155–176. Durham, N.C.: Duke University Press.

Holston, James, and Arjun Appadurai. 1999. "Introduction: Cities and citizenship." In *Cities and citizenship.* J. Holston, ed., 1–18. Durham, N.C.: Duke University Press.

Honorable Alcaldía Municipal (HAM). 1985. *Plan director de la región urbana de Cochabamba.* Cochabamba: Honorable Alcaldía Municipal.

——. 1987. *Plan director de la región urbana de Cochabamba 2.* Cochabamba: Honorable Alcaldía Municipal.

Howard, Ebenezer. 1902. *Garden cities of tomorrow.* London: Swan Sonnenschein.

Hubert, Henry, and Marcel Mauss. 1964. *Sacrifice: Its nature and function.* W. D. Halls, trans. Chicago: University of Chicago Press.

Huggins, Martha K., ed. 1991. *Vigilantism and the state in modern Latin America: Essays on extralegal violence.* New York: Praeger.

Instituto Nacional de Estadística (INE). 1992. *Censo nacional de población y vivienda.* Cochabamba: INE.

——. 2001. *Censo nacional de población y vivienda.* Cochabamba: INE.

Isbell, Billie Jean. 1985. *To defend ourselves: Ecology and ritual in an Andean village.* 3rd ed. Prospect Heights, Ill.: Waveland.

Izko, Xavier. 1986. *Tiempo de vida y muerte: Estudio de caso en dos contextos andinos de Bolivia.* La Paz: Consejo Nacional de Población.

Janes, Regina. 1993. "Beheadings." In *Death and representation.* S. W. Goodwin and E. Bronfen, eds., 242–262. Baltimore: Johns Hopkins University Press.

Jelin, Elizabeth, ed. 1990. *Women and social change in Latin America.* London: Zed Books.

Jelin, Elizabeth, and Eric Hershberg, eds. 1996. *Constructing democracy: Human rights, citizenship, and society in Latin America.* Boulder, Colo.: Westview.

Johnston, Les. 1996. "What is vigilantism?" *British Journal of Criminology* 36(2): 220–236.

Joseph, Gilbert M., and Daniel Nugent, eds. 1994. *Everyday forms of state formation: Revolution and the negotiation of rule in modern Mexico*. Durham, N.C.: Duke University Press.

Joseph, May. 1999. *Nomadic identities: The performance of citizenship*. Minneapolis: University of Minnesota Press.

Kagan, Richard L. 2000. *Urban images of the Hispanic world: 1493–1793*. New Haven: Yale University Press.

Keatinge, Elsie B. 1973. "Latin American peasant corporate communities: Potentials for mobilization and political integration." *Journal of Anthropological Research* 29: 37–58.

Kertzer, David I. 1988. *Ritual, politics and power*. New Haven: Yale University Press.

Klein, Herbert S. 1969. *Parties and political change in Bolivia 1880–1952*. Cambridge, England: Cambridge University Press.

———. 1992. *Bolivia: The evolution of a multi-ethnic society*. Oxford: Oxford University Press.

Knaudt, Gustavo. 1947. "Problemas del urbanismo de Cochabamba." 19 August. *Los Tiempos* (Cochabamba).

Kohl, Benjamin. 2003. "Restructuring citizenship in Bolivia: El Plan de Todos." *International Journal of Urban and Regional Research* 27(2): 337–351.

Kristal, Efrain. 1987. *The Andes viewed from the city: Literary and political discourse on the Indian in Peru*. New York: Peter Lang.

" 'Los ladrones están matando para evitar que los linchen.' Habla el director de la Policía Técnica Judicial." 2002, 8 May. *La Voz* (La Paz).

Lagos, María L. 1993. " 'We have to learn to ask': Hegemony, diverse experiences and antagonistic meanings in Bolivia." *American Ethnologist* 20(1): 52–71.

———. 1994. *Autonomy and power: The dynamics of class and culture in rural Bolivia*. Philadelphia: University of Pennsylvania Press.

———. 1997. " 'Bolivia la nueva': Constructing new citizens." Paper presented at the meetings of the Latin American Studies Association (LASA), Guadalajara, Mexico.

Larson, Brooke. 1988. *Colonialism and agrarian transformation in Bolivia: Cochabamba, 1550–1900*. Princeton: Princeton University Press.

———. 1998. *Cochabamba, 1550–1900: Colonialism and agrarian transformation in Bolivia*. Expanded ed. Durham, N.C.: Duke University Press.

Larson, Brooke, and Olivia Harris, eds. 1995. *Ethnicity, markets, and migration in the Andes*. Durham, N.C.: Duke University Press.

Laserna, Roberto. 1995. "Coca cultivation, drug trafficking and regional development in Cochabamba, Bolivia." PhD diss., University of California.

———. 1997. *Twenty (mis)conceptions on coca and cocaine*. La Paz: Plural Editores, Clave.

Lazarus-Black, Mindie. 2001. "Law and the pragmatics of inclusion: Governing domestic violence in Trinidad and Tobago." *American Ethnologist* 28(2): 388–416.

Lechner, Juan. 1981. "El concepto de 'policía' y su presencia en la obra de los primeros historiadores de Indias." *Revista de Indias* 41: 390–404.

Le Corbusier (Charles-Edouard Jeanneret). [1929] 1996. "A contemporary city." In *The city reader.* R. T. LeGates and F. Stout, eds., 367–375. London: Routledge.

Ledebur, Kathryn. 2003. "Bolivia: Una crisis violenta." *Ideele* 153: 73–76.

Ledo García, Carmen. 1993. *Cochabamba y su problemática urbana.* Cochabamba: CERES.

———. N.d. *Urbanización y migración en la ciudad de Cochabamba.* Cochabamba: IESE.

Lee, Wayne E. 2001. *Crowds and soldiers in revolutionary North Carolina: The culture of violence in riot and war.* Gainesville: University of Florida Press.

Leeds, Anthony. 1994. *Cities, classes, and the social order.* R. Sanjek, ed. Ithaca: Cornell University Press.

Lehm Ardaya, Zulema. 1998. *Milenarismo y movimientos sociales en la amazonia boliviana: La búsqueda de la loma santa y la marcha indígena por el territorio y la dignidad.* Santa Cruz: APCOB-CIDDEBENI-OXFAM.

Léons, Madeline Barbara, and Harry Sanabria. 1997. "Coca and cocaine in Bolivia: Reality and policy illusion." In *Coca, cocaine, and the Bolivian reality.* M. B. Léons and H. Sanabria, eds., 1–46. Albany: State University of New York Press.

Lewis, Oscar. 1966. *La vida: A Puerto Rican family in the culture of poverty.* New York: Vintage.

Liebson, Miguelina. 1995. *Los migrantes altiplánicos en Cochabamba: Persistencia y cambio en sus costumbres y patrones alimentarios (el caso de Sebastián Pagador).* Cochabamba: Universidad Mayor de San Simon, IESE.

"Linchadores y linchados quedan en la impunidad." 2001, 27 July. *Los Tiempos* (Cochabamba).

"Linchamiento: Atacan a instituciones sociales." 2001, 30 March. *Los Tiempos* (Cochabamba).

"Linchamiento: Más de 100 sospechosos en lista." 2001, 24 April. *Los Tiempos* (Cochabamba).

"Linchamientos e impunidad." 2002, 10 April. *Opinión* (Cochabamba).

"Los linchamientos no son actos salidos de la cultura ni tradición." 2001, 10 May. *Los Tiempos* (Cochabamba).

"Los linchamientos se repiten porque las autoridades no hacen nada para evitarlos." 2002, 21 June. *Opinión* (Cochabamba).

"Linchar: Señal de barbarie." 2001, 13 April. *Los Tiempos* (Cochabamba).

"Lincharían por histeria y estrés." 2001, 29 March. *Los Tiempos* (Cochabamba).

Lloyd, Peter. 1979. *Slums of hope? Shantytowns of the third world.* New York: St. Martin's.

———. 1980. *The "young towns" of Lima: Aspects of urbanization in Peru.* Cambridge, England: Cambridge University Press.

Lobo, Susan. 1982. *A house of my own: Social organization in the squatter settlements of Lima, Peru*. Tucson: University of Arizona Press.

Lomnitz, Larissa Adler. 1977. *Networks and marginality: Life in a Mexican shantytown*. New York: Academic.

Lopez G. de Page, María Cristina. 1993, 10 February. "El crecimiento de Cochabamba." *Los Tiempos* (Cochabamba).

Low, Setha M. 1996. "Spatializing culture: The social production and social construction of public space." *American Ethnologist* 23(4): 861–879.

——. 2000. *On the plaza: The politics of public space and culture*. Austin: University of Texas Press.

Luján, Abdelardo. 1994, 7 June. "Sebastián Pagador." *Los Tiempos* (Cochabamba).

Lukacs, John. 1993. *The end of the twentieth century and the end of the modern age*. New York: Ticknor and Fields.

Luykx, Aurolyn. 1999. *The citizen factory: Schooling and cultural production in Bolivia*. Albany: State University of New York Press.

MacAloon, John J. 1984. "Olympic games and the theory of spectacle in modern societies." In *Rite, drama, festival, spectacle: Rehearsals toward a theory of cultural performance*. J. J. MacAloon, ed., 241–280. Philadelphia: Institute for the Study of Human Issues.

"Una madre y tres de sus hijos casi linchados en V. Pagador." 1995, 12 March. *Opinión* (Cochabamba).

Mallon, Florencia E. 1983. *The defense of community in Peru's central highlands*. Princeton: Princeton University Press.

Malloy, James M. 1989. *Bolivia: La revolución inconclusa*. La Paz: CERES.

Mangin, William. 1954. "The cultural significance of the fiesta complex in an Indian hacienda in Peru." PhD diss., Yale University.

——. 1969. "Latin American squatter settlements: A problem and a solution." *Ekistics* 27: 37–39

——. 1970. *Peasants in cities: Readings in the anthropology of urbanization*. Boston: Houghton-Mifflin.

Mannheim, Bruce, and Dennis Tedlock. 1995. Introduction to *The dialogic emergence of culture*. B. Mannheim and D. Tedlock, eds., 1–32. Urbana: University of Illinois Press.

Mariategui, José Carlos. [1928] 1985. *Siete ensayos de interpretación de la realidad peruana*. Lima: Amauta.

Marinkovic Uzqueda, Vezna. 2002, 20 June. "Nerviosos y delincuentes." *Los Tiempos* (Cochabamba).

Martínez, Gabriel. 1987. *Una mesa ritual en Sucre: Aproximaciones semióticas al ritual andino*. La Paz: Hisbol-Asur.

Martínez, Héctor. 1959. "Vicos: Las fiestas en la integración y desintegración cultural." *Revista del Museo Nacional* 28: 235–250.

Mayer, Enrique. 1991. "Peru in deep trouble: Mario Vargas Llosa's 'Inquest in the Andes' reexamined." *Cultural Anthropology* 6(4): 466–504.

McDonogh, Gary. 1993. "The geography of emptiness." In *The cultural meaning of urban space.* R. Rotenberg and G. McDonogh, eds., 3–15. Westport, Conn.: Bergin and Garvey.

Medeiros, Carmen. 2001. "Civilizing the popular? The law of popular participation and the design of a new civil society in 1990's Bolivia." *Critique of Anthropology* 21(4): 401–425.

Mendoza, Zoila S. 2000. *Shaping society through dance: Mestizo ritual performance in the Peruvian Andes.* Chicago: University of Chicago Press.

Merry, Sally Engle. 1993. "Sorting out popular justice." In *The possibility of popular justice: A case study of community mediation in the United States.* S. E. Merry and N. Milner, eds., 31–66. Ann Arbor: University of Michigan Press.

——. 1996. "Urban danger: Life in a neighborhood of strangers." In *Urban life: Readings in urban anthropology.* 3rd ed. G. Gmelch and W. P. Zenner, eds., 47–59. Prospects Heights, Ill.: Waveland.

——. 2001. "Spatial governmentality and the new urban social order: Controlling gender violence through law." *American Anthropologist* 103(1): 16–29.

Ministerio de Justicia y Derechos Humanos. 1997. *Justicia comunitaria.* Vols. 1–10. La Paz: Sierpe.

Mitchell, W. J. T. 1994. *Picture theory.* Chicago: University of Chicago Press.

Morales, Waltraud Queiser. 1992. *Bolivia: Land of struggle.* Boulder, Colo.: Westview.

Mullings, Leith. 1987. "Introduction: Urban anthropology and U.S. cities." In *Cities of the United States.* L. Mullings, ed., 1–15. New York: Columbia University Press.

Mumford, Lewis. 1961. *The city in history: Its origins, its transformations, and its prospects.* New York: Harcourt, Brace and World.

Murillo Vacareza, Josermo. 1987. "Identidad y semblanza de Sebastián Pagador." In *Perfiles de Oruro.* Vol. 1. E. Delgado Morales, ed., 53–59. Oruro: Biblioteca Orureña.

Nagel, Beverly Y. 1999. "'Unleashing the fury': The cultural discourse of rural violence and land rights in Paraguay." *Comparative Studies in Society and History* 41(1): 148–181.

Nas, Peter J. M. 2002. "Masterpieces of oral and intangible culture: Reflections on the UNESCO World Heritage List." *Current Anthropology* 43(1): 139–143.

Nash, June. 1979. *We eat the mines and the mines eat us: Dependency and exploitation in Bolivian tin mines.* New York: Columbia University Press.

——. 1992. "Interpreting social movements: Bolivian resistance to economic conditions imposed by the International Monetary Fund." *American Ethnologist* 19(2): 275–293.

Navarro, Marysa. 1989. "The personal is political: Las madres de la Plaza de Mayo." In *Power and popular protest: Latin American social movements*. S. Eckstein, ed., 241–258. Berkeley: University of California Press.

Newman, Simon P. 1997. *Parades and the politics of the street: Festive culture in the early American republic*. Philadelphia: University of Pennsylvania Press.

"No lo lincharon, pero ¡como! lo golpearon." 2001, 19 April. *Los Tiempos* (Cochabamba).

Nugent, Daniel. 1993. *Spent cartridges of revolution: An anthropological history of Namiquipa, Chihuahua*. Chicago: University of Chicago Press.

"Ojo con los linchamientos dice PTJ." 2001, 20 April. *Los Tiempos* (Cochabamba).

Orlove, Benjamin S. 1993. "Putting race in its place: Order in colonial and post-colonial Peruvian geography." *Social Research* 60(2): 301–336.

———. 1994. "The dead policemen speak: Power, fear, and narrative in the 1931 Molloccahua killings (Cusco)." In *Unruly order: Violence, power, and cultural identity in the high provinces of southern Peru*. D. Poole, ed., 63–96. Boulder, Colo.: Westview.

———. 1997. "Meat and strength: The moral economy of a Chilean food riot." *Cultural Anthropology* 12(2): 234–268.

Ortner, Sherry B. 1995. "Resistance and the problem of ethnographic refusal." *Comparative Studies in Society and History* 37(1): 173–193.

"Oscar Terceros: 'Antes que sea tarde debemos reconducir el desarrollo urbano.'" 1993, 7 February. *Opinión* (Cochabamba), 7B.

Osiel, Mark. 1997. *Mass atrocity, collective memory, and the law*. New Brunswick, N.J.: Transaction.

Paerregaard, Karsten. 1994. "Conversion, migration, and social identity: The spread of Protestantism in the Peruvian Andes." *Ethnos* 59: 168–186.

———. 1997. *Linking separate worlds: Urban migrants and rural lives in Peru*. New York: Berg.

Paley, Julia. 2001. *Marketing democracy: Power and social movements in post-dictatorship Chile*. Berkeley: University of California Press.

Palmer, Gary B., and William R. Jankowiak. 1996. "Performance and imagination: Toward an anthropology of the spectacular and the mundane." *Cultural Anthropology* 11(2): 225–258.

"¿Paranoia? Casi linchan à dos inocentes." 2001, 26 April. *Los Tiempos* (Cochabamba).

Pardo, Italo, ed. 2000. *Morals of legitimacy: Between agency and system*. New York: Berghahn.

Park, Robert E. 1928. "Human migration and the marginal man." *American Journal of Sociology* 33(6): 881–898.

Patterson, Orlando. 1998. *Rituals of blood: Consequences of slavery in two American centuries*. Washington, D.C.: Civitas/Counterpoint.

Paulson, Susan. 1996. "Familias que no 'conyugan' e identidades que no conjugan: La vida en Mizque desafía nuestras categorías." In *Ser mujer indígena, chola, o birlocha en la Bolivia postcolonial de los años 90*. S. Rivera Cusicanqui, ed., 85–162. La Paz: Subsecretaria de Asuntos de Género.

Paulson, Susan, and Pamela Calla. 2000. "Gender and ethnicity in Bolivian politics: Transformation or paternalism?" *Journal of Latin American Anthropology* 5(2): 112–149.

Peattie, Lisa R. 1968. *The view from the barrio*. Ann Arbor: University of Michigan Press.

———. 1974. "The concept of 'marginality' as applied to squatter settlements." In *Latin American urban research*, Vol. 4: *Anthropological perspectives on Latin American urbanization*. W. A. Cornelius and F. M. Trueblood, eds., 101–109. Beverly Hills: Sage.

———. 1987. *Planning: Rethinking Ciudad Guyana*. Ann Arbor: University of Michigan Press.

Peña Cazas, Waldo. 2001, 9 May. "El crimen como recurso de subsistencia." *Los Tiempos* (Cochabamba).

Peñaloza Chej, Teresa. 1991. *Proceso migratorio a Cochabamba entre 1987–1990: El caso de los mineros relocalizados*. Cochabamba: Centro de Estudios de Población, Universidad Mayor de San Simón.

Perlman, Janice E. 1976. *The myth of marginality: Urban poverty and politics in Rio de Janeiro*. Berkeley: University of California Press.

Pezzoli, Keith. 1987. "The urban land problem and popular sector housing development in Mexico City." *Environment and Behavior* 19(3): 371–397.

Piccato, Pablo. 2001. *City of suspects: Crime in Mexico City, 1900–1931*. Durham, N.C.: Duke University Press.

Pinheiro, Paulo Sérgio. 1999. "The rule of law and the underprivileged in Latin America: Introduction." In *The (un)rule of law and the underprivileged in Latin America*. J. E. Mendéz, G. O'Donnell, and P. S. Pinheiro, eds., 1–15. Notre Dame: University of Notre Dame Press.

"El plan de serenazgo vecinal empieza con fallas de coordinación." 2002, 30 April. *La Razón* (La Paz).

Platt, Tristan. 1982a. *Estado boliviano y ayllu andino*. Lima: Instituto de Estudios Peruanos.

———. 1982b. "The role of the Andean ayllu in the reproduction of the petty commodity regime in northern Potosí." In *Ecology and exchange in the Andes*. D. Lehmann, ed., 27–69. Cambridge, England: Cambridge University Press.

———. 1987. "Entre cháwxa y muxas: Para una historia del pensamiento político Aymara." In *Trés reflexiones sobre el pensamiento andino*. T. Bouysee-Cassagne, O. Harris, T. Platt, and V. Cereceda, eds., 61–132. La Paz: HISBOL.

Poole, Deborah. 1990a. "Accommodation and resistance in Andean ritual dance." *Drama Review* 34(2): 98–126.

———. 1990b. "Ciencia, peligrosidad y represión en la criminología indigenista peruana." In *Bandoleros, abigeos y montoneros: Criminalidad y violencia en el Perú, siglos XVIII–XX.* C. Aguirre and C. Walker, eds., 335–367. Lima: Instituto de Apoyo Agrario.

——, ed. 1994. *Unruly order: Violence, power, and cultural identity in the high provinces of southern Peru.* Boulder, Colo.: Westview.

Postero, Nancy. 2000. "Bolivia's indígena citizen: Multiculturalism in a neoliberal age." Paper presented at the meetings of the Latin American Studies Association (LASA), Miami, Fla.

Powell, Elwin H. 1962. "The evolution of the American city and the emergence of anomie: A culture case study of Buffalo, New York: 1810–1910." *British Journal of Sociology* 12: 15–166.

"Una práctica condenable." 2002, 25 March. *Los Tiempos* (Cochabamba).

Quinones, Sam. 2001. *True tales from another Mexico: The lynch mob, the Popsicle Kings, Chalino, and the Bronx.* Albuquerque: University of New Mexico Press.

Quiroga Oblitas, Jorge Hugo. 2002, 12 April. "Perdonados de ser linchados." *Opinión* (Cochabamba).

Radcliffe, Sarah A., and Sallie Westwood, eds. 1993. *"Viva": Women and popular protest in Latin America.* London: Routledge.

——. 1996. *Remaking the nation: Place, identity, and politics in Latin America.* London: Routledge.

Rama, Angel. 1996. *The lettered city.* Durham, N.C.: Duke University Press.

Rasnake, Roger. 1989. *Autoridad y poder en los Andes: Los kuraqkuna de Yura.* La Paz: Hisbol.

"Reyes Villa proclamó política urbana para una defensa del medio ambiente." 1993, 20 January. *Los Tiempos* (Cochabamba).

Rivera, Alberto P. 1992. *Los terratenientes de Cochabamba.* Cochabamba: CERES, FACES.

Rivera Cusicanqui, Silvia. 1986. *Oprimidos pero no vencidos: Luchas del campesinado aymara y quechwa de Bolivia, 1900–1980.* Geneva: Instituto de Investigaciones de las Naciones Unidas para el Desarrollo Social.

——, ed. 1996. *Ser mujer indígena, chola o birlocha en la Bolivia postcolonial de los años 90.* La Paz: Ministerio de Desarrollo Humano.

Roberts, Bryan R. 1978. *Cities of peasants: The political economy of urbanization in the Third World.* London: Edward Arnold.

——. 1995. *The making of citizens: Cities of peasants revisited.* London: Edward Arnold.

Rocha, José Antonio. 1990. *Sociedad agraria y religión: Cambio social e identidad en los valles de Cochabamba.* La Paz: Hisbol.

Rodgers, Susan. 2002. "The dead body on the front page: The coverage of death in Medan's 'Batak press' during the New Order." Paper presented at the Workshop on Art, Media and Violence in Southeast Asia, Harvard University, Cambridge, Mass.

Rodríguez Ostria, Gustavo, and Humberto Solares. 1990. *Sociedad oligárquica, chicha, y cultura popular*. Cochabamba: Editorial Serrano.

Rogers, Mark. 1999. "Spectacular bodies: Folklorization and the politics of identity in Ecuadorian beauty pageants." *Journal of Latin American Anthropology* 3(2): 54–85.

Roseberry, William. 1989. *Anthropologies and histories: Essays in culture, history and political economy*. New Brunswick, N.J.: Rutgers University Press.

Rosenbaum, H. Jon, and Peter Sederberg. 1976. *Vigilante politics*. Philadelphia: University of Pennsylvania Press.

Rosenthal, Anton. 2000. "Spectacle, fear, and protest: A guide to the history of urban public space in Latin America." *Social Science History* 24(1): 33–73.

Rotenberg, Robert. 1993. "On the salubrity of sites." In *The cultural meaning of urban space*. R. Rotenberg and G. McDonogh, eds., 17–29. Westport, Conn.: Bergin and Garvey.

Rotker, Susana, ed. 2002. *Citizens of fear: Urban violence in Latin America*. New Brunswick, N.J.: Rutgers University Press.

Rouse, Roger. 1991. "Mexican migration and the social space of postmodernism." *Diaspora* 1: 8–23.

Rowe, William, and Vivian Schelling. 1991. *Memory and modernity: Popular culture in Latin America*. London: Verso.

Saignes, Thierry. 1995. "Indian migration and social change in seventeenth-century Charcas." In *Ethnicity, markets, and migration in the Andes: At the crossroads of history and anthropology*. B. Larson, O. Harris, and E. Tandeter, eds., 167–195. Durham, N.C.: Duke University Press.

Salomon, Frank. 1981. "Killing the Yumbo: A ritual drama of northern Quito." In *Cultural transformations and ethnicity in modern Ecuador*. N. J. Whitten, ed., 162–208. Urbana: University of Illinois Press.

Sanabria, Harry. 1993. *The coca boom and rural social change in Bolivia*. Ann Arbor: University of Michigan Press.

——. 1997. "The discourse and practice of repression and resistance in the Chapare." In *Coca, cocaine, and the Bolivian reality*. M. B. Léons and H. Sanabria, eds., 169–194. Albany: State University of New York Press.

Sanchez-Albornoz, Nicolás. 1978. *Indios y tributos en el Alto Perú*. Lima: Instituto de Estudios Peruanos.

Sandoval Z., Godofredo, Xavier Albó, and Thomas Greaves. 1987. *Chukiyawu: La cara Aymara de La Paz*. Vol. 4 (Cuadernos de investigación, No. 29). La Paz: CIPCA.

Santivañez Soria, Marco. 2002, 10 March. "Ley andina: La violencia para reponer el orden." *Los Tiempos* (Cochabamba).

Sarat, Austin. 2001a. *Law, violence, and the possibility of justice*. Princeton: Princeton University Press.

——. 2001b. *When the state kills: Capital punishment and the American condition.* Princeton: Princeton University Press.

Sarat, Austin, and Thomas R. Kearns. 1996. "Legal justice and injustice: Toward a situated perspective." In *Justice and injustice in law and legal theory.* A. Sarat and T. R. Kearns, eds., 1–34. Ann Arbor: University of Michigan Press.

Sassen, Saskia. 1999. "Whose city is it? Globalization and the formation of new claims." In *Cities and citizenship.* J. Holston, ed., 177–194. Durham, N.C.: Duke University Press.

Scarry, Elaine. 1985. *The body in pain: The making and unmaking of the world.* Oxford: Oxford University Press.

Schechner, Richard. 1988. *Performance theory.* New York: Routledge.

——. 1993. *The future of ritual: Writings on culture and performance.* New York: Routledge.

Scheper-Hughes, Nancy. 1992. *Death without weeping: The violence of everyday life in Brazil.* Berkeley: University of California Press.

Schultz, Jim. 2000. "Bolivia's war over water." http://www.democracyctr.org/waterwar/. Accessed 18 December 2003.

——. 2001. "Taking the census—Bolivian style." Democracy Center Newsletter. Vol. 40. http://www.democracyctr.org. Accessed 18 December 2003.

Scott, Alison MacEwen. 1994. *Divisions and solidarities: Gender, class and employment in Latin America.* New York: Routledge.

Scott, James C. 1998. *Seeing like a state: How certain schemes to improve the human condition have failed.* New Haven: Yale University Press.

"Se salvaron de ser linchados." 2002, 18 June. *Opinión* (Cochabamba).

Secretaría Nacional de Participación Popular. 1995. *Ley de Participación Popular y su reglamentación.* La Paz: Ministerio de Desarrollo Sostenible y Medio Ambiente.

Seligmann, Linda. 1989. "To be in between: The cholas as market women." *Comparative Studies in Society and History* 31(4): 694–721.

Serulnikov, Sergio. 1994. "When looting becomes a right: Urban poverty and food riots in Argentina." *Latin American Perspectives* 21(3): 69–89.

Shaw, Peter. 1981. *American patriots and the rituals of revolution.* Cambridge, Mass.: Harvard University Press.

Sheriff, Robin E. 1999. "The theft of carnaval: National spectacle and racial politics in Rio de Janeiro." *Cultural Anthropology* 14(1): 3–28.

Shirley, Robert W. 1990. "Recreating communities: The formation of community in a Brazilian shantytown." *Urban Anthropology* 19(3): 255–276.

Simmel, Georg. 1950. "The metropolis and mental life." In *The sociology of Georg Simmel.* K. H. Wolff, ed. New York: Free Press.

Singer, Milton. 1959. *Traditional India: Structure and change.* Philadelphia: American Folklore Society.

Skar, Sarah Lund. 1994. *Lives together, worlds apart: Quechua colonization in jungle and city.* Oslo: Scandinavian University Press.

Smith, Gavin. 1989. *Livelihood and resistance: Peasants and the politics of land in Peru.* Berkeley: University of California Press.

Solares Serrano, Humberto. 1986. *Movimientos urbanos en Cochabamba.* Cochabamba.

———. 1990. *Historia, espacio, y sociedad: Cochabamba 1550–1950: Formación, crisis y desarrollo de su proceso urbano.* Cochabamba: CIDRE.

Souza Martins, José de. 1991. "Lynchings—Life by a thread: Street justice in Brazil, 1979–1988." In *Vigilantism and the state in modern Latin America: Essays on extralegal violence.* M. K. Huggins, ed., 21–32. New York: Praeger.

Spalding, Karen. 1984. *Huarochirí: An Andean society under Inca and Spanish rule.* Stanford: Stanford University Press.

Speed, Shannon, and Alvaro Reyes. 2002. "'In our own defense': Rights and resistance in Chiapas." *Political and Legal Anthropology Review* 25(1): 69–89.

Spitzer, Leo. 1998. *Hotel Bolivia: The culture of memory in a refuge from Nazism.* New York: Hill and Wang.

Staples, Anne. 1994. "*Policía y buen gobierno:* Municipal efforts to regulate public behavior, 1821–1857." In *Rituals of rule, rituals of resistance: Public celebrations and popular culture in Mexico.* W. H. Beezley, C. E. Martin, and W. E. French, eds., 115–126. Wilmington, Del.: Scholarly Resources.

Starn, Orin. 1991. "Missing the revolution: Anthropologists and the war in Peru." *Cultural Anthropology* 6(1): 63–91.

———. 1999. *Nightwatch: The politics of protest in the Andes.* Durham, N.C.: Duke University Press.

Stein, William. 1961. *Hualcan: Life in the highlands of Peru.* Ithaca: Cornell University Press.

Stephenson, Marcia. 1999. *Gender and modernity in Andean Bolivia.* Austin: University of Texas Press

Stern, Steve J. 1982. *Peru's Indian peoples and the challenge of Spanish conquest: Huamanga to 1640.* Madison: University of Wisconsin Press.

Ströebele-Gregor, Juliana. 1996. "Culture and political practice of the Aymara and Quechua in Bolivia: Autonomous forms of modernity in the Andes." *Latin American Perspectives* 23(2): 72–90.

Sunstein, Cass R. 1996. *Legal reasoning and political conflict.* Oxford: Oxford University Press.

"Supuesto ladrón de ganado se salva por un pelo de ser linchado: En la comunidad de Calli Pampa." 2002, 24 April. *La Patria* (Oruro).

Suttles, Gerald D. 1972. *The social construction of communities.* Chicago: University of Chicago Press.

Swaney, Deanna, and Robert Strauss. 1992. *Bolivia: A travel survival kit.* Hawthorne, Victoria, Canada: Lonely Planet Publications.

Szuchman, Mark D. 1996. "The city as vision: The development of urban culture in

Latin America." In *I saw a city invincible: Urban portraits of Latin America*. G. M. Joseph and M. D. Szuchman, eds., 1–31. Wilmington, Del.: Scholarly Resources.

Taller de Información y Formación Académica y Popular (TIFAP). 1988. *"Relocalizados": Ex-trabajadores de la minería asentados en Sucre (TDMAS)*. Sucre: Secretariado Arquidiocesano de Pastoral Social.

Tamayo, Franz. 1975. *Creación de la pedagogía nacional*. La Paz: Editorial El Diario.

Tarrow, Sidney. 1994. *Power in movement: Social movements, collective action, and politics*. Cambridge, England: Cambridge University Press.

Taussig, Michael. 1997. *The magic of the state*. New York: Routledge.

Taylor, Diana. 1997. *Disappearing acts: Spectacles of gender and nationalism in Argentina's "Dirty War."* Durham, N.C.: Duke University Press.

Thompson, E. P. 1971. "The moral economy of the English crowd in the eighteenth century." *Past and Present* 50: 76–136.

Ticona, Esteban, Gonzalo Rojas, and Xavier Albó. 1995. *Votos y wiphalas, campesinos y pueblos originarios en democracia*. La Paz: Fundación Milenio-CIPCA.

Tolnay, Stewart E., and E. M. Beck. 1995. *A festival of violence: An analysis of southern lynchings, 1882–1930*. Urbana: University of Illinois Press.

Tórres, Yuri. 2001, 14 April. "El linchamiento, expression de la degradación social." *Los Tiempos* (Cochabamba).

Trouillot, Michel-Rolph. 2001. "The anthropology of the state in the age of globalization: Close encounters of the deceptive kind." *Current Anthropology* 42(1): 125–138.

Turino, Thomas. 1993. *Moving away from silence: Music of the Peruvian altiplano and the experience of urban migration*. Chicago: University of Chicago Press.

Turner, Terence. 1991. "Representing, resisting, rethinking: Historical transformations of Kayapo culture and anthropological consciousness." In *Colonial situations: Essays on the contextualization of ethnographic knowledge*. G. W. Stocking, ed., 285–313. Madison: University of Wisconsin Press.

——. 1992. "Defiant images: The Kayapo appropriation of video." *Anthropology Today* 8(6): 5–16.

Turner, Victor. 1957. *Schism and continuity in an African society: A study of Ndembu village life*. Manchester, England: Manchester University Press.

——. 1986. *The anthropology of performance*. New York: PAJ Publications.

UNESCO. 2001. "Masterpieces of the oral and intangible heritage of humanity: Proclamation." http://www.unesco.org/culture/heritage/intangible/masterp/html_eng/declar.shtml. Accessed 3 September 2003.

"Urbanismo evitará loteamiento de áreas verdes." 1993, 2 February. *Los Tiempos* (Cochabamba).

"Urge la conservación de las áreas de reserva urbana." 1974. *Los Tiempos* (Cochabamba).

Urquidi, José Macedonio. 1949. *El origen de la "Noble Villa de Oropesa" (Cochabamba)*. Cochabamba: Imprenta Universitaria, Sección Comercial.

Urquidi Zambrana, Jorge E. 1967. *La urbanización de la ciudad de Cochabamba: Síntesis del estudio.* Vol. 1: *Antecedentes.* Cochabamba: Editorial Universitaria.

——. 1986. *La urbanización de la ciudad de Cochabamba y el desarrollo regional y urbano: Examen crítico.* Vol. 2. Cochabamba: Colegio de Arquitectos de Bolivia, Filial Cochabamba.

——. 1995. *Evolución urbana de la ciudad de Cochabamba: A través de ordenanzas y reglamentos municipales 1786–1982.* Cochabamba: Genial S.R.L. Cbba.

——. 1999. *Anécdotas de un pasado cochabambino.* Cochabamba: Colegio de Arquitectos de Cochabamba.

"Valle Hermoso cansado de delincuencia." 1999, 7 May. *Gente* (Cochabamba).

Van Cott, Donna, ed. 1994. *Indigenous peoples and democracy in Latin America.* New York: St. Martin's.

——. 2000. *The friendly liquidation of the past: The politics of diversity in Latin America.* Pittsburgh: University of Pittsburgh Press.

Van den Berg, Hans. 1985. *Diccionario religioso Aymara.* Iquitos, Puno: CETA-IDEA.

Van den Berg, Hans, and Norbert Schiffers, eds. 1992. *La cosmovisión Aymara.* La Paz: Hisbol/UCB.

Van den Berghe, Pierre L. 1974. "Introduction." *International Journal of Comparative Sociology* 15(3–4): 121–131.

"Vecinos carbonizan el 'taxi del delito.'" 2001, 20 July. *Los Tiempos* (Cochabamba).

"Vecinos entregan vivos a ladrones pero dicen que será la última vez." 2002, 9 April. *Opinión* (Cochabamba).

Velez-Ibañez, Carlos G. 1983. *Rituals of marginality: Politics, process, and culture change in urban central Mexico, 1969–1974.* Berkeley: University of California Press.

Vilas, Carlos M. 2001a. "(In)justicia por mano propia: Linchamientos en el México contemporáneo." *Revista Mexicana de Sociología* 63(1): 131–160.

——. 2001b. "Tristezas de Zapotitlán: Violencias e inseguridad en el mundo de la subalternidad." *Bajo el Volcán* 2(3): 123–142.

"Villa S. Pagador quiere organizar su propia policía." 1995, 14 March. *Los Tiempos* (Cochabamba).

Vogt, Evon. 1969. *Zincantan: A Maya community in the highlands of Chiapas.* Cambridge, Mass: Belknap.

"Voto resolutivo." 1995, 22 March. *Los Tiempos* (Cochabamba).

Wacquant, Loic J. D. 1995. "The comparative structure and experience of urban exclusion: 'Race,' class, and space in Chicago and Paris." In *Poverty, inequality and the future of social policy.* K. McFate, R. Lawson, and W. J. Wilson, eds., 543–70. New York: Russell Sage Foundation.

——. 1999. "Urban marginality in the coming millennium." *Urban Studies* 36(10): 1639–1647.

Warren, Kay B. 1996. "Reading history as resistance: Mayan public intellectuals in

Guatemala." In *Maya cultural activism in Guatemala*. E. Fischer and M. Brown, eds., 89–106. Austin: University of Texas Press.

——. 1997. "Narrating cultural resurgence: Genre and self-representation for Pan-Mayan writers." In *Auto/ethnography: Rewriting the self and the social*. D. E. Reed-Danahay, ed., 21–46. Oxford: Berg.

Weber, Max. [1918] 1958. "Politics as a vocation." In *Max Weber: Essays in sociology*. C. W. Mills and H. H. Gerth, eds. Oxford: Oxford University Press.

Weisberg, Robert. 1992. "Private violence as moral action: The law as inspiration and example." In *Law's violence*. A. Sarat and T. R. Kearns, eds., 175–210. Ann Arbor: University of Michigan Press.

Weismantel, Mary. 2001. *Cholas and pishtacos: Stories of race and sex in the Andes*. Chicago: University of Chicago Press.

White, Walter. [1929] 2002. *Rope and faggot: A biography of Judge Lynch*. Notre Dame: University of Notre Dame Press.

Williams, Raymond. 1973. *The country and the city*. Oxford: Oxford University Press.

——. 1976. *Keywords: A vocabulary of culture and society*. Oxford: Oxford University Press.

Wilson, Elizabeth. 1991. *The sphinx in the city: Urban life, the control of disorder, and women*. Berkeley: University of California Press.

Wolf, Eric R. 1955. "Types of Latin American peasantry." *American Anthropologist* 57: 452–471.

——. 1957. "Closed corporate peasant communities in Mesoamerica and central Java." *Southwestern Journal of Anthropology* 13: 1–18.

Wolff, Robert Paul. 1971. "Violence and the law." In *The rule of law*. R. P. Wolff, ed., 54–72. New York: Simon and Schuster.

Wright, Timothy. 2000. "Gay organizations, NGOs, and the globalization of sexual identity: A Bolivian case." *Journal of Latin American Anthropology* 5(2): 89–111.

Yampara Huarachi, Simón. 1992. "La sociedad aymara: Sistemas y estructuras sociales de los Andes." In *La cosmovisión aymara*. H. Van den Berg and N. Schiffers, eds., 221–240. La Paz: Hisbol/UCB.

Zimmerman, Arthur Franklin. 1938. *Francisco de Toledo: Fifth Viceroy of Peru, 1569–1581*. Caldwell, Idaho: Caxton Printers.

Zuidema, R. Tom, and Ulpiano Quispe. 1973. "A visit to God." In *Peoples and cultures of native South America*. D. R. Gross, ed., 358–373. Garden City, N.Y.: Natural History Press.

Zulawski, Ann. 2000. "Hygeine and 'the Indian problem': Ethnicity and medicine in Bolivia, 1910–1920." *Latin American Research Review* 35(2): 107–129.

Index

Cochabamba, 2–5, 10–12, 15–16, 22, 93; agrarian economy of, 57–60; climate of, 34, 57, 106–7, 149, 230 n.13; founding of, 56–57; as Garden City, 185; growth of, 13, 26, 57–63, 70, 97–99, 184; indigenous people in, 230 n.15; mestizaje in, 138; as modernist utopia, 54–56; population of, 70–71; public identity of, 58, 63; violence in, 24, 184, 211

Collective action, 3, 106, 127, 231 n.5; potential for, 139, 199; reputation for in Villa Pagador, 220; violence as, 194. *See also* Community; Solidarity, collective

Collective identity. *See* Identity: collective

Collusion, 18, 37–38, 227 n.4

Comité de Festejos, 49, 146

Community, 3, 37, 94–96, 120, 194–95, 219–20; construction of, 20, 27, 106–8, 115, 125, 139; diversity within, 105, 177, 218; fiesta de San Miguel and, 158–60, 164–65, 172; indigenous, 94–95, 135, 231 n.4; performance of, 138, 143, 197, 218, 224; reputation of Villa Pagador for, 122, 132; studies of, 46, 95; urban, 164. *See also* Unity

Compadrazgo, 37–39, 76; in fiesta de San Miguel, 147, 150–51, 155–56; loteadores and, 119; in politics, 103–4, 131

Concubinage, 159

Convite, 144

Cooperativa Agraria Alalay, 100

Coronil, Fernando, 235 n.3

Coronil Rivas, Humberto, 97

Corruption: accusations of, 155, 163; city officials and, 98; defined, 195–96; of police, 179–81, 187, 193–95, 200, 205–6, 210, 216, 227 n.1, 236 n.2

Costumes, 142, 147–48, 153

Crime, 12, 23, 185, 190; rising levels of, 180, 183; vulnerability to, 24, 216, 223. *See also* Violence

Criminalization: of the poor, 12, 27; of settlement process, 97; of urban migrants, 14

Cultural capital, 91

Dagnino, Evelina, 235 n.3

DaMatta, Roberto, 17

Dancing, 92, 149, 165, 168; folkloric, 25–27, 218; fraternities and, 146, 151–53, 157, 164; styles of, 142–45, 152

Dandler, Jorge, 62

Davis, Susan G., 4

Death penalty, 211, 217

Debord, Guy, 237 n.1

Debt: fiesta sponsorship and, 158; foreign, 21–23, 71; loteadores and, 119, 131

Decentralization: of alcaldia, 81–84, 122; of national state, 80, 88, 91

Delinquency. *See* Crime

Democracy, 12, 22–23, 29, 84, 130, 180; and the Casa Comual/Taller Zonal, 124–27, 131; citizenship and, 130, 220; failures of, 182, 221–22; lynching as attack on, 185–88; transition to, 88, 227 n.13

Demostración, in fiesta de San Miguel, 137, 143–45, 161, 172–74

Descartes, René, 8

Desconfianza, 26, 32–33, 37–45, 48, 52; and lynching, 187

Development, 27, 30–32, 36, 40–41, 105, 121, 228 n.7; community organization and, 172, 192; self-help, 84, 94, 107–8, 126. *See also* Infrastructure

Diablada, 1, 140–41, 145, 168, 172, 233 n.6

Douglas, Mary, 12

Dramas, 16; of citizenship, 5, 19. *See also* Performance; Spectacle

Nas, Peter J. M., 233 n.1
Neighborhood Security Brigades, 211–12
Neoliberalism, 2–5, 18, 21, 29, 80; crime and, 180; democratic failure under, 221–22; NGOs and, 30; reforms of, 13, 22, 89, 181; as state ideology, 227 n.13; violence and, 223
The Netherlands, 40
Neufert, Ernst, 66
New Penal Procedural Code (Nuevo Código de Procedimiento Penal), 196, 209, 236 n.13
Nongovernmental organizations (NGOs), 30, 41, 94, 121; barrio reputation and, 108, 192
Nueva Fuerza Republicana (NFR), 235 n.5
Nueva Política Económica, 22, 227 n.13
Nugent, Daniel, 89

Office of Barrio Management, 82
Opinión, 214, 235 n.5, 236 n.9
Organization of American States, 136
Orlove, Benjamin, 8
Oruro, 3, 59–61, 71, 97, 104, 137–38, 146–48; folklore in 134–36, 142–45, 165–66, 174; local identity and, 112, 116; migration to Villa Pagador from, 94, 98, 107, 169, 232 n.8; national significance of, 108, 135, 143, 167–68, 172, 233 n.2; Sebastián Pagador and, 109; tourism in, 169–70. See also Carnaval de Oruro
Osorio, Captain Gerónimo, 56

Pachamama, 50, 148
Padres de Familia, 114, 160
Pagador, Sebastián, 108–10
Paraguay, 62
Paris, 9, 65
Participación Popular. See Law of Popular Participation

Participant-observation, 26, 32, 46–48. See also Ethnography
Pasantes, 140, 144–46, 153, 161; motivations for becoming, 158–65; qualities of, 160; reciprocal obligations of, 155
Patron-client relationships, 105, 124, 207; in Andes, 103; loteadores and, 116, 127; state and, 131
Paz Estenssoro, Victor, 71
Performance, 3–4, 16, 25–26, 33, 42, 51, 134; of citizenship, 5, 18–20; of community, 138, 143, 197, 218, 224; folkloric, 108, 136–38; of identity, 31–32, 108, 176, 218; violence as, 4–5, 21, 214. See also Events, public; Ritual; Spectacle
Peru, 8, 60
Picota, 8, 226 n.7
Piqueros, 59
Plan for Citizen Security, 211
Plano aprobado, 85–88; citizenship and, 85, 122, 130
Plano Regulador, 63–70, 77, 229 n.7; goals of, 82; modernist basis of, 85; rationality of, 72–74; violations of, 76, 100, 185
Plan Regional, 67–69, 99–100, 229 n.7
Police, 2, 8–9, 14, 23–24, 180, 190, 212; inadequacy of, 179, 199, 209; justice and, 194; lynching and, 187, 208; mistrust of, 32, 46, 195–97; privatization of, 30. See also Corruption
Policía, 7, 223, 226 n.6, 226 nn.8–9; definition of, 56; lynching and, 188
Policía Técnica Judicial, 210
Political parties, 105, 128
Pongueaje, 62
Potosí, 57–59, 71, 142, 148
Prestige, 160–63, 166–68, 177
Primer Grupo, 101, 114, 120, 124; fiesta sponsorship and, 162; land legalization in, 102, 117

Daniel M. Goldstein is Assistant Professor
in the Department of Sociology and Anthropology
at College of the Holy Cross.

Library of Congress Cataloging-in-Publication Data
Goldstein, Daniel M.
The spectacular city : violence and performance in
urban Bolivia / Daniel M. Goldstein.
p. cm. — (Latin America otherwise)
Includes bibliographical references and index
ISBN 0-8223-3360-0 (cloth : alk. paper)
ISBN 0-8223-3370-8 (pbk. : alk. paper)
1. Social action—Bolivia—Cochabamba—Political
aspects. 2. People with social disabilities—Bolivia—Cochabamba—
Political activity. 3. Festivals—Bolivia—Cochabamba. 4. Lynching—
Bolivia—Cochabamba. 5. Violence—Bolivia—Cochabamba. 6. Political
participation—Bolivia—Cochabamba. 7. Villa Sebastián Pagador
(Cochabamba, Bolivia) I. Title. II. Series.
HN280.C63G65 2004   306'.0984'23—dc22   2004001305